# GLOBAL SECURITY BEYOND THE MILLENNIUM

*Also by Sharyl Cross*

THE NEW CHAPTER IN UNITED STATES–RUSSIAN RELATIONS
Opportunities and Challenges (*co-editor*)


*Also by Igor A. Zevelev*

RUSSIA AND THE NEW RUSSIAN DIASPORAS: The Road to
Domination in Eurasia?


*Also by Victor A. Kremenyuk*

INTERNATIONAL NEGOTIATIONS: Analysis, Approaches and Issues

CONFLICTS IN AND AROUND RUSSIA

# Global Security Beyond the Millennium

## American and Russian Perspectives

Edited by

**Sharyl Cross**
*Associate Professor of Political Science*
*San Jose State University, USA*

**Igor A. Zevelev**
*Head Research Associate*
*IMEMO*
*Russian Academy of Sciences, Moscow*
*and*
*Senior Fellow*
*United States Institute of Peace, Washington, DC*

**Victor A. Kremenyuk**
*Deputy Director*
*Institute of USA and Canada Studies*
*Russian Academy of Sciences, Moscow*

and

**Vagan M. Gevorgian**
*Senior Editor*
*USA: Politics, Economy and Ideology*
*Russian Academy of Sciences, Moscow*

First published in Great Britain 1999 by
**MACMILLAN PRESS LTD**
Houndmills, Basingstoke, Hampshire RG21 6XS and London
Companies and representatives throughout the world

A catalogue record for this book is available from the British Library.

ISBN 0–333–68899–6

First published in the United States of America 1999 by
**ST. MARTIN'S PRESS, INC.,**
Scholarly and Reference Division,
175 Fifth Avenue, New York, N.Y. 10010

ISBN 0–312–22055–3

Library of Congress Cataloging-in-Publication Data
Global security beyond the millennium : American and Russian
perspectives / edited by Sharyl Cross ... [et al.].
p.   cm.
Proceedings of a conference held July 1997, Institute of USA and
Canada Studies of the Russian Academy of Sciences, Moscow.
Includes bibliographical references (p.       ) and index.
ISBN 0–312–22055–3 (cloth)
1. National security—United States.   2. United States—Defenses.
3. National security—Russia (Federation)   4. Russia (Federation)–
–Defenses.   5. United States—Military relations—Russia
(Federation)   6. Russia (Federation)—Military relations—United
States.   7. World politics—1989–   8. Security, International.
I. Cross, Sharyl.
UA23.G6474   1999
355'.033073—dc21                                         98–42209
                                                              CIP

We Dedicate this Book to Our Parents —

Jerry and Christine Cross

Aleksandr Zevelev and Irina Zeveleva

Aleksandr and Klavdiya Kremenyuk

Mamikon and Sirush Gevorgian

The authors also dedicate this book to the next generation of students of American-Russian security relations.

# Contents

# Preface

The end of the Cold War brought closure to the twentieth-century confrontation between the United States and the USSR. The threat of thermonuclear war between East and West diminished. The collapse of the bipolar world system implied that international politics no longer must be a zero-sum competition in which victory for one side would result in loss for the other. Yet, despite expectations that the end to the East-West stand-off would usher in an era of reduced international tensions and conflicts, both the United States and Russia continue to confront a global security environment fraught with serious challenges as the two countries approach the next millennium.

This book is devoted to analyzing the evolution of the US-Russian post-Cold War security relationship, obstacles and opportunities in bilateral cooperation and critical security challenges for the two countries on the threshold of the twenty-first century. American and Russian contributors discuss prospects for managing a range of issues encompassing both traditional military aspects of security, as well as in-depth exploration of the broader non-military dimensions of international security. The contents of this book will provide readers with an understanding of the complexities and potential perils within the global environment as human civilization begins the transition from the twentieth to the twenty-first century. The book is designed to challenge readers to think about some of the most pressing security issues of our time and the roles and responsibilities of the United States and Russia in preserving global stability and peace.

In July 1997, our contributors gathered for a three-day conference held at the Institute of USA and Canada Studies of the Russian Academy of Sciences in Moscow. The conference participants were asked to address a range of questions and issues. The discussion moved from exploring fundamental assumptions concerning international security to assessing the influence, behavior and future roles of the United States and Russia in the world arena. Several sessions of the meeting focused on defining and analyzing the most critical contemporary and future security challenges of the post-Cold War era.

The central questions explored at the conference and throughout this book include: In what fundamental ways will the emerging security environment of the twenty-first century differ from that of the twentieth century? In the aftermath of the Cold War, are traditional definitions of "security" measured primarily in "military" terms still appropriate or should "security" be understood increasingly in "economic," "technological" or "human" terms? Given the increasingly "transnational" nature of security challenges, is it reasonable to continue to think in terms of promoting "national security" interests or is it more appropriate to think of preservation of "security" in "regional" or "global" terms? What are the major contemporary and potential future security threats for the United States and Russia? Is US-Russian cooperation vital for responding to these challenges? What role might the United States and Russia play in the future world community as "partners," "adversaries" or "enemies?" Are the two countries, by virtue of geostrategic location, history or culture inevitably locked into an adversarial relationship?

A major objective in undertaking this project was to produce a genuinely US-Russian collaborative collection capturing different perspectives and exchanges between specialists of both countries. During the conference held in Moscow, American and Russian participants presented draft versions of manuscripts and exchanged constructive and substantive feedback concerning arguments and illustrative cases and evidence. American and Russian contributors continued to confer throughout the various phases of the writing process. Such a collaborative product could not have been achieved by simply compiling existing essays or including articles produced in isolation from the collective American-Russian review process. In the end, it is our hope that by enlisting specialists from both countries we have provided a more comprehensive treatment of these critical bilateral and global security issues.

We also believe that our readers will benefit by our encouraging the expression of different points of view. Obviously, the specialists participating in this project are products of different cultural backgrounds, academic traditions and professional experiences. Also of interest is that the perspectives represented in this collection span three generations or four decades in terms of age differences among contributors. The fact that some authors were directly affected by the Second World War or the Cuban missile crisis, while several other contributors have no personal recollection of such key historical events is perhaps an important factor in shaping thinking concerning the issues examined in this book. In short, this book represents a forum for the expression of diverse perspectives.

In terms of structure, these original contributions address questions, issues and problems that will continue to be of central concern into the twenty-first century. The first section contains chapters devoted to analyzing the evolution of the US-Russian post-Cold War security relationship and potential for creating a security partnership from the point of view of a Russian scholar; and the changing nature of the global security environment and the significance of the US-Russian security relationship from the perspective of an American scholar. Subsequent chapters provide American and Russian perspectives on a range of bilateral and regional and global security issues including: the initiation and evolution of US-Russian post-Cold War military cooperation; the impact of new developments in information technology; proliferation challenges and nonproliferation opportunities focusing especially on the issues created by the post-Soviet transition; development of Russia's post-Soviet identity and implications for regional and international security; environmental security; the problems of democratization, economic integration, drugs and migration; the sources of regional conflicts and consequences of intervention; and military strategy and future warfare.

*Global Security Beyond the Millennium: American and Russian Perspectives* is primarily intended for use in university courses or seminars. The wealth of primary source material contained within this book as well as analysis of contemporary policy issues suggest that it should also be of interest to the scholarly and policy communities and the general public. It is our firm conviction that students who will have to function in the increasingly interdependent global society of the twenty-first century will benefit from exposure to perspectives from both the West and the East contained in this book. Students will have an opportunity to examine these controversial and complex issues by considering and discussing the assumptions, arguments and analyses advanced by both American and Russian specialists. Also, the rapid changes in the post-Cold War security environment and US-Russian relations have made it difficult to obtain up-to-date material for university courses. The book is designed to provide a comprehensive and substantive background inclusive of recent developments and the necessary foundation to encourage readers to think about challenges and opportunities likely to be presented in the future.

We would like to extend our appreciation to our colleagues and the staff at the Institute of USA and Canada Studies of the Russian Academy of Sciences for hosting the conference for participants in this project. We extend a special thanks to Dr. Sergei A. Rogov, Director of the Institute of USA and Canada Studies, for supporting this effort. We would like to express our appreciation to the San Jose State University Foundation for providing grant funds for this project. We also thank Dr. Lela Noble, Dean of the College of Social Sciences and Dr. Terry Christensen, Chairman of the Political Science Department, San Jose State University, for their support of this project. Sharyl Cross thanks the International Research and Exchanges Board (IREX) for providing grant support for travel to Russia contributing to the completion of this book. Igor Zevelev thanks the Woodrow Wilson International Center for Scholars and the United States Institute of Peace for providing generous institutional support facilitating his involvement in this project.

The editors have benefited from countless discussions with many individuals of the scholarly, policy, and military/defense communities in both the United States and Russia in formulating the questions for exploration in this book. Beyond recognizing the significance of ongoing interactions with each of our contributors, we would also like to acknowledge several of our colleagues who have been valuable resources to us in discussing developments in post-Cold War US-Russian security relations and contemporary security challenges. We extend our thanks to Dr. Harley Balzer (Georgetown University); Dr. Sally Blair (US Institute of Peace); Dr. Michael Boll (George C. Marshall Center for European Security); Dr. George Breslauer (University of California, Berkeley); Dr. Herbert Ellison (Jackson School of International Studies, University of Washington); Dr. Gregory Gleason (University of New Mexico, Albuquerque); Dr. Robert Litwak (Woodrow Wilson International Center for Scholars); Dr. Diane C. Marozas (Sandia Laboratories); Dr. Sergo A. Mikoyan (Institute of Peace); Dr. Irina A. Modnikova (Institute of USA and Canada Studies); Dr. Deborah Anne Palmieri (Russian-American Chamber of Commerce); Dr. Peter Pavilionis (US Institute of Peace); Admiral William Pendley (Air War College/Air University); Colonel Vladimir Razumenko (Russian Federation Air Force); Dr. Blair Ruble (Kennan Institute of Advanced Russian Studies); Dr. Nodari Simonia (Institute of World Economy and International Relations/IMEMO); Dr.

Victor Sumsky (IMEMO); and Suzanne Thompson (Moscow Times). We would also like to acknowledge our students at San Jose State University, the United States Air Force, Air War College, Air University and the University of California at Berkeley for providing dynamic seminar atmospheres for exploring many of the issues contained in this book.

The editors are grateful to T. M. Farmiloe, Publishing Director, Macmillan Press, for his support and interest in this project. We also express our appreciation for the dedicated efforts of our research assistants, Carolina Fernandez, Daniil Rosental and Marcelus Suciu. The editors are grateful to Molly Molloy of the Hoover Institution at Stanford University for her generous assistance in obtaining primary source materials for this project. We thank John A. Lee and Professor Richard L. Dinardo for their assistance with the translation of General Larionov's contribution. The editors owe a deep debt of gratitude to Professor Roy Christman and Vanetia Johnston of San Jose State University for their editorial and technical contributions in preparing the manuscript. We thank the staff of the Political Science Department at San Jose State University, Victoria Rodriguez and Gloria Rios, for their valuable support. Finally, we would like to offer a special word of thanks to Vagan, Anya and Sergei Gevorgian, Suzanne Thompson, Vladimir and Tatyana Razumenko and Sergei Vasiliev and Larissa Vasilieva for hosting American contributors in Moscow.

This book represents the culmination of a two-year effort of our contributors who share the common objective of heightening awareness and enhancing understanding of US-Russian bilateral security issues and contemporary and future global security challenges. We thank each of our colleagues who participated in this project for taking time from demanding schedules to prepare the contributions contained in this book. We are grateful for the commitment and patience of all those involved in completing this project. The fact that the American and Russian specialists managed to overcome the cultural, linguistic and distance barriers presented in preparing this book demonstrates that cooperation is possible when there is mutual recognition of the importance of promoting US-Russian dialogue and understanding concerning these critical security issues.

*Sharyl Cross and Igor A. Zevelev*

# 1

## The United States and Russia: Partnership in the Next Century?

*Victor A. Kremenyuk*

The question of the desirability and feasibility of US-Russian partnership in matters of international security is still a subject for debate in both countries. The subject of US-Russian partnership also attracts attention in other countries; such a partnership would influence not only the global security strategy of the United States and Russia, but would also be important for the development of strategies of many other countries.

In considering global post-Cold War security issues, both government and non-government experts in Russia and the United States initially devoted attention to the subject of US-Russian partnership, although both countries have become increasingly reluctant to discuss the topic in security and foreign policy deliberations. One explanation for this shift is that the widely discussed "strategic partnership" proclaimed as a policy goal by both sides in 1993 has failed to materialize. As a result, there is an understandable skepticism in both countries regarding the desirability of such a US-Russian relationship.

The concept of "strategic partnership," as originally conceived, was rather vague.[1] It simply reflected a desire of the leaders of both nations to move away from Cold-War confrontation toward more positive mutual attitudes. The new relationship would incorporate agreements accumulated in the late 1980s in bilateral arms control and other areas of security cooperation. Unfortunately, neither side expended serious effort in making the concept of security cooperation concrete, workable and structured.

The discussions concerning the post-Cold War US-Russian relationship created unrealistic expectations in both Moscow and Washington. Russian policy makers anticipated that their demonstrative friendliness toward the United States would result in substantial US assistance in support of Russian reforms.[2] At the same time, their counterparts in Washington expected that Russia would move quickly through the reform stage to be transformed into a developed market economy and institutionalized democracy in a matter of two or three years.[3]

Neither side was correct. The Clinton Administration, though it had verbally pledged to raise significant money for what it dubbed as a "Marshall Plan for Russia," was not successful in its endeavor. The actual US assistance rendered to Russia has been much less than anticipated.[4] In turn, President Boris Yeltsin's government has not managed to stage consistent and meaningful economic reform. Further, in the midst of economic and structural crisis, the Yeltsin government undertook such risky actions as the dissolution of the Supreme Soviet in 1993 and the war in Chechnya in 1994. Either of these actions might have easily put an end to democracy in Russia.

In the meantime, while opting for a totally new type of relationship with the United States, Russia agreed to significant concessions, such as accelerating the withdrawal of Russian forces from the Baltic states and supporting the US-sponsored United Nations Security Council resolution on Yugoslavia, promptly labeled as "unilateral disarmament" by critics of President Yeltsin's foreign policy in Russia.[5] Russian concessions were never adequately reciprocated by Washington, creating the perception that the US-Russian relationship was unbalanced or favored the interests of the United States. This perception, coupled with growing real asymmetry in economic and military capability between the United States and Russia, alarmed many government officials and non-government experts in Russia. Such developments created and fueled anti-US sentiment, especially since the decision to enlarge NATO was made public.[6]

In 1996, President Yeltsin had to dismiss Andrei Kozyrev, one of the proponents of the US-Russian "strategic partnership," and to appoint the much more conservative centrist Yevgeny Primakov as his new Foreign Minister. Subsequently, Russia has changed its style and tone toward the United States and has initiated a serious anti-NATO campaign.[7]

Whatever impact this transition had on US policy, it at least signaled that Russia was moving away from "strategic partnership" as it was developed in 1993-96. This change has not raised any serious policy debate in Washington, but, of course, was not unnoticed. The consequence has been a discernible difference in US attitudes concerning "partnership" with Russia.

As a result of these developments, the notion of US-Russian partnership has become compromised in the view of many in Moscow and Washington. In terms of actual policy, the American-Russian relationship has reached a point of bifurcation. While both the United States and Russia have applied much effort to avoid a possible confrontation over the issue of NATO enlargement that would incorporate Poland, Hungary and the Czech Republic into the alliance, they have also come to a standstill on the future of their bilateral relations. Building on the NATO-Russia Founding Act of 1997 and inclusion of Russia into the G-7 group, the relationship could develop in the direction of a new attempt to build a partnership. However, equally likely, Washington and Moscow could choose a path of mutual irritation and dissatisfaction and move in the direction of another type of global, this time non-ideological, confrontation between the US-led West and a Russia-China-India triangle of the non-Western world.

## FACTORS IMPEDING "STRATEGIC PARTNERSHIP"

The history of Russian-US contacts from the period of the emergence of the United States as an independent nation in late eighteenth century has not borne anything similar to a desirable "pattern" of relations between two nations. There are other nations, like the United Kingdom or France, that have worked over many years to develop relations with Russia and have managed to sustain such a pattern. Russia and the United States vacillated between extremes of total indifference to instances in which they made mutually beneficial agreements such as the United States' purchase of Alaska in 1867. In the twentieth century, the relations between the two nations continued to span extremes, from the World War II alliance against the Axis powers to subsequent Cold War confrontation. Therefore, when the Cold War finally came to an end, as the result of efforts by both nations, and the communist regime in Russia was defeated, there was no clear view shared by both Washington and Moscow concerning the future direction of relations between their two countries.[8]

Russia had greater latitude in formulating a post-Cold War foreign policy. Following the collapse of the Soviet Union, Russia embarked upon a new course in nation-building and turned over a completely clean sheet in its foreign policy. In contrast, the United States has preserved its vast system of Cold War era alliances, placing limitations on its foreign policy choices in the new period. Russia could not return to its role during the Cold War, not only because of disarray in its economy, but also because of strong consensus in a society that had grown weary of endless ideological confrontations from 1917 forward. Equally, Russia could not broach the question of forming a new alliance with the United States. In the immediate post-Soviet circumstances, such an initiative would have been regarded as completely inappropriate even by the most pro-American circles in Moscow.

Moscow was in a position, however, to suggest a new type of relationship that might have been friendly, cooperative and rather close, while providing Russia the necessary time to reassess its new position in the world and to identify its foreign policy interests. Russia's priorities included gaining agreement by the United States to distinguish Russia from other former Soviet republics, to take into account its nuclear super-power status, and to recognize Russia's great power status as a permanent member of the UN Security Council. In essence, these factors would serve as basic prerequisites for entering into a "strategic partnership" with the United States.

Although such a relationship failed to materialize, it should be emphasized that this does not rule out the fact that there is a sound basis for creating a special sort of partnership between the two countries. Russia has inherited some highly valuable assets from the Soviet Union, including size, territory, industrial and scientific capabilities, a nuclear arsenal and established international commitments. Among the latter, the USSR and the United States shared several commitments for many years that were readily assumed by the Russian leadership. These included firm convictions to avoid nuclear war, to prevent nuclear proliferation in a conflict-ridden world, to achieve either nuclear disarmament or significant reductions in weapons of mass destruction, and to support the UN as a mechanism for protecting international security. The new Russian leadership has indicated its interest in preserving these shared values and has expressed the desire to proceed much further in expanding these established areas of cooperation through some sort of partnership.[9]

Several factors have worked against creating a new type of US-Russian partnership. First, Russia's proclaimed goal of building a democratic society and preventing the return of communists to power provided a basis for anticipating that the United States—leader of the free world—would serve as Russia's partner in combating communists of the former Soviet Union. While concentrating on this interpretation, Russian leaders ignored widespread Western ideas summed up by Francis Fukuyama in his 1989 publication "The End of History?" which was based on the assumption that the end of the Cold War was not simply a victory of liberal democracy over the totalitarian model, but also represented the victory of the West over the East.[10] In Russia, the downfall of the communist regime and the desire to build a democratic society were regarded primarily as a victory of opponents of the communist regime, a victory of the Russian people. In the United States, the majority regarded it as an American triumph, which implicitly incorporated the idea that Russia was a "defeated nation." Insignificant as it may have seemed at the early stage of relationship, this difference in attitude has acquired tremendous importance with time. In approaching the new Russian Federation, the President of the United States had to assume a "victorious" posture because this was expected by the US public.[11] The tone and the style of US policy proclamations toward Russia sometimes sounded like statements concerning Japan and Germany in the late 1940s, while the Russian President and the Russian public could not even think of being a "defeated side" and certainly considered such attitudes inappropriate and improper. The US approach generated suspicions that its policy was aimed at unilaterally exploiting Russian weakness and Russian readiness to cooperate to advance the "global role" of the United States.

Second, those who constituted the leading group in the Russian government in late 1991-early 1992 had practically no foreign policy experience. Vice-Premier Yegor Gaidar and his team — with all due respect to their expertise in economics (which has also become increasingly questionable) — had no substantial knowledge of US politics, society or economics. Because of political considerations, they were not inclined to rely on the existing expertise in Russia concerning the United States, which could have been helpful in devising a realistic approach to building Russia's relationship with Washington. Instead, they accepted a widely shared myth among Russian intellectuals of American omnipotence. They expected that public promises by American leaders of considerable financial assistance to Russia (President Bush in 1992 and President Clinton in 1993) were backed by sufficient resources. They believed that the United States government could allocate the necessary resources to facilitate completion of the Russian reform project in a matter of two to three years. Expectations of forthcoming aid from the United States became a vital factor in their policy planning and an important component of the pro-reform propaganda. The realistic assessments offered by non-government experts suggesting that the US economy had lost much due to the Cold War effort and that the United States had become the largest borrower in the world were ignored and regarded as an attempt by communists to subvert US-Russian partnership. The government's initial pro-US policy created unrealistic expectations among many Russians. The result of the failure to meet these expectations has been a predictable anti-American backlash. [12]

Third, contrary to basic rules of standard international conduct, Russian foreign policy makers in 1992-93 were voluntarily yielding one position after another. Instead of hard bargaining on every issue, consistent with standard norms of international conduct, be it withdrawal of troops from Europe, policy towards Iraq, or relations with historically close Serbia, the Russian government ultimately accepted some of the most unfavorable and counterproductive policy initiatives proposed by the West. This created the wrong impression in the West. It appeared that the new government in Moscow rejected all traditional Russian geopolitical interests and would be inclined to accept any deal if it came from Washington. This conduct was also perceived as a sign of weakness, indecisiveness, and lack of political experience and will on the part of the Russian president. In Russia, it provided the climate for the rise of xenophobia.

The style of Russian diplomacy introduced by Andrei Kozyrev was misleading and deceptive because it ignored a vast segment of Russian public opinion that remains suspicious of the West and reluctant to entertain any notion of cooperation. Furthermore, Russia's behavior provoked the West into some ill-conceived decisions such as NATO enlargement. The decision to enlarge NATO would never have been made had there been a better understanding of both Russian readiness to cooperate with the West and its ability to defend itself in the event that its legitimate interests were in any way jeopardized.

In assessing the factors that worked for and against US-Russian partnership, it should be recognized that while there was and still is a vast and partially untapped reserve for bilateral cooperation, the style and the manner in which it was promoted in 1992-96 were counterproductive and contributed to compromising the idea rather than to advancing it. There was no serious attempt to negotiate the subject and mode of partnership, to establish working mechanisms (with one significant exception being the Gore-Chernomyrdin Commission), to turn the concept of partnership into reality, or to consider how such a relationship could be developed in the context of existing alliance structures and international commitments. Thus, the entire concept of "strategic partnership" remained nothing more than a statement of good intentions and was grudgingly recognized as a failure.

At the same time, it would be premature to conclude that the thought of some sort of US-Russian partnership is buried altogether. First,the mere fact that both nations have been able to prevent a crisis that could have resulted from the decision on NATO enlargement and to sign the NATO-Russia Founding Act, which created opportunities for further dialogue, provides ample evidence that the prospects for partnership are much stronger than may seem. Second, both sides have agreed on certain areas in which cooperation could be enhanced, though progress has not been even or sufficient, perhaps most clearly illustrated in the striking inadequacy of development in US-Russian economic relations. Certainly, additional bilateral cooperation could be achieved with removal of more of the barriers inherited from the Cold War era. Third, these potential but unrealized "partners" have not yet devoted sufficient attention to exploring the possibility of forming a new type of relationship or to defining the full range of possible new areas for cooperative engagement.

To explain why this is the case, one should consider several problems in both countries. One of the most important is the residue of the Cold War. Even when both sides declared the Cold War over, when they agreed to reduce the numbers of nuclear weapons and to de-target the remainder, deep suspicions and mistrust remain. Phobias exist on both sides: Russophobia in the United States on the part of prominent figures such as Zbigniew Brzezinski or Henry Kissinger and US-phobia in Russia shared by hard-line communists and newly born Russian chauvinists. Even if both nations were able to identify this problem and make the eradication of these phobias high-priority long-term political goals — in the same way that inculcating mutual animosities was a priority for both governments in the 1940s — it would still take years of sustained effort before the policy making communities of both countries could overcome the memories of nearly a half century of bitter confrontation. The problem of overcoming these mutual negative perceptions is critical for the future evolution of US-Russian relations, but neither side has even attempted to address the issue.

The other explanation has a more operative nature, though it is equally important. There never should have been expectations that once the Cold War was over, all the differences, disputes and conflicts between the two countries would no longer exist. Fortunately, there were no disputed borders in US-Russian relations. However, there have always been disputes involving third countries, in the areas, both geographical and functional, where the interests of both the United States and Russia come into contact or where there is a threat to the interests of each nation. Both countries must make sincere and sustained effort to identify not only spheres of common interest, or where the interests of the two parties are not in contradiction and a high likelihood of achieving cooperation is possible, but also to identify spheres where such cooperation is impossible, at least at present, or areas where there is a high risk of rivalry.

It is clear enough that US-Russian relations will develop within a framework of "conflict-cooperation," just as the relationship developed in the days of the Cold War. Even relations among nations that are close allies, such as the United States and Japan, function within such a framework. It is unrealistic to expect to eliminate all conflicts among nations. The object should be to shift the balance between "conflict" and "cooperation" increasingly in favor of the latter by establishing a conflict resolution mechanism in the form of a partnership.

It was only reasonable to expect that the United States-Russian relationship would be challenged with significant controversies. The real trouble is that, so far, only a few of these issues have been negotiated with the purpose of finding a mutually acceptable solution. A number of these contentious issues were negotiated during the Soviet era, some prior to the accession of Mikhail Gorbachev, but most primarily during the period when Gorbachev was directing Soviet foreign policy. In the last few years, aside from the "partnership" rhetoric, there has been almost no progress in working through difficult issues, while the friction and divergence of interests continue to be obviously significant.

## PROSPECTS AND ADVANTAGES FOR BUILDING PARTERNSHIP

International security is the most important and established area in which both the United States and Russia have already expressed a strong desire and intention to cooperate.[13] The fact that both nations possess huge nuclear arsenals and share the desire to avoid confrontation either between their two countries or in other areas of the world provides a solid foundation for continued cooperation. These common interests can serve as the pillars of a US-Russian bilateral partnership and cooperative engagement in international security matters. Both sides have agreed, on several occasions, and as recently as the Helsinki Summit in March 1997, that they should proceed to negotiate further cuts of their arsenals and to support nonproliferation and to cooperate in other areas, including anti-ballistic weapons and conventional arms control. It seems that not withstanding all the problems and controversies that have and may continue to occur in US-Russian relations, the robust commitment of both nations to preventing nuclear war, combating nuclear terrorism, and supporting the nonproliferation regime may play an important role in bringing about a much closer relationship between the two countries, with cooperation in both bilateral and multilateral aspects of international security.

It would be premature to assume that the US-Russian relationship either will not change or will evolve toward greater cooperation. The first signal that the relationship might be changing surfaced in 1993 when the draft of the new Russian military doctrine was published.[14] This draft proclaimed that Russia could resort to first-use of nuclear weapons in defending its interests if threatened by nuclear or non-nuclear nations. The new statement was received rather skeptically in the West and was treated primarily as a sign of military weakness rather than as a change in nuclear policy. Nevertheless, the existing state of Russian military capabilities suggests that the nuclear first-use option demands much more serious attention in the West. The war in Chechnya revealed the striking weakness of Russia's conventional forces, a fact that had already been recognized by experts. Following the disintegration of the Soviet military machine, inadequate funding and political turmoil had a disastrous effect on the morale of the military. It may require a considerable amount of time, perhaps a decade, before the Russian military reform effort will bring visible changes and transform Russian conventional forces once again into a reliable and credible foreign policy resource. Until that time, it can only be expected that the Russian government will have to rely on its strategic nuclear force as an ultimate source of influence in circumstances threatening vital interests.

It is certainly possible that the Russian attitude with respect to strategic arms control, including negotiated reductions, could move toward reluctance to cooperate with the United States, which remains the world's largest nuclear and conventional military power. Such a Russian perspective would be fueled by strong support from anti-government opposition, with significant backing in both political and military circles. Opposition forces have already managed to block ratification of the Strategic Arms Reduction II (START II) Treaty. Should Russia become increasingly insecure in the current international situation, in which military manpower continues to play a significant role, diminished interest in achieving additional strategic arms reductions should be anticipated.

The tendency toward resisting cooperation cannot be ruled out until at least two factors change: 1) the current Russian strategic arsenal wears out due to the natural aging process and thereby is no longer a credible deterrent; 2) the military reform finally results in reestablishing a highly sophisticated, flexible and effective conventional force with the capacity to serve as the power arm of Russian foreign policy. If these changes occur, the inclination toward cooperation will increase because the Russian government will be interested in ensuring some sort of control over the US strategic force through negotiated arms control agreements.

Since both countries presently share a mutual interest in strategic arms control, it is important to use this area of agreement as the central foundation to develop an institutionalized US-Russian security partnership as soon as possible.[15] The US-Russian security agreement can be widened beyond strategic arms control to include agreements on destruction of chemical weapons, conventional weapons control in Europe, and joint peace-keeping operations, primarily in former Yugoslavia. The NATO-Russia Founding Act provides some hope that security cooperation between the two nations may also move into new spheres of regional conflict management, arms transfers and other areas of mutual security interest.[16]

The lack of any sort of dynamic progress in US-Russian cooperation in the last few years has promoted other negative trends. Of particular concern is the emergence of clearly definable differences in approaches to nuclear nonproliferation. Two nearly simultaneous events occurred in

1996 demanding particular attention: the Russian agreement with Iran on nuclear power plant construction and the US agreement with North Korea on nuclear reactors. Undoubtedly, Russia must have markets for its nuclear power industry. As the trend to limit Russian access to markets in Eastern Europe (possibly with the exception of Slovakia and Bulgaria) has developed, Russian nuclear plant producers are increasingly forced to seek out new markets. As a result, there will be an area of friction with the United States as Russia's search for new markets leads to the development of ties with countries labeled as "rogue states" by the Clinton Administration. Russia will never agree to exclusion from the markets where it was the first-comer as in North Korea. The problem here is not in the lack of negotiations on market activities. The real problem is that the two nations, given their commercial interests and anxieties, have overlooked their failure to cooperate in matters of primary political importance, and this failure could potentially undermine traditional consensus in the critical area of nuclear weapons nonproliferation.

Both sides have also been reluctant to establish additional rules and procedures to build upon the cooperation in nuclear and non-nuclear proliferation established during the Cold War era. The lack of progress in enhancing partnership in nonproliferation has contributed to growth of controversies, suspicions and misunderstandings with potential adverse consequences in this important area of security cooperation. The same may be said of the US-Russian relationship within the UN Security Council. Russia has indicated rather strongly its dissatisfaction with the conduct of UN-NATO cooperation in the Bosnian crisis. In witnessing the shift of power from the UN Security Council to NATO headquarters, Russia was justified in concluding that its own interests were either neglected or ignored. That bitter experience only added to Moscow's skepticism concerning the fairness of the Western, particularly US, role in the Security Council. This experience increased both Russia's desire to activate Russian-Chinese cooperation and its resistance to plans to incorporate Germany and Japan into the UN Security Council within the forthcoming reform of that organization.[17] Such aspects of the US-Russian relationship suggest that without progress in the establishment of a partnership agreement, cooperation in prevention of nuclear war and nuclear arms control, nonproliferation and activities of the UN Security Council could be jeopardized.

Paradoxical as it may seem, the less the threat of direct confrontation between the United States and Russia, the less is the concern by the leaders of both sides to work together in order to regain even the level of cooperation that existed between the United States and USSR during the period of Mikhail Gorbachev and *New Thinking* in the late 1980s. This is undoubtedly dangerous, and, without meaningful effort devoted to reversing this trend, the security environment in the world may change significantly for the worse and to such an extent that even the US "global force" will be unable to check it.

Much will depend on US-Russian cooperation and not on the enlargement of NATO or on promotion of other US-led alliances, which either have become ineffective or are quickly nearing that stage.[18] One should keep in mind that the advancement of US-led alliances, including NATO enlargement, will only encompass what is now recognized as the Western community — either in the Euroatlantic or Pacific areas. Given current US capabilities, it is questionable whether the US will be able to finance deeper engagement in these areas because of potential resistance by the US Congress to undertake additional spending commitments. Furthermore, this leaves vast areas of the world, regions of greatest instability and potential for conflict, ignored or remaining unattended on the margins of these security mechanisms.

The United States has attempted to exert its influence in regional conflicts in a few cases, including the Persian Gulf, Somalia, Haiti and Zaire (primarily through the UN). However, because of the residual of the "Vietnam syndrome," with the reluctance to become too deeply involved in these situations, results were less than optimal. Major challenges to international security, both regional and global, will not come from Russia in the foreseeable future, but from these areas, especially in the regions of "rogue states." In the absence of a partnership between the United States and Russia, each will be tempted to exploit events in those areas for unilateral advantage.

Some extremist Russian political leaders would champion a strategy directed toward fueling turmoil by proxy in order to exert significant pressure on US global and regional policy while avoiding any sort of direct confrontation.[19] But the majority of responsible Russian politicians share another view. They would argue that a strong US-Russian cooperative relationship should be established, closely approximating the joint cooperation in Bosnia, to increase the capabilities of both powers and the UN to contain and resolve regional conflicts. This is not because they have any special sympathy toward the United States, but because Russia must consider national security threats coming from some parts of the

Islamic World, the Korean peninsula and other neighboring areas, such as the Transcaucasus and Balkans. Without such cooperation, there will always be a threat that extremist movements such as the Taliban in Afghanistan may be used by other nations (including the United States) and thus pose a security threat to Russia and its allies, or to US allies in neighboring areas. [20]

In the conditions of disintegration of the bipolar system, it would be short-sighted and naive to think that a single "victorious" side might supplant the role of international "anchor," which had previously been performed by two major powers. It is simply not possible for any single power to amass such influence on a wider global scale. To a limited extent, this may occur, possibly in Central and Eastern Europe. An attempt by the United States to achieve influence in Central and Eastern Europe, while ignoring the interests of Russia, will inevitably return the region to a battleground. Overextension of US global commitments may become both a source of security concern for its allies and an opportunity for those who regard the United States as a threat to their security. In order not to overburden US capabilities, and to avoid the risk of the outbreak of global chaos that could follow the collapse of US-led alliances, a strong and multi-purpose partnership with Russia may be a necessity. Such an agreement is becoming a prerequisite for global stability, Western security and the preservation of the security environment in Eurasia, where Russia continues to play a central role. [21]

The future constellation of power relations in the world will inevitably center on the United States, which has alliance relationships with countries in the Western Hemisphere, Euroatlantic, and Asia-Pacific areas, and plays an important role in the UN Security Council. Within this constellation, the Moscow-Washington axis acquires special importance primarily because of the nuclear factor, but also because of Russia's special role in the post-Soviet neighboring areas.

Russia's importance also derives from its leading position in post-communist transformations progressing throughout the former communist world, and because of its significant influence for future developments in China and Vietnam. The success or failure of democratic changes in Russia will figure decisively in the development of power and ideological alignments in the twenty-first century. Developments in Poland, Hungary, Czech Republic or any other Central European nations will not alter the balance between the West and the rest of the world. However, developments in Russia will have significant consequences for the global distribution of power into the next century.

Even if humanity enters the twenty-first century free from global confrontation (not to exclude, of course, the age-old confrontation between the rich and the poor),[22] the fate of the West and liberal democracy will continue to depend on the number of new nations that will adhere to the values of democracy and free-market economics. The success of the Western model will depend largely on the future of the Russian reform project. The Russian experience will be studied thoroughly in China, Korea, Vietnam, Syria, Libya, Afghanistan and many other countries in the throes of struggle between traditional values and cultures and the Western democratic/free-market model. Depending on their assessment of the results of the Russian experiment, the general situation in the world could evolve either in the direction of liberal democracy or toward revitalization of traditional and nationalistic values.

The next century may continue to see wars and revolutions not because of ideas such as Marxism-Leninism, but because of the inability of certain nations to proceed along the Western path of development and unfulfilled material expectations.   This is likely to result in resurgent traditionalism, to be manifested in different forms of fundamentalism. It may become a problem both for individual states and for the West as a whole to incorporate the "damned of the Earth" in their social security or international mechanisms. The reluctance of NATO to hear the pleas of some of the least developed East European nations and resistance to incorporate Russia into Western international institutions stems from concern that these nations could jeopardize these precariously devised Western structures.[23]

The only realistic solution for this imminent crisis for the West is partnership with Russia based both on conflict-control and support-to-modernization policies. Given its current status and level of political and economic development, Russia stands somewhere between the North and the South. In this intermediate position, Russia has much in common with both worlds. Russia may move in the direction of the North and increase its resources and adaptive capabilities, or it could move in the direction of the South, providing strong leadership and the protection of a nuclear superpower.[24]   The future course will be contingent not only on the Russian domestic effort, but also on reciprocity of the West.   Only the United States that can provide the political, security and economic momentum to forge a consistent and sensible Western position that reflects sufficient appreciation of Russia's legitimate security and economic interests.

## A STRATEGY FOR PARTNERSHIP IN THE NEXT CENTURY

Both Russia and the United States have learned some important lessons from the period 1992-97. There is no basis to suspect that either of them were not sincere when they agreed that their relationship should be centered on the creation of a "strategic partnership." Unfortunately, both countries have concluded that partnership has not become the pattern of their relationship.

The first lesson for the two countries was that their relations are rather shaky and unstable and to a large degree depend on actions of third countries or unanticipated developments emerging from within these countries. The second lesson was that without a consistent attempt to introduce some structure into their relationship, they cannot hope for a sound basis for creating an enduring institutionalized partnership. The third lesson consisted in shared understanding that there should be no lengthy periods of inactivity or idle time because the rapid dynamics of the international arena are bound to generate unpredictable events between annual US-Russian summits. The final lesson was that US-Russian relations should grow in depth in order to make them more resistant to the impact of controversial and accidental happenings.

Two things must be done. First, a new attempt should be made to salvage the concept of US-Russian partnership and to make it a reality. Second, a concrete plan should be set forth defining a consistent and systematic strategy to establish such a partnership. Any spontaneous decisions, improvisations and ad hoc solutions should, to the extent possible, be abandoned. The two sides should instead work to create a mutually acceptable model for partnership. They should outline the specific steps and a clear time-frame required to create this relationship. Otherwise, the inertia of the previous period, unresolved issues and interference on the part of third parties are likely to thwart another attempt to build a US-Russian partnership.

It would be inappropriate to draft a detailed and structured schedule or program; that is a subject for governments and their staffs. However, one might suggest general guidelines for creating a legal document to provide the foundation for the US-Russian partnership. Neither the American nor the Russian leadership devoted adequate consideration to the notion that the end of the Cold War would require some general treaty to establish the basis for a new relationship.  In the current international practice, it is a recognized rule that nations seeking to establish a certain type of relationship negotiate formal agreements (alliance, friendship, cooperation or mutual assistance).  Somehow, the United States and Russia have failed to negotiate such an agreement, preferring instead an ad hoc process.

The Basic Principles Agreement between the United States and the Soviet Union (1973) might provide a pattern for the agreement.  The NATO-Russia Founding Act, representing the first attempt to draft a broad legal document between Russia and the West in the aftermath of the Cold War, is actually more useful for this purpose.  That document is related to a specific case and specific type of relationship.  Evidently, its purpose is the creation of Russian-NATO partnership in matters of European security, and it contains specific terms to achieve this stated aim.  A similar document should be negotiated, signed and ratified by the legislatures of both nations defining their diplomatic agendas for at least the next decade.

The document should contain several major items.  It should include a joint statement on the principles of relations between the two nations.  Apparently there is no place for something like "peaceful coexistence," which was the formula for a peaceful relationship between ideologically divergent or even hostile societies.  In the contemporary period, both the United States and Russia share the same basic values and principles of social organization.  The document should emphasize this point in order to confirm that the era of ideological confrontation is past and that both countries can develop their relationship within the same ideological framework.  The other rationale for inclusion of a statement on joint principles is to establish clearly the vision of equality in the relationship.  There are people on both sides who believe that the US-Russian relationship cannot be based on principles of equality.  In the United States, one frequently encounters writings insisting that US "leadership" should be regarded as a basis for relations with any foreign nation.  In Russia, there are parties and individuals who regard US-Russia asymmetry as jeopardizing Russian autonomy in national security matters.  This statement would alleviate anxieties and simultaneously avoid the development of any type of asymmetry that could become disastrous for the partnership.

The second part of such a document should define the areas where the interests of both nations coincide and specify ground rules for developing cooperation in these areas. This should not present a serious problem; at nearly every US-Russian summit there is a reiteration of the commitment of both sides to cooperate in matters of mutual concern and to develop collaboration in those areas. This has included principles and general guidelines in arms control (strategic, conventional, means of mass destruction) with specific reference to the shared goals and means for achieving objectives. They include expression of mutual concern on some of the most threatening international developments, with reference to nuclear weapons proliferation, nuclear and conventional terrorism, regional and local conflicts, drugs and environmental problems. This also involved statements of mutual agreement on means of dealing with these security challenges, with praise for mechanisms that have already contributed to peacekeeping and problem-solving, such as the UN, Organization for Security and Cooperation in Europe (OSCE), and rather cautious appreciation of NATO and its role in Europe.[25]

Third, and perhaps most important, the document should provide for a joint mechanism for problem-solving, an inseparable component of any such cooperative agreement. Reflecting on the history of US-Soviet cooperation during the Cold War, one can easily identify more than a dozen joint documents specifying the details for the establishment of mechanisms to prevent unauthorized launches of strategic and non-strategic missiles, prevention of incidents at and above high seas, mutual inspections, exchange of sensitive information, and many other written statements facilitating resolution or avoidance of conflicts. The United States and Russia can now proceed much further if they undertake measures to turn prior and newly emerging understandings into a standard practice embodied in new standing institutions, exchange of personnel and information, regular consultations and other measures that would turn the words "partnership" and "cooperation" into a daily routine. Coupled with a significant surge of business investment and other economic activities, exchanges in culture and research, and visits of private persons, this could lay solid ground for instituting a substantive US-Russian partnership.

One of the most important aspects of the potential partnership is the dual nature of such an agreement. It is definitely a bilateral relationship, but it would also have a global dimension. While the bilateral dimension might be achieved rather painlessly, the global dimension may be much more complicated. In this respect, Russia is in a better position because it is in the process of restructuring its international commitments. Russia is maintaining former Soviet commitments that it prefers to continue (UN, OSCE, relations with the West), abrogating those that it does not consider necessary (former Communist "brothers"), and looking for new relationships, in both the political and economic spheres: G-7, NATO, IMF, World Bank, World Trade Organization, European Council, European Union and Pacific Cooperation Council.

It is much more difficult for the United States to manage its existing commitments and obligations while trying to cultivate a partnership with Russia. The possibility of a deeper US-Russian relationship has already produced some negative undercurrents with close allies of the United States (with Japan in the G-7) and may produce even more tensions in the future. There is some concern that concentration of US interest in developing partnership with Russia would result in diminished US interest elsewhere. The greatest concern, and even jealousy, has surfaced among some Central European countries, believing that any improvement of relations between the United States and Russia constitutes a setback for their interests and any problem in the relationship as serving their advantage. Considering the influence of various forces within the wider international context, such as the role of China, India, Iran, some Arab nations and Balkan states, it is understandable that the issues of constructing a US-Russian partnership are not likely to be resolved easily and smoothly.

The US-Russian partnership may become one of the major cornerstones of the global security structure in the twenty-first century. This structure could be something genuinely global, with space-based monitoring, transnational information systems and databases, with highly sophisticated weaponry and qualified personnel. The structure would be based on the principles of universal security in the spirit of the UN Charter. In part, that system may be controlled by the Western alliances and US-led groups in the Pacific and Western hemisphere. However, partnership with Russia may well be one of the primary means to extend this global security system to encompass the vast Eurasian "heartland" that has played such a visible role in human history.

## NOTES

1.   "A Deal That Nobody's Heard Of," *Los Angeles Times,* News Fax, Moscow Edition (6 July 1992).

2. "Debt Moratorium Tops Yeltsin's Wish List," *Los Angeles Times,* News Fax, Moscow Edition (1 June 1992).

3. "Russia Bades Bold Economic Reforms," *Los Angeles Times*, News Fax, Moscow Edition (26 June 1992).

4. "Yeltsin Arrives, Gets Aid Assurance," *Los Angeles Times,* News Fax, Moscow Edition (16 June 1992).

5. "Yeltsin Gets Mixed Reviews At Home," *Los Angeles Times*, News Fax, Moscow Edition (19 June 1992).

6. A. Konovalov, S. Kortunov and S. Oznobishchev, "Rossiya i NATO: Vremya Diskussiy Konchilos" (Russia and NATO: Time for Discussions Has Ended), *Nezavisimaya gazeta* (29 September 1996).

7. "Zayavleniye rabochey grupy Soveta po vneshney i oboronnoy politike po politike v otnoshenii NATO" (Statement by the Working Group of the Council on Foreign and Defense Policy on NATO), *Nezavisimaya gazeta* (12 May 1997).

8. "Congress Applauds Speech by Yeltsin," *Los Angeles Times*, News Fax, Moscow Edition (18 June 1992).

9. "Arms Pact: An End to Nuclear Fears," *Los Angeles Times*, News Fax, Moscow Edition (17 June 1992).

10. F. Fukuyama, "The End of History?" *The National Interest* (Summer 1989), pp. 3-18.

11. "Old Lending Rules Are Thwarting Russia," *Los Angeles Times*, News Fax, Moscow Edition (18 June 1992).

12. A. Bogaturov and V. Kremenyuk, "Sami amerikantsky ne ostanoviatsya nikogda" (The Americans Never Stop on Their Own, They Have to be Stopped), *Nezavisimaya gazeta* (26 June 1996).

13. D. M. Abshire, *Preventing World War III: A Realistic Ground Strategy*, (New York: Harper and Rowe, 1988).

14. "Osnovy voennoy doktriny Rossii. Proekt" (Basics of the Russian Military Doctrine. A Draft) (Moscow: Krasnaya Zvezda Publishers, July 1993).

15. J. R. Azrael and E. A. Payin, eds., *US and Russian Policymaking With Respect to the Use of Force*, RAND Conference Paper Series (Santa Monica: RAND Corporation, 1996).

16. "Osnovopolagayushchiy Akt. O vzaimnykh otnosheniyakh, sotrudnichestve i bezopasnosti mezhdu NATO i Rossiyskoy Federatsiyey" (Founding Act. On Mutual Relations, Cooperation and Security between NATO and the Russian Federation), (Brussels: NATO Office of Information Press, 1997).

17. S. Rogov, "Neizbezhen li krizis v rossiysko-amerikanskikh otnosheniyakh?" (Is a Russian-American Crisis Inevitable?), *Nezavisimaya gazeta* (20 March 1997).

18. A. S. Lodkin, "Ratifikatsiey dogovora SNV-2 speshit nelzya" (There Is No Need To Speed up START-2 Ratification), *Nezavisimaya gazeta* (17 October 1996).

19.  S. Hoffmann, "The Crisis of Liberal Internationalism," *Foreign Policy*, No. 98 (Spring 1995), pp. 159-179.

20.  K. Borovoy, "Budushchee rossiyskogo dialoga s NATO" (Russia's Future Dialogue with NATO), *Nezavisimaya gazeta* (28 May 1997).

21.  V. Kremenyuk, "Vneshniaya politika administratsii Klintona: na novy srok so starym bagazhom" (Clinton Administration's Foreign Policy: New Term, Old Baggage), *SShA: ekonomika, politika, ideologiya*, No. 5 (May 1997), pp. 20 - 32.

22.  V. Kremenyuk, "International Security: A New Old Paradigm?," *Arms Control: Contemporary Security Policy*, Vol. 14, No. 2 (August 1993), pp. 206-15.

23.  "NATO-Russia Relations: A Key Feature of European Security," *NATO Review*, No. 3 (May-June 1997).

24.  A. Ignatenko, "Islamskiy faktor v mirovikh i rossiyskikh delakh" (Islamic Factor in World and Russian Politics), *Nezavisimaya gazeta - Tsenarii*, No. 8 (21 November 1996).

25.  Madeleine Albright Statement Before SFRC 8 January 1997, *US Embassy Information Bulletin*, Moscow (January 1997)

# 2

# United States-Russian Security Relations on the Threshold of the Twenty-First Century

## *Sharyl Cross*

As the United States and Russia approach the next millennium, the two nations confront enormous security challenges and uncertainties. Policy makers, East and West, have yet to come to terms with the vast scope and significance of change brought about by the collapse of the Soviet empire.

The end of the Cold War offered unprecedented opportunity for shaping a more peaceful and cooperative global community. The response to these new circumstances will determine the global security configuration into the next century. The United States, possessing the largest economy and military force among nations in the contemporary international system, must make the "right" choices, not only for the United States, but for the forging of a post-Cold War order that will facilitate the preservation of the security of the global community into the next century.

Initially, the enormous transformations throughout the former communist world ushered in a period of euphoric expectations in the West. Dramatic scenes such as the tearing down of the Berlin Wall or that of Russia's first elected leader, Boris Yeltsin, positioned atop a tank speaking in support of continued democratic transition are likely to remain indelibly embedded in the minds of many who witnessed these events. Both American and Russian leaders proclaimed that the Cold War was over. Though NATO and the Warsaw Pact never engaged in direct combat, the prospect for confrontation was so potentially apocalyptic that the end to this conflict could only be expected to be followed by a reduction of tension within the world community.

However, as Victor Kremenyuk suggests, initial proclamations of "partnership" and even "friendship" have not been matched by an equivalent level of substantive progress in developing a US-Russian security partnership. The initiative to expand the NATO alliance is the single issue that places perhaps the greatest strain on the US-Russian post-Cold War relationship and stands as the most significant barrier to bringing the US-Russian security partnership to complete fruition.

This chapter explores critical questions for the United States as the nation approaches the twenty-first century: Has the United States succeeded in crafting a long-term policy strategy toward Russia best suited to serve US interests in the realities of the contemporary and future international security environment? Is United States policy sufficiently focused on the future, or is the policy still driven by perceptions formulated during the Cold War? How might the United States and Russia deepen their bilateral security relationship, and how might this facilitate the preservation of global security into the twenty-first century?

## THE EMERGING TWENTY-FIRST CENTURY GLOBAL SECURITY ENVIRONMENT

In considering the formulation of the post-Cold War US relationship with Russia, it is essential to attempt to envision the characteristics of the future global security environment. What are the primary security threats to US interests? How might Russia figure in aiding US efforts in responding to these challenges?

Both pessimistic and optimistic prognoses abound regarding the post-Cold War international security environment. Samuel Huntington advanced the "clash of civilizations" thesis arguing that the future international system would be characterized by conflicts between civilizations rather than ideologies.[1] Huntington sees a future in which the West may be pitted against the Islamic world, Eastern Orthodox Slavic civilization or others. John Mearsheimer argued that the shift from a bipolar to multipolar system in Europe was likely to be destabilizing leading to conflicts among major powers in Europe or resulting in disintegration into regional rivalries previously contained by the United States or the former Soviet Union.[2] For Mearsheimer, there is no evidence that "Europeans believe that war is obsolete," and it requires "only one country" to "decide that war is thinkable to make war possible." Robert D. Kaplan argues that ethnic strife, crime, resource scarcity and environmental maladies will come to engulf much of the planet.[3]

To counter the forecasts of pessimists, Francis Fukuyama cites the strength and growth of the US economy, projected increases in wealth for many of the poor in today's world (especially in Asia) and the fact that Europe is now free from great power rivalry negating the assertion that "Just as in 1914... the Balkans in our own day may serve as the tinderbox for a larger European conflict."[4]

One can identify several significant immediate and longer-term potential challenges to US interests in the contemporary and emerging post-Cold War security environment. These include:

- Territorial, resource, ethnic, racial, religious and cultural conflicts leading to interstate wars and nation-state implosion;

- Greater vulnerability as a result of the increasingly transnational and interdependent global environment;

- Proliferation of weapons of mass destruction;

- New complexities in warfare due to developments in information technology;

- Greater incidence of security threats originating from non-state-sponsored sources (terrorism, international crime);

- Growing economic disparity between the nations of the developed and developing worlds;

- Threats to the quality of human life (population growth, poverty, environmental degradation);

- Nation-state challenges including strains in relations with existing allies, emerging major power contenders or threats from rogue states.

The outbreak of several conflicts following the collapse of communism in the former Soviet Union in part explains the reluctance of some observers to accept visions of transition to a more peaceful world society. The unanticipated war in the former Yugoslavia among Serbs, Croats and Bosnian Muslims resulted in widespread devastation and dislocation. The post-Cold War world community has witnessed conflict throughout the territory of the former Soviet empire in Georgia, Moldova, Azerbaijan, Armenia and Tadjikistan, and violent struggles in Somalia, Rwanda and elsewhere. Russia has been threatened with impulses toward further disintegration most clearly illustrated in the Chechen secessionist struggle. The growing prominence of multicultural education and post-modern thought in American institutions of higher learning is indicative of pressures the United States could face on the part of marginalized groups for greater political and economic equality and influence in the coming years.[5]

While one might argue that such tensions both within and between nations have been a constant in international politics and does not necessarily portend a global future of larger-scale clashes, other critical trends will fundamentally alter the nature of the international system in the twenty-first century.

First, the global environment continues to evolve toward greater interdependence. Developments in transportation and communication and the explosion in information technology will continue to make the international community more interwoven. Borders and distances between nation-states will be of lesser significance leaving nations of the world arena increasingly vulnerable.

The United States and other nations will be forced to deal with a host of existing security threats that can only be expected to become more serious unless current trends are reversed. The global community suffers from the proliferation of weapons of mass destruction (WMD): nuclear, biological and chemical weapons. Concerted international efforts so far have not been adequate for preventing proliferation of destructive weapons and agents.

It will no longer be so simple to define the "enemy" as this or that nation-state. Rather, enemies will also take the form of group or individual, rather than state-sponsored terrorist and criminal organizations operating across state borders. Even if all nations did begin to adhere to international agreements restricting the sale or transfer of weaponry and technology, this would not necessarily prevent such tools of destruction from falling into the hands of terrorists or criminal organizations. The United States faces the threat that such destructive weaponry could be unleashed on its soil in the future, not only by rogue states, but also by organized terrorist groups or individuals harboring unresolved grievances.

Continued advancement in information technology promises to render the United States and other nations vulnerable to threats of "cyber" warfare. Military forces as well as security and financial organizations have become susceptible to penetration. Not only will such technology complicate the battlefields of the future, but information warfare will not necessarily be restricted to use by nation-states. The possibility of "hackers" interrupting communications in warfare or disrupting intelligence or commerce must be included in forming the picture of the future security environment. Concerted international efforts to govern such technology remain rudimentary.

Projections indicate that by 2025 the Earth will number nearly 8 billion inhabitants, and most of them will reside in the lesser- or non-industrialized poorer nations. The widening gap in wealth between North and South, poverty and disease plaguing nations experiencing the most rapid population growth suggest that a global future marked by the pervasive presence of the so-called "damned of the Earth" may not be far from reality. The movement of migrants and refugees originating from regions of growing scarcity in search of improved economic conditions or fleeing protracted conflicts, wars and violence is likely to place greater pressures on the advanced industrialized nations. Environmental degradation and resource scarcity threaten the existing quality of human life and will continue to present significant challenges for the next century. If current trends are not reversed, the United States and other major powers of the developed world are likely to be increasingly affected by dismal conditions threatening human well-being throughout vast areas of the world.

Even if Francis Fukuyama is correct in citing the strength of the US economy as a key factor in support of an optimistic future global prognosis, does Francis Fukuyama or anyone else really believe that the United States, even given its wealth and overwhelming military capability, will be able to unilaterally manage the security environment of the next century? World history suggests that hegemonic powers rise and decline within the international system as new contenders gain influence relative to the major power. The United States risks dissipating its resources in assuming sole responsibility for attempting to respond to these challenges.

US policy makers may be suffering an illusion of invulnerability resulting from previous successes including the "victory in the Cold War" or the impressive display of force in the Persian Gulf. The United States would be remiss to assume that its current predominant status will inevitably remain into the twenty-first century. The United States cannot become complacent. It must be vigilant in thinking long-term and pursuing initiatives and crafting strategy based upon realistic understanding of the coming security environment.

Where are the potential future antagonists that might be tempted to challenge US interests or compound the security threats within the international system? If one is to accept the proposition that the United States will be unable to singularly manage the global security challenges of the future, then what nations will be critical in this effort?

The United States enjoys longstanding diplomatic, security, economic and cultural ties with nations of Western Europe and its NATO allies. However, since the end of the Cold War, US influence in Europe has not been unchallenged. Influential figures among the nations of Western Europe have questioned the appropriateness of US leadership and presence in Europe. Protestations abound in these countries concerning US claims to predominance on the world stage. While United States associations with nations of Western Europe are likely to remain close, these relationships will not be free from some strains. The United States cannot necessarily expect that nations of Western Europe will readily support all US foreign policy initiatives, nor that US influence in Europe will remain uncontested in the future. Absent the unifying Soviet threat, previously providing a cohesive focus for the alliance, conflicts have emerged within NATO itself. The war ravaging the former Yugoslavia, for example, has tested the integrity of the alliance. Greece and Turkey tended to favor the interests of Serbs or Bosnian Muslims respectively because of shared religious traditions.

While Fukuyama's observation concerning the absence of great power rivalry in Europe today may be correct, the historical record of the twentieth century, the two major wars and numerous other lesser conflicts suggests that it is a leap of faith to believe that the relative calm among major powers will continue into the next century. Differences were already evident in the assessments of the sources of conflict and policy prescriptions among members of the Contact Group (United States,

Russia, Germany, Britain and France) in responding to the war in former Yugoslavia.

China, a burgeoning economic giant with a vast population and growing military capability, may challenge US security interests in the future. The global democratization wave has yet to consume China. China will enter the next century as an oppressive regime with a long-standing record of human rights violations. The question of relations with Taiwan, tensions with Japan and many other longer-term issues could test future Sino-US relations. While China's ties to the global economy might eventually be accompanied by some liberalization of its political system, and desire to avoid conflict with the West, still, the future objectives and international behavior of this nation remain unknowns.

Furthermore, obviously, a nation does not have to be a great power to threaten US interests. Nations throughout the Third World could demand US attention and resources including Iran, Iraq, North Korea, Libya, Cuba or other nations. The situation in the Middle East appears particularly problematic. There is scant evidence that resolution of the Israeli-Palestinian conflict is in sight. The Clinton Administration unexpectedly received less than enthusiastic support for its initiatives even from regional allies Kuwait and Saudi Arabia in the most recent crisis with Saddam Hussein concerning expulsion of UN weapons inspectors. US relations with Iran, Iraq and other potential rogue states may become increasingly difficult to manage as these countries gain access to more sophisticated weaponry. Even in today's world, questions remain about the capacity of the United States to manage two simultaneous major regional conflicts. What challenges might the United States face in 2020 in regional conflict settings in the Middle East or elsewhere if the global community is no more successful than it has been in reversing the proliferation of nuclear, biological and chemical weapons?

In short, trends indicate that the world community of the twenty-first century will be far more complex, interconnected and potentially dangerous. Furthermore, meeting the security challenges of the emerging system is likely to increasingly demand multilateral coordination among nations.

As the international community undergoes the transition from the Cold War era into the twenty-first century, US policy makers would be well served to remain focused on major power centers. After all, the future global security configuration and rules and norms for governing the international system will, for the most part, be determined by forces in

Washington, Moscow, major centers in Western Europe, Tokyo and perhaps Beijing.

Against the global security environment outlined above, the United States relationship with Russia takes on enormous significance. Russia, by virtue of sheer physical size as the largest nation in the world, geopolitical location and nuclear capability, will be critical not only for stability in Eurasia, but arguably for preservation of security throughout the global community. The United States will need Russia's cooperation in meeting the security challenges beyond the millennium. A strong and cooperative Russia would support US efforts in promoting international stability and security. However, if American-Russian relations move toward renewed confrontation and hostility; if conditions within Russia deteriorate toward anti-Western authoritarianism; then Russia could greatly complicate the aforementioned security challenges.

The democratic transition underway in Russia and desire to cooperate with the United States offer a tremendous opportunity. The consequences of failing to respond appropriately could spell peril in the future. Add to the equation outlined above a nuclear-armed "rogue Russia" or a Russian-Chinese or Russian-Iranian alliance pitted against the United States in 2010. The long-term consequences of failure to prevent increasing official or even unofficial sales of Russian weaponry and technology to US adversaries is just one more possible serious consequence.

## THE LEGACY OF THE PAST: A CRITICAL PROBLEM FOR POST-COLD WAR POLICY

If the United States and Russia share an interest in building a lasting security partnership, what explains the fact that such a relationship has yet to fully develop? The Gore-Chernomyrdin Commission, established in 1993 to promote the expansion of bilateral cooperation in defense conversion, business, space, science, environment and other areas, represents a significant positive step forward in building ties for the next century. However, lingering remnants of the Cold War era have created obstacles for realizing the potential of the commission. Also, the existence of the commission cannot necessarily be taken as indication that the United States has thus far assigned the highest priority to building such ties with Russia; the United States put forth initiatives to establish similar commissions with South Africa, Egypt and Ukraine.

The generational factor has been at play in the formulation of US post-Cold War thinking with respect to Russia. The legacies of the antiquated Cold Warrior mind-set continue to surface. Influential figures who have shaped US foreign policy in the past, and remain important voices on US policy within the United States, Zbigniew Brzezinski and several others have been unable to move beyond the image of Russia as enemy. Also, the Sovietological academic community in the United States attracted many individuals with origins in East-Central Europe and the former Soviet Union who suffered the oppression and brutality of authoritarian communist regimes. As a result, animosities have been implanted in American thinking about the former Soviet Union and now Russia. Finally, many Soviet specialists in the United States within the policy and academic communities were attracted to studying the former Soviet Union, not necessarily for any great interest in the unique features of the nation's history, culture, or society, but because of the appeal of focusing on the primary US "strategic enemy" during the years of the Cold War. Despite the monumental changes of the past decade both within the USSR/Russia, and in its foreign policy, several of these scholars continue to adhere to the same negative assumptions concerning Russia: Russia cannot be trusted; Russia's intentions and interests contradict the interests of the West; Russia has and will continue to threaten its neighbors; the United States will be unable to form a relationship with Russia that in any way approximates its relationship with nations of Western Europe. These individuals and their students continue to speak, write and thereby influence US perceptions of Russia.

Institutional inertia is also a significant operative factor. There are limits to the pace that the institutions tasked with countering the Soviet threat during the Cold War can be transformed. The roles and missions of US security and defense organizations have been undergoing redefinition and reorganization to adjust to the realities of the post-Cold War security environment. However, though this transition is underway, the changes are incremental, and these institutions remain overwhelmingly staffed by individuals who formulated their views about the USSR/Russia during the pre-Gorbachev Soviet era.

The legacies and images of the past are evident in the statements of key figures formulating US thinking and policy toward Russia. The centerpiece of US post-Cold War strategy—the initiative to enlarge the NATO alliance—perhaps best exemplifies backward, rather than forward thinking. Though the US Administration has attempted to present the initiative as representing a futuristic strategy aimed at consolidating democracy throughout the former communist bloc, the underlying fear of a potential resurgent Russia is undeniable. In a 1997 *New York Times* editorial entitled "Russia Has Nothing to Fear," Strobe Talbott writing in the capacity as Deputy Secretary of State explains why NATO enlargement will not threaten Russia's interests emphasizing the US desire to promote democracy and stability in Europe. Despite Talbott's reassurances, the remnants of old thinking emerge even in this article when Talbott states that a decision not to enlarge NATO would "send an unwelcome and unhelpful message to the Central Europeans...It would imply that they are consigned to a permanent *buffer zone between East and West*" [emphasis added].[6] Testifying before the Senate Foreign Relations Committee in support of NATO enlargement, US Secretary of State Madeleine Albright stated outright: "...One should not dismiss the possibility that Russia could return to the patterns of its past..."[7] Influential voices within the US Congress have offered even more blatant statements of suspicion. For example, US Senate Majority Leader Trent Lott states: "I think to enlarge NATO to include Hungary, Poland and the Czech Republic is a natural extension of having won the Cold War. We allowed the Soviet Union to come in and take over Eastern Europe once. We should not allow that again."[8]

Even with significant American sentiment against or indifferent to NATO expansion, arguably due in large part to the continued influence of individuals carrying legacies of the past, the Administration has been persuaded to proceed with expansion of the Western security alliance toward the East. Given the vast scope and magnitude of change that confronted US policy makers as a result of the collapse of communism in the former Soviet Union, the temptation to fall into old patterns of belief and behavior in attempting to comprehend and respond to a new reality was overwhelming. Thus, the US posture toward Russia continues to reflect past perceptions that may no longer represent a realistic or accurate assessment of present-day realities or potentialities with respect to the *new Russia*.

## RUSSIA'S TRANSITION AND THE UNITED STATES

Russia stands at a critical juncture as it approaches the next century. The July 1996 presidential election demonstrated that despite the severe dislocation, economic hardship and uncertainty unleashed by the reform process, Russians remain committed to charting a new course for the future. This sentiment is especially strong among the younger generation rejecting resurrection of the past. Russia's President Boris Yeltsin has been committed to continued democratization, transition to a free-market economy and to cultivating ties with the West and the United States. In terms of international behavior, Gorbachev and Yeltsin cooperated with the United States in bringing about the most dramatic nuclear arms reductions in history, not only in terms of cutting existing arsenals, but also in eliminating entire classes of weapons systems. Both leaders worked in unprecedented fashion with Western nations in dealing with regional conflicts in Central America, the Middle East, Bosnia and elsewhere. The fact that US and Russian peacekeeping forces worked side by side in Bosnia and that US and Russian forces have participated in joint exercises on American and Russian soil provide visible manifestation of the dramatic changes in recent years.

At the same time, Russia's society still faces a difficult transition for many years ahead. The individuals occupying positions of authority, including the nation's president, members of parliament, and the military-security structures and industrial managers, are products of the Soviet system. It will take time to eradicate the patterns of governance and management inculcated during the many years of the authoritarian command system of the past. The vast bulk of Russia's population has yet to realize improvements in living conditions as a result of the reform effort. The inability of the state to overcome lawlessness, the growth of Russian organized crime and corruption compound the pain of transition for ordinary citizens and reflect the problems encountered by Russia's embryonic democratic government, and its periodically ailing leader, in managing this transitional society.

The Russian military is demoralized and plagued by insufficient salaries (several months in arrears), poor housing and lack of adequate equipment and training.[9] Russia faces the challenge of downsizing its military force, while creating a strong and efficient mobile force suitable for meeting future security challenges, all the while lacking sufficient resources in the cash-starved economy. The political appeal of former and current military officers such as General Alexander Lebed or General Lev Rokhlin within the ranks of the military is symptomatic of the deep-felt dissatisfaction within the former premier Soviet military force.

Russia's future remains uncertain. From the perspective of US interests, in the best case, Russia will continue to make strides in developing a democratic system of government and civic society, to begin to elevate the overall standard of living throughout the society and to provide markets and greater opportunities for US investment. However, if the reform process is derailed, if Russia disintegrates further, if anti-Western and/or ultra-nationalist elements are able to capture political control, then the West can expect renewed hostility and a nation that may be more difficult to manage than was the former Soviet Union.

Despite the concerns expressed by Senator Lott and others regarding Russia's designs on retaking East-Central Europe, it should be noted that even the most extreme ultra-nationalist or anti-Western fringe elements in Russia do not hold such expansion as a priority. However, halting continued progress in arms control, working against the United States in regional conflict situations, stepping up sales of weapons of mass destruction to rogue states, cultivating alliances with US adversaries, undertaking efforts to reassert Russian control throughout the Newly Independent States (NIS), reversing political and social freedoms within Russia, chaos, disorder, violence and dissolution within Russian society are within the realm of the possible should the political balance shift in the coming years. The threat is not from a resurgent Russian military force poised for expansion, but from an unstable and disintegrating superpower force lashing out as a result of the perception of being cornered and alienated.

It is only reasonable that US observers should be cautiously optimistic concerning Russia's future. The challenges are formidable and it is the Russians themselves who will determine their future. However, the United States can do much to promote the best possible outcome in Russia. Perhaps most important, US leaders must avoid the danger of the self-fulfilling prophecy in approaching the new Russia: one expects the worst, prepares for resurgent threat, and thereby creates such a reality.

The temptation exists for some to discount Russia because of its current domestic malaise or lack of capacity to challenge US claims to dominance in the post-Cold War world. However, the realities of the transnational global community certainly imply that Russia's problems are or will become problems for the United States. The thought that the United States can afford to ignore this troubled giant of the East again simply demonstrates the inability to comprehend the realities of present-day international conditions.

The collapse of the Soviet Empire was accompanied not only by the relinquishment of many Third World client states and Warsaw Pact nations, but also territories previously included within the borders of the USSR. Absent sufficiently substantive reciprocal US initiatives toward building a genuinely cooperative relationship with Russia, there has been a growing sense that Gorbachev and Yeltsin sold out the nation to the West. Moreover, US policy makers have tended to be insensitive to Russia's need to continue to be dealt with as a nation of "great power" status.

Russians have become aware of the limits to US economic capacity and do not necessarily expect large-scale aid. However, what does and will matter in the future is whether the United States has consistently offered an adequate level of respect to Russia during the current *smutnoye vremya* (time of troubles) and that US intentions are genuinely devoted to promoting, rather than thwarting, Russia's restoration. The critical question will be whether US policy makers effectively managed the opportunity offered during the Yeltsin period so as to solidify a deep, stable and cooperative US-Russian bilateral relationship for the next century.

It will take time and mutual cooperative initiatives on the part of both nations to overcome the negative images of the past. The problem is that global security challenges are so pressing that sufficient time may be lacking. US policy makers would be well served to recognize exactly what is at stake in Russia. The focus should move from the past to current realities and the security concerns of the next century. A serious US effort to build a deeper long-term security relationship could help to create the necessary ties and incentives to make a cooperative US-Russian relationship irreversible and even unthinkable in the future. This would do much to defuse the arguments and credibility of ultra-nationalist and anti-Western forces in Russia and further shift the political equation in favor of Yeltsin's potential successors who would seek continued cooperation with the West. [10]

Given Russia's history, location and geostrategic interests, it was unrealistic to believe that there would be a complete compatibility between US and Russian global interests. The emergence of tactical differences concerning NATO's air strikes against Bosnian Serbs in 1995 or regarding the US resolve to use military force in responding to Bagdhad's failure to comply with UN weapons inspections, Russian sale of a nuclear reactor to Iran and other issues demonstrate that the two countries will not always act in complete unison. At the same time, the common security interests shared by the United States and Russia suggests that the deepening of the US-Russian post-Cold War security relationship is not unrealistic.

## NATO ENLARGEMENT:     ADVANCING US SECURITY INTERESTS?

Enlargement of the NATO alliance is central to the post-Cold War US relationship with Russia.   At the June 1997 Madrid Summit, NATO members announced the initiative to extend invitations to three East-Central European nations, Poland, the Czech Republic and Hungary, to become full alliance members by 1999.   Forthcoming invitations to Slovenia and Romania and even the Baltic states have also been discussed.

The proposal for a dramatic expansion in membership of an organization founded to confront a no longer existing Soviet threat required the articulation of some tangible advantages.   The initiative is consistent with the *US National Security Strategy of Engagement and Enlargement* in that it is viewed as a means to advance US interests in the post-Cold War community by promoting the proliferation and consolidation of democracies and free-market economies in East-Central Europe and the Soviet successor states.[11]   Advocates of NATO enlargement argue that expansion would stabilize the post-Cold War "security vacuum" in East-Central Europe.[12]

The initiative also represents a response on the part of NATO members to the appeals of these countries for membership in the alliance. Poland, Hungary and other aspiring member states in East-Central Europe and the former Soviet Union view membership in NATO as a means of gaining the advantages accompanying inclusion under the Western security and economic umbrella.  Also, understandably, given their past relationship with Russia, fear of resurgent threat from the East prompts these countries to appeal for membership.  Finally, many of these nations, by virtue of religion, ethnicity or language, have always more closely identified with the West.

While many see advantages to NATO expansion, there is good reason that no less a significant figure than the architect of the US containment strategy, George Kennan, referred to the initiative as the "most fateful error of American policy in the entire post-Cold War era."[13] Several former American diplomats, political leaders and scholars have voiced opposition to NATO enlargement largely because of concern with the implications of the initiative for the US-Russian relationship.[14]

The initiative has been received with sustained objections from President Boris Yeltsin, Prime Minister Victor Chernomyrdin, Foreign Ministers Andrei Kozyrev and Yevgeny Primakov, with even stronger opposition being voiced from more conservative and nationalistic military/security and legislative leaders.[15] Despite efforts of the Clinton Administration to downplay Russia's opposition to NATO enlargement, as Russia's Ambassador, Yuli M. Vorontsov, made quite clear writing recently in *The Washington Post:*

> ...Russia's attitude toward NATO enlargement has been and remains unequivocally negative...
>
> Naturally we do not expect a NATO attack now. But NATO is a military alliance, and its military machine is getting closer to the boundaries of Russia...Whether we want it or not, we shall be obliged to react to these developments if the process goes on.
>
> Few people take account of the psychological factor—the historic memory of Russians. It was from the West that real threats continuously came to Russia, bringing to our people immeasurable losses and destruction.[16]

Writing in *Foreign Affairs* in 1993, Ronald Asmus, Richard Kugler and F. Stephen Larrabee, advocating NATO enlargement, stated that "extending the alliance eastward should be seen as the West taking a step toward Russia, not against it."[17] Given that many Russians still remain gripped with the memory of the loss of life suffered during the Second World War, and the fact that NATO was originally established for the purpose of countering the Soviet threat, how could the Russians be expected to believe this? The discussion of extension of the NATO alliance eastward through East-Central Europe, and especially to include Ukraine or the Baltic nations, will only rekindle deep Russian concerns and anxieties regarding the intentions of the West.

The proposed expansion has prompted serious reconsideration within the Russian foreign policy and security establishments concerning what to anticipate from the United States and other Western powers in the coming years. For example, during his visit to NATO headquarters in late 1996, former Defense Minister Igor N. Rodionov discussed Russia's perceptions of the consequences of NATO enlargement for altering the geostrategic military balance in Europe. Rodionov opened the exchange with an argument often advanced to express Russia's disillusionment with NATO enlargement. Rodionov stated:

> When Mikhail Gorbachev made his decision to withdraw Soviet forces from Eastern Europe, the West verbally guaranteed never to expand the North Atlantic Alliance toward the East...Soviet troops are gone from Europe, whereas clearly we are here discussing the issue of NATO expansion right up to Russia's borders. [18]

Some of the adverse results cited by Rodionov include significantly reducing the early-warning time available to Russia's anti-ballistic missile systems; providing NATO with the option of carrying out a surprise air strike on strategic Russian assets such as Kursk, Bryansk and Smolensk; hemming in Russia's Baltic fleet as a result of NATO assuming control of Poland's strategic Baltic ports; and that NATO's tactical nuclear weapons could be deployed in these "new territories" for combat use leaving Russia "completely exposed to nuclear attack." Rodionov said that NATO's expansion would "require Russia to take adequate countermeasures." He continued stating that the "logic here is simple. NATO expansion deprives Russia of the ability to defend herself with existing anti-missile and anti-aircraft systems. The only remaining defense option in the event of an irreconcilable conflict of interests between NATO and Russia is to plan for a crippling first strike." [19] As confirmation of Russia's concerns, in late March-early April 1997, Russia staged military exercises involving nuclear forces against a hypothetical NATO attack. The simulation involved invading NATO, Lithuanian and Polish military forces, with counterattacks using nuclear weapons. [20] Furthermore, members of Russia's Duma have repeatedly cited NATO enlargement as justification for unwillingness to approve the Strategic Arms Reduction II (START II) Treaty or to begin to entertain the possibility of agreeing to the deeper cuts in the strategic nuclear arsenals of the United States and Russia proposed in the Strategic Arms Reduction III (START III) Treaty. [21]

The NATO initiative has been interpreted by many Russians as rejection from the West or even as an effort by the West to take advantage of Russia's present turmoil and weakness. This has led to discussions within Russia's foreign and military/security policy circles concerning the formation of counter alliances among the Commonwealth of Independent States (CIS). More realistic, and potentially more threatening in the long-term, are recent Russian and Chinese overtures for cooperation in security matters. Russia's concern with NATO enlargement contributed to prompting Boris Yeltsin to sign a joint declaration in 1997 with China's President Jiang Zemin obviously directed toward the United States calling for a "multipolar" world where no country "should seek hegemony..."[22]

The proposition that NATO enlargement is the key to stability in the aftermath of the Cold War must be viewed with skepticism. NATO enlargement, rather than serving as a deterrent, may result in only unnecessarily provoking the Russians — to again divide the world, and thus imply a long-term destabilizing effect. The initiative might represent the optimal approach only if one is convinced that Russia is destined by virtue of its past political traditions and geostrategic position and interests inevitably to return to a confrontational relationship with the West. If Western nations seek to demonstrate their support and provide incentive for continued transition in East-Central Europe, they can do so by channeling resources toward investment and aid in support of democratic and economic reform in these countries, rather than initiating an expansion of the Western security alliance to the East at this critical juncture.

Zbigniew Brzezinski has argued that raising the question of the cost of expansion is a "deliberate exclusionary tactic."[23] The truth is that the cost will be substantial, and there is no agreement on what nations will shoulder the burden for the expense.[24] US taxpayers and their elected representatives in Congress are likely to balk at assuming a substantial portion of these costs. It seems clear that aspiring member countries, in the throes of economic reform, will have difficulty in garnering the resources required to convert their military forces for membership in NATO.

NATO enlargement represents policy predicated upon historical fears. The initiative demonstrates the absence of sufficient appreciation for contemporary international realities and long-term US security interests. Before putting forth this initiative, did US planners really stop to consider the nature of the future security environment? Who is America's "enemy?" How will including Poland or Estonia in NATO aid the United States in preserving its interests in the future security environment? Should US taxpayers devote resources to NATO enlargement when the United States has been downsizing its own military force over the past several years? If Russia is a critical factor for security in East-Central Europe, Eurasia and the wider global community in the next century, does NATO enlargement represent the optimal approach to advance US interests?

## FOUNDATIONS FOR ENHANCING US-RUSSIAN SECURITY COOPERATION FOR THE TWENTY-FIRST CENTURY

Though the announcement issued at the Madrid Summit created the impression that the admission of new member states would be a *fait accompli*, these invitations must be approved by the legislative bodies of each NATO member nation. Even if all 16 member nations decide to confirm the first-tier invitations, there is still time to reconsider further NATO enlargement and to tailor a strategy more advantageous to long-term US interests. The broaching of the initiative to enlarge NATO has already placed a serious strain on US-Russian relations, and continued expansion to the East, especially beyond the first-tier nations (Poland, Hungary and Czech Republic), may jeopardize all that has been accomplished in the West's relationship with the former Soviet Union and Russia since the end of the 1980s.

NATO does not have to "expand or die" as Brzezinski and others have argued.[25] NATO remains the most powerful, credible security force in a turbulent post-Cold War security environment. The UN has not proven itself as capable of providing effective operational control or coordination of military operations and is clearly not a viable alternative to NATO. The Organization for Security and Cooperation in Europe (OSCE) has no military force capability. The political benefits of the NATO alliance are obvious. The alliance provides a mechanism for maintaining ongoing diplomatic contact and coordination among members of a tried and tested alliance.

There is no reason that NATO should not remain, for at least the next several years, as the chief guarantor of security for Western nations. In fact, NATO enlargement is only likely to strain and test the cohesion of the alliance. NATO members differ concerning sequence of admission of aspiring member states and means for financing the admission of new members. Moreover, future disputes may erupt between NATO members regarding security obligations to new member nations.

Rather than channeling resources toward expansion of the alliance, NATO should continue to enhance the capacity of the existing alliance structure to respond to the security challenges of the post-Cold War world community, as in dealing with regional conflicts in Bosnia and elsewhere.

Greater resources might be directed in support of NATO's Combined Joint Task Forces (CJTF) for use of multinational forces in specific contingency operations including peacekeeping and enforcement, humanitarian relief operations and for other in- or out-of-area purposes. NATO members can continue to build ties with nations of the former Warsaw Pact via Partnership for Peace (PfP). Eventually, such ties will provide the foundation for moving toward the creation of an all-inclusive US-Russian-European security structure for the twenty-first century.

Though political considerations may present serious obstacles in bringing about a reversal of the proposed NATO enlargement, there are ways to ameliorate the adverse consequences of the initiative with respect to Russia. Expansion should be limited to first-tier NATO nations, including only Hungary, Poland and the Czech Republic. It seems that the Russians have resigned themselves to accepting the membership of these three nations, but additional invitations to incorporate other East/Central European countries or especially Ukraine or the Baltics cannot but be expected to thwart continued Russian cooperation with the West. The United States should move to strengthen security ties with Russia within the context of the existing NATO-Russia Founding Act and preferably also by advancing a bold initiative aimed toward significantly deepening US-Russian security cooperation for the twenty-first century.

Though the NATO-Russia Founding Act may help to offset some of Russia's concerns, it can also be as potentially damaging to NATO's relationship with Russia. One can readily identify several problem areas in interpretation of the existing agreement. The document creates a Permanent Joint Council (PJC), in which Moscow is to be "consulted" on all security issues affecting its interests.[26] However, in another section, the agreement states that such consultation confers no authority and will not enable Russia to veto NATO decisions. Yet, President Yeltsin stated following the Madrid Summit that the agreement would give Moscow a decisive voice in inter-NATO councils.[27] President Yeltsin also claimed that NATO had agreed not to expand its forces or to construct bases on the territory of new member states. In turn, NATO representatives maintain that the agreement does not preclude such moves.

The establishment of the Permanent Joint Council (PJC), chaired jointly by the Secretary General of NATO, rotational representation of one of the NATO member states and a representative of Russia, creates a forum for ongoing dialogue and consultation and joint decisions and actions on security matters between NATO and Russia.[28] The PJC will meet at the level of foreign and defense ministers twice each year and monthly at the level of ambassadors. Military representatives and chiefs of staff will meet regularly, and it was also agreed that senior Russian military liaison officers would be attached to NATO's military command structures, with provision for reciprocal NATO representation in Russia. [29]

It should be recognized however that institutionalization of permanent exchanges will be counterproductive if the Russians are marginalized within NATO's decision-making structures. The constant aim should be to foster a sense of inclusion, rather than exclusion, of Russia from Western military/security structures. In approaching this issue from the perspective of NATO's past mission and functional operation, integrating Russian participation in NATO's decision-making structure may seem untenable, but working toward inclusion of Russia is much more desirable considering post-Cold War realities and contemporary and emerging security challenges.

Additionally, mechanisms should be established for achieving deeper integration of Russian participation in peacekeeping operations with Western nations as pledged in the NATO-Russia Founding Act. Continued promotion of military-to-military cooperation initiated under PfP involving routine joint exercises, visits and educational exchanges have and will continue to be a vital component for constructing the future Western-Russian security relationship.

Furthermore, the United States would be well served to proceed with advancing a separate initiative to substantially deepen its existing bilateral security relationship with Russia. If Russia's concerns regarding NATO enlargement could be resolved, this would remove the major barrier to forging the US-Russian post-Cold War security partnership. Such an initiative on the part of the United States would constitute meaningful and substantive recognition of the monumental changes in Russia as well as Russia's vital importance to future world security. This would greatly improve the climate in bilateral relations facilitating cooperation in resolving issues of contention in security relations and establishing the foundation for mutual conflict management into the twenty-first century. This shift could unleash a transition toward a complete and permanent departure from the traditional adversarial US relationship in dealing with the Soviet Union of the past, toward a new mode of interaction with Russia based upon mutual security interests and perception of partnership. It would constitute an original and innovative posture toward Russia focused on the twenty-first century free from the baggage and verbiage of the past.

At the summit meeting held in Helsinki in 1997, President Clinton and President Yeltsin reaffirmed the commitment to the ongoing development of the US-Russian partnership mentioning the desire for continued cooperation in a number of areas including strategic arms reductions, weapons proliferation and cooperation with NATO.[30] In May 1997, the two countries signed an agreement pledging to deepen ties in the development of cooperation in military reorganization, counterproliferation, peacekeeping and to increase routine military-to-military contacts.[31] US officials have repeatedly reiterated the desire to continue with the arms reductions cuts proposed in START II and have urged Russian officials to work to gain ratification for the treaty.[32] Yet, NATO enlargement still remains the single most significant factor that could thwart the realization of these stated objectives.

The removal of the NATO enlargement barrier could provide renewed impetus for continued compliance and progress in bilateral arms reductions under the START II and III initiatives. The successful US-Russian joint engagement in peacekeeping in Bosnia provides a foundation for building future military ties. An improved atmosphere in US-Russian security relations would assure that the two countries could continue to work together to contain regional conflicts and to cooperate at the operational level in peacekeeping and enforcement. United States and Russian cooperation will be critical for strengthening the resolve of the global community to limit proliferation of WMD and for combating international terrorism and crime. The United States and Russia could begin to cooperate in managing the critical weapons technologies of the future, possibly even including space and information technologies. The US-Russian security partnership should also include provision for assigning greater attention to critical non-military security challenges including the environment. In short, a deep institutionalized multi-dimensional security partnership between the two countries could help to establish the basis of trust and cooperation required so that the two countries can combine diplomatic influence and other resources to deal effectively with the most pressing security challenges likely to plague the international community into the next century.

## THE UNITED STATES, RUSSIA AND SECURITY BEYOND THE MILLENNIUM

The end of the East-West conflict might have been accompanied by some reevaluation both within the United States and Russia, and perhaps joint policy and academic assessment of global security challenges of the future and the fundamental assumptions for guiding relations among nations into the twenty-first century. Former Soviet leader and Nobel Peace Prize recipient Mikhail Gorbachev frequently speaks of unconventional prescriptions for governing international behavior. For example, Gorbachev has argued that "global human values" should take precedence over "national interests" in guiding contemporary foreign policy makers or that leaders of nations should approach conflict situations placing "respect for the sanctity of human life" as a first priority.[33] While such assertions would seem unrealistic, or even ridiculous, to many political leaders, seasoned foreign policy advisors and international relations specialists, what are the consequences of continuing to function in accordance with the maxims of the past?

The realist tradition, so dominant in thinking concerning international politics in the West, and influential in contemporary Russian foreign policy circles, is predicated upon negative assumptions of insecurity, fear and dogged pursuit of self-interest, control and power.[34] Realism provides a world vision of zero-sum competition and constant threat. The central concept of power is defined in overwhelmingly negative terms throughout the literature: "coercion," "compelling actors to do what they otherwise would not do..." The realist literature stresses the separation and clashes of interests among actors while minimizing or discounting the interconnection and common interests among humanity. The focus of the realist paradigm on the nation-state as the primary unit of analysis seems outmoded in a world community of burgeoning security and economic interdependence.

Several questions might be considered as humanity approaches the next century with respect to the appropriateness of the assumptions of the realist tradition for contemporary international conditions: Do such negative world views on the part of policy makers and those formulating thinking about international relations limit human potential? Will it not be necessary to cultivate manifestations of the more positive side of human nature and potential in relations among nations if in fact humankind is to overcome the pressing security challenges of the coming century? Should there be so much pessimism regarding the potential for building trust and cooperation in the international environment? Is it correct to assume that traditional realist prescriptions for peace such as deterrence and maintenance of equilibrium will continue to prevent calamities in this increasingly complex and militarized world system?

In the interconnected twenty-first century global community, in which the fates of all nations are linked more so than ever in human history, nations may no longer be able to approach the world stage thinking solely in terms of serving "national interests." "National security interests" are increasingly tied to "global security interests." Furthermore, the traditional focus on the military aspects of security in the twentieth century will not be adequate in a global community in which human life is increasingly threatened by transnational non-military challenges—the environment, migration, poverty, crime and other problems.

Exclusive reliance on military force, or the threat of military force, will not be sufficient for managing the security environment of the next century. While situations will continue to emerge that may ultimately necessitate a military response, policy makers must appreciate the limits of the application of military force as a means of achieving ends in a world community composed of greater numbers of nations possessing tools of mass destruction. The business of statecraft will demand greater sophistication, insight and skill in negotiation and diplomacy derived from a deep understanding of the history, culture, society, interests and perhaps even psychological profiles of individual leaders of other nations.

The influence of the United States, Russia and other major powers will be critical for shaping the standards of conduct for global politics into the twenty-first century. The realities of the next century suggest the necessity for concerted multilateral action among nations holding the preservation of global security as a priority. The United States and Russia cannot afford to be reluctant parties to limiting the proliferation of weapons of mass destruction. The two countries should be at the forefront of initiatives to address global environmental ills and recognize the vital importance of devoting attention and resources toward lessening the physical and material deprivation of so many citizens of this interconnected global society.

The United States, Russia and other nations of the international community could seize upon the opportunity created by the end of the Cold War to forge a more cooperative global order. The failure to craft strategies consistent with the realities of the emerging security environment suggests that the technological achievements of humanity may usher in a twenty-first century of yet unparalleled destruction and human suffering.

The author would like to thank Igor A. Zevelev and Deborah Anne Palmieri for their valuable comments on this article.

## NOTES

1.   Samuel P. Huntington, "The Clash of Civilizations?" *Foreign Affairs* (May-June 1993).

2.   John Mearsheimer, "Why We Will Soon Miss the Cold War," *The Atlantic Monthly*, Vol. 266, No. 2 (August 1990).

3.   Robert D. Kaplan, "Anarchy," *The Atlantic Monthly* (February 1994).

4.   Francis Fukuyama, "Against the New Pessimism," *Commentary*, Vol. 97, No. 2 (February 1994), p. 25.

5.   For one of the most interesting discussions concerning this issue see James Kurth's analysis of the "clash" between Western civilization and the "grand alliance" composed of multicultural and feminist movements in the United States. See James Kurth, "The Real Clash," *The National Interest*, No. 37 (Fall 1994).

6.   Strobe Talbott, "Russia Has Nothing to Fear," *The New York Times* (18 February 1997).

7.   Testimony by Secretary of State Madeleine K. Albright before the Senate Foreign Relations Committee on NATO Enlargement, *United States Information Agency* (7 October 1997) and "The East: Senate Concerned About Consequences of NATO Expansion," *RFE/RL* (8 October 1997). Similarly, Dr. Henry Kissinger, arguing for NATO enlargement and reflecting on the potential threat posed by Russia, made the following statement in the *Washington Post*: "It is not wise to defer obtaining fire insurance until the house is actually on fire." See Henry A. Kissinger, "Expand NATO Now," *The Washington Post* (19 December 1994) and Henry A. Kissinger, "Be Realistic About Russia," *The Washington Post* (25 January 1994).

8.   Interview with Senate Majority Leader Trent Lott (R-Miss), *Meet the Press* (22 March 1998).

9.   See Bejamin Lambeth, "Russia's Wounded Military," *Foreign Affairs*, Vol. 74, No. 2 (March-April 1995); Sergei A. Rogov, "The Future of Military Reform in Russia," unpublished paper provided to the author (1995); and Pavel Felgenhauer, "Army Moral at a New Low," *Moscow Times* (12 March 1998).

10.  For discussion of the struggle between the executive branch of Russia's government and ultra-nationalist, communist and anti-Western forces in the development of contemporary foreign policy see Igor A. Zevelev and Sharyl Cross "Moscow and the Yugoslav Secession Crisis," in Constantine P. Danopoulos and

Kostas G. Messas, eds., *Crisis in the Balkans: Views from the Participants* (Boulder: Westview Press, 1997), pp. 265-270.

11. *A National Security Strategy of Engagement and Enlargement* (Washington DC: US Government Printing Office, 1994).

12. For discussion of arguments in support of NATO enlargement see Strobe Talbott, "Why NATO Should Grow," *The New York Review* (10 August 1995) and Ronald D. Asmus, Richard L. Kugler and F. Stephen Larrabee, "Building a New NATO," *Foreign Affairs* (September-October 1993).

13. George F. Kennan, "NATO, A Fateful Error," *The New York Times* (5 February 1997).

14. For example, see "Former Policy Makers Voice Concern Over NATO Expansion," Washington DC (26 June 1997), *Washingtonian Magazine* (August 1997); "NATO: Albright Meets Congressional Skepticism on Expansion," *RFE/RL* (6 March 1997); and *The New York Times* staff editorial supporting the assertion that "It remains hard to see how the expansion of a cold-war military alliance will help consolidate democracy and free markets in Russia, which should be the primary concern of Europe and America..." in "NATO Expansion, Ready or Not," *The New York Times* (15 May 1997).

15. For further discussion of views within Russia on NATO enlargement see Sharyl Cross, "The Question of NATO Expansion: Searching for the Optimal Solution," *Mediterranean Quarterly*, Vol. 7, No. 1 (Winter 1996).

16. Yuli M. Vorontsov, "One Thing All Russians Agree On," *The Washington Post* (10 March 1998).

17. Asmus, Kugler and Larrabee, "Building a New NATO," p. 37.

18. "Rodionov to NATO: Don't Bait a Wounded Bear," *Moscow News*, No. 51 (26-31 December 1996).

19. Ibid. and Mikhail Pogorely, "Russia's Defense Minister Presents a Tough but Principled Position to NATO," *Krasnaya zvezda* (20 December 1996).

20. "Moscow Held Nuke Military Exercises," *Associated Press* (8 July 1997) and "Russian Nuclear Forces Used in Test Exercise," *The Record* (9 July 1997).

21. See "NATO Pact Clouds Fate of Arms Cuts, A Yeltsin Aide Says," *The New York Times* (16 May 1997).

22. See "Russia-China Theme: Contain the West," *The New York Times* (24 April 1997); "Moscow and Beijing Want to Live as Friends," *Izvestia* (24 April 1997); and "West Frowns on Russia-China Rapprochement," *Nezavisimaya gazeta* (26 April 1997).

23. Zbigniew Brzezinski, "NATO: Expand or Die?" *The New York Times* (28 December 1994); Zbigniew Brzezinski, "A Plan for Europe," *Foreign Affairs* (January-February 1995); and Keynote Address to the Political Committee, North Atlantic Assembly Political Committee, Washington DC (15 November 1994)

published in *North Atlantic Assembly 1994 Political Committee Report*, Brussels (November 1994), pp. 41-42.

24. A 1996 Congressional Budget Office report estimated the cost ranging from $21 billion to $125 billion depending on numbers of new states, repositioning of forces and so forth. See "The Costs of Expanding the NATO Alliance," *Congressional Budget Office* (March 1996). A study by the RAND Corporation was somewhat more conservative with a low estimate of $10 billion to a high of $110 billion. These reports suggest that the "most likely" cost will range from $42 billion to $60+ billion. See "Rancorous Debate Emerges on Cost of Enlarging NATO," *The New York Times* (13 October 1997).

25. See Brzezinksi, "NATO: Expand or Die?"

26. See *Founding Act on Mutual Relations, Cooperation and Security Between NATO and the Russian Federation*, issued in Paris (21 May 1997), *NATO Review*, No. 4 (July-August 1997), pp. 7-10.

27. "Former Enemies Speak of Peace," *The New York Times* (28 May 1997) and "Yeltsin, Clinton Receive Different Draft Accords?" *Komsomolskaya pravda* (16 May 1997).

28. See *Founding Act on Mutual Relations* and Ulrich Brandenburg, "NATO and Russia: A Natural Partnership," *NATO Review*, Vol. 45, No. 4 (July-August 1997), pp. 20-21.

29. Brandenburg, "NATO and Russia," pp. 20-21.

30. "Clinton, Yeltsin find common ground; Make Progress on NATO growth, START," *The Washington Times* (22 March 1997) and *Press Conference of President Clinton and President Yeltsin*, Helsinki (21 March 1997).

31. "Russia and USA Agree to Expand Bilateral Military Cooperation," *ITAR-TASS* (14 May 1997); *British Broadcasting Corporation* (15 May 1997); and "US, Russia to Increase Military Cooperation," *The Financial Post* (14 May 1997).

32. *Press Conference of President Clinton and President Yeltsin* and "Russia Vows to Push Pact Cutting Arms," *The New York Times* (12 March 1998).

33. Mikhail S. Gorbachev, participant in panel entitled "Challenges to Democracy, State of the World Forum," San Francisco, California (6 October 1996) *The CSPAN Archives at Purdue University* (1997) and Mikhail Gorbachev, Interview with Brian Lamb, *CSPAN* (24 November 1996).

34. For some of the most significant and more recent and classical writings of the realist tradition see Kenneth N. Waltz, *Theory of International Politics* (Menlo Park: Addison Wesley, 1979); Hans J. Morgenthau, *Politics Among Nations, The Struggle for Power and Peace* (New York: Alfred A. Knopf, 1948); Henry A. Kissinger, *A World Restored* (Boston: Houghton Mifflin, 1957); Thomas Hobbes, *Leviathan* (New York: Washington Square Press, 1964); and Niccolo Machiavelli, *The Prince and the Discourses* (New York: Random

House, 1940). Andrei Tsygankov explains that Russia's realists accept many of the propositions of the Western realists: "Security results from balancing [power] rather than international cooperation; it is based on a state's individual strength rather than collective efforts; and its major goals are the maintenance of individual strength rather than collective efforts..." Consistent with the philosophical orientation of Gorbachev's *New Thinking*, and in contrast to the realist school, the "international institutionalist" school assigned first priority to international cooperation. Tsygankov argues that international institutionalism remained the dominant school of thought for a period of five to six years following the introduction of Gorbachev's *New Thinking*. However, he argues that the failure to realize the international institutionalist's objective of building a partnership with the West, combined with the inability of this school to offer a strategy for dealing with military conflicts on Russia's periphery, the war in Chechnya, NATO expansion and other issues, resulted in a resurgent influence of realism in Russia's intellectual and policy communities. At the same time, Tsygankov does not completely discount the international institutionalist school in Russia. He concludes: "Increasingly Russian politicians are coming to accept that, in today's interdependent world, cooperation is a prima facie of international politics...If global trends toward peace and cooperation prevail, it is possible that the limitations of the realist balance of power thinking will be acknowledged and that the ongoing foreign policy debates will produce a better elaborated version of Gorbachev's *New Thinking* for Russian foreign policy to take." See Andrei P. Tsygankov, "From International Institutionalism to Revolutionary Expansionism: The Foreign Policy Discourse of Contemporary Russia," *Mershon International Studies Review*, Vol. 41 (November 1997).

# 3

# The Politics of US-Russian Military Cooperation in the Post-Cold War Era

*Constantine P. Danopoulos, Anna S. Bukharova,*
*Vagan M. Gevorgian and Sergei A. Baburkin*

The end of the Cold War and the geopolitical changes that followed the dissolution of the Warsaw Pact and the Soviet Union, as well as the democratic processes in Russia, created new conditions and a seemingly more cooperative environment for the development of US-Russian relations. A sense of euphoria was created by those changes, and optimistic expectations about the beginning of a new era in East-West relations prevailed in both countries. A host of conferences and seminars, involving civilian and military participants, dealt with issues of cooperation between yesteryear's mortal enemies. For purposes of clarity, cooperation occurs "when the policies followed by one government are regarded by its partners as facilitating realization of their own objectives, as the result of a process of policy coordination."[1]

Ironically, though not surprisingly, one of the areas that received significant attention was military cooperation. Uniformed and civilian security officials from both sides began to meet regularly and discussed military-related issues from reducing nuclear weapons to visiting each other's hitherto closed military installations and facilities. There was open discussion of inviting Russia to join the ranks of an expanded NATO.

However, the initial euphoria soon gave way to a certain degree of skepticism. The Bosnian quagmire, and particularly the bombing of Sarajevo's market in August 1995, opened a gulf between Washington and Moscow. Talk of returning to the Cold War reverberated through both capitals. The recent and on-going flare-up involving the issue of United Nations' weapons-inspection in Iraq furnished additional evidence of the rift between the United States and Russia. Did the two sides miss a golden opportunity or were the initial expectations of harmony in US-Russian relations unrealistic? This chapter analyzes the evolution of military-to-military cooperation between the United States and Russia, and focuses on assessing the repercussions of two regional conflict flashpoints for US-Russian bilateral cooperation.[2]

## THE GENESIS AND EVOLUTION OF THE POST-COLD WAR BILATERAL MILITARY RELATIONSHIP

The advocates and formulators of cooperation between Washington and Moscow were influenced by the positive climate created by the policies of *perestroika* and *glasnost* set in motion in the mid-1980s by former Soviet leader Mikhail Gorbachev. They sought to apply the perception of the relationship between the United States and the Soviet Union to that of the United States and Russia, and it was this new type of relationship that was labeled "strategic partnership." The strategic competition between the United States and the Soviet Union during the long period after World War II would be replaced by strategic cooperation between the two countries. That formula for cooperation was accepted at the Vancouver Summit by Presidents Bill Clinton and Boris Yeltsin in April 1993. The two leaders agreed to broaden and deepen the US-Russian strategic relationship and declared "their firm commitment to a dynamic and effective US-Russian partnership that strengthens international stability."[3]

A central component of the US-Russian post-Cold War strategic partnership was military cooperation, coupled with broader cooperation in the spheres of security and defense. The military establishments in both countries, fulfilling the directives of their political leadership, began to formulate specific plans for US-Russian military cooperation. The US Department of Defense (DOD) considered the post-Soviet situation to be favorable for changes in the relationship between the United States and Russia. Defense Secretary Les Aspin spoke for the Clinton

Administration when he stated that "this partnership will stress areas of common interests with the same vigor with which they previously emphasized their differences."[4]

DOD's formula for military cooperation with Moscow aimed to support the reform process in Russia. The emphasis was placed upon contributing to reforming Russia's armed forces by instilling democratic values, demonstrating that in a market economy adequate levels of military preparedness could be maintained, promoting the reduction of nuclear and conventional forces and developing cooperation in resolving regional crises. In the minds of DOD policy makers, accomplishing these goals would contribute to meeting US security interests. To realize these goals, DOD sought to initiate and maintain regular contacts and dialogue at the highest levels of leadership, and to undertake joint practical actions such as military exercises.

US military leaders were under no illusions that these tasks could be accomplished simply or speedily. They admitted that building a new relationship would be a difficult and lengthy undertaking. They also believed that the main obstacles for this task were the psychological remnants of the Cold War. Secretary Aspin summed up the problems and prospects by saying:

> It is clear ... that this transition from the hostility of the Cold War will be neither instantaneous nor easy. It will be a defining challenge for the decade ahead. Views and prejudices, habits and procedures developed over the past decades pose major obstacles to these new relationships. A steady, continued engagement is called for in which each party seeks to clarify to the other its fundamental national security interests — one that is not disheartened by inevitable setbacks.[5]

The official approach of the Russian Ministry of Defense was not altogether different from Washington's. It, too, emphasized support for the development of military cooperation with the United States. Public statements by Russian military leaders, especially Defense Minister General Pavel Grachev, presented the strategic partnership with the United States in the military sphere as the means for strengthening the security of Russia and its allies. In September 1993, he spoke, for example, about the strategic partnership as a relationship that had already been achieved.[6]

Supporters of US-Russian military cooperation among the Russian military pointed out that "radical changes in the system of international relations raise in a new manner the problems of interaction between

Russia and the United States in the cause of safeguarding their national security and strengthening international security in general."[7] At the same time, they understood from the very beginning that changes in Russia's political landscape and in the general geopolitical order would not lead automatically to the formation of a wide and fruitful partnership between the two countries in the sphere of security. Echoing Aspin's remarks, Major General Viktor Mironov affirmed that "by itself, the removal of causes that provoked conflicts and acute crises between the former USSR and the United States does not mean the automatic establishment of a wide zone of constructive interaction and cooperation in the sphere of international security."[8]

Trying to identify coinciding interests and the parameters of the post-Cold War security relationship, Russian military officers emphasized such issues as proliferation of weapons of mass destruction — primarily nuclear weapons. They stressed that the effective enforcement of nonproliferation could be assured only under conditions of close cooperation between the United States and Russia. The same Russian officials also considered joint efforts for peaceful settlement of territorial and ethnic conflicts as very important aspects of the new US-Russian cooperation. Major General Mironov expressed optimism concerning future military-to-military ties when he said that "the sphere of US-Russian cooperative interests now has a tendency toward expansion."[9]

The post-Cold War US-Russian military-to-military relationship was founded on contacts between the United States and Soviet military that began in the 1980s, particularly after 1988. By 1993, US-Russian interaction had reached new levels that involved the establishment of a new organizational structure for the military relationship between the two countries and the widening of the range of joint actions. The number of mutual contacts also increased. An important initial step in the development of mutual cooperation was the Memorandum of Understanding and Cooperation on Defense and Military Relations, signed during Defense Minister Grachev's visit to Washington in September 1993. This document affirmed the readiness of both sides to cooperate militarily and established the framework for future dialogue. The memorandum inaugurated an annual exchange of visits and the establishment of six bilateral working groups composed of military and civilian specialists from Russia and the United States. The program of exchanges involved the Joint Chiefs of Staff, the Russian General Staff, and other military officials. Special emphasis was placed on peacekeeping as an area of joint action. The memorandum promoted plans for joint education and exercises of peacekeeping forces.[10]

In this September 1993 agreement, Aspin and Grachev established a Bilateral Working Group to facilitate "new areas of cooperation" with the purpose of "broadening and deepening" relations between the two erstwhile enemies. The Group reached an agreement in 1995 defining 19 types of military-to-military contacts, including five senior-level visits, and a host of sports and cultural exchange activities.

Perhaps the most visible manifestations of cooperation to come out of the 1993 Vancouver meeting was the initiation of joint training in peacekeeping. Two joint US-Russian ground force training exercises, "Peacekeeper 94" and "Peacekeeper 95," were held following the meeting. The first took place in Totskoye, Russia, in September 1994, and the second at Fort Riley, Kansas, between 23 October to 2 November 1995. "Peacekeeper 95," marking the first instance that Russian troops trained on US soil, involved participation of the 1st Infantry Division at Fort Riley with the Russian 27th Guards Motorized Rifle Division in training exercises to prepare for peacekeeping tasks.

The agreements signed between the United States and Russia bore fruit in establishing the foundation for the initiation of routine military-to-military contacts. For example, in September 1995, a US Long Range Surveillance Detachment, 25th Infantry Light Division, was deployed to the Russian Far East Military District to train on Russian soil with a Russian Army Airborne battalion. Servicemen from both countries participated in parachute packing, an air assault, weapons training classes, and company-level field exercises. Beginning in 1994, the United States and Russia stepped up the numbers of joint exercises at sea expanding the theater of joint naval operations. For example, "Cooperation from the Sea 94, 95 and 96" established a basis for routine exercises to improve interoperability between US and Russian sailors and marines in carrying out humanitarian and disaster relief missions, and to build measures of trust and confidence.[11]

American and Russian forces have also participated in combined multinational exercises under the auspices of the NATO Partnership for Peace Program ("BALTOPS" and "Cooperative Venture 94") focusing on increasing operational cooperation capability including enhancing communication and command in humanitarian, peacekeeping and rescue operations. For example, "BALTOPS 95, 96 and 97" involved the participation of naval and air forces of the United States, Russia, and several NATO and non-NATO European nations. In conjunction with the "BALTOPS 95" exercises, US ships visited ports at Baltiysk and St. Petersburg, Russia.

Joint search and rescue exercises have also been held between the American, Russian and Canadian air forces. The first such "SAREX" exercise took place in April 1993 followed by subsequent exercises in Alaska "SAREX 94" and Alberta Canada "SAREX 95." In July 1995, Russian jet fighters visited military bases in Alaska to demonstrate operational capabilities and to become acquainted with American facilities. There have been a number of air force "Sister Base" exchanges over the past few years. From the Russian side, units stationed in Ryazan, Lipetsk, and Tver Bases, and affiliates of the Gagarin Higher Air Force College have participated in such exchanges with their counterparts in the United States.

The ceremonial component of US-Russian military-to-military exchanges forms a vital element in constructing the post-Cold War relationship. For example, Russian and American naval ships participated in the 50th Anniversary Commemoration of the end of the Second World War held in Hawaii in 1995, an important symbolic gesture emphasizing shared cooperation against a common threat in the past and the desire to work toward the betterment of contemporary US-Russian military-to-military relations.

Military officers of both countries have displayed enthusiasm and interest in such cooperation. For example, a Russian naval officer participating in "Cooperation from the Sea 96" held in Vladivostok, stated: "It is good to work together like this...Not only for our two countries, but for our neighbors as well. Our teamwork sends a positive message around the world...And it is something that we must continue to do to maintain stability throughout the region."[12] US Marine Cpl. Dale R. Strunks, a participant on the US side, made this observation: "I really didn't know what to expect, but I was impressed. It was the opportunity of a lifetime to see Russian Marines in their daily routine on their own turf."[13] Russian Colonel Nicolas Malyshev, a participant in "Peacekeeper 95," offered the following comment: "We never hated the American people... We see them with our own eyes, and we see that they are friendly. We don't hate them. It was politics."[14]

The initiation of US-Russian post-Cold War military-to-military contact had three significant implications. First, the establishment of this direct military link signaled a shift from confrontation to cooperation based on mutual understanding of the importance of peacekeeping and other joint US-Russian military-to-military cooperation to the preservation of international security. Second, this provided the opportunity for both countries to exchange technical as well as conceptual knowledge on matters relating to war and peace. Without question, the two countries have accumulated valuable experience in the conduct of joint military operations as a result of such exchanges. Third, this contact contributed to fostering a more positive atmosphere enabling both countries to begin to put aside the feelings of fear, animosity and mistrust that had characterized their relationship during the Cold War.[15]

Recently, the two sides renewed their commitment to promoting military-to-military cooperation. In a meeting held in May 1997, Defense Secretary William Cohen and his Russian counterpart, General Igor Rodionov, signed the Joint Declaration on Future Cooperation, pledging commitment to continuing to develop cooperation in a number of military-related areas and US-Russian military-to-military activities. The agreement made provisions for additional military exchanges, regular leadership contact, and joint exercises and events involving more than 100 activities.[16] Areas of focus for development of future US-Russian military-to-military cooperation include:

- Analysis of military doctrines and programs;
- Exploring prospects for cooperation on reform of Russia's armed forces;
- Promotion of high level military/defense and senior officer exchanges;
- Exchanges of views concerning issues of international security;
- Strengthening efforts in arms control, disarmament, non-proliferation of weapons of mass destruction;
- Exploring means for deepening military-to-military ties;
- Examining means for enhancing cooperation in peacekeeping;
- Port calls, unit exchanges and joint exercises;
- Military educational exchanges.[17]

In addition, Washington and Moscow began to seek cooperation in the less traditional military, but equally important, aspects of national security including combating terrorism, corruption and organized crime. The demise of the Soviet Union and the advent of democratization removed the authoritarian mechanisms associated with the Soviet state, weakening its successors' extractive, resource-mobilization, and conflict resolution capacities. As a result, mafia-like paramilitary gangs have surfaced in many parts of Russia and other Soviet successor states, threatening public and national security. The annual increase in contract killings reached 100 per cent between 1990 and 1994. In 1993 alone, 650 explosions occurred that took the lives of 116 people.[18] According to one report, more than 40 leading Russian bankers were killed during the period 1994-95. According to the Russian Ministry of Internal Affairs, there were approximately 5,700 groups of organized criminals operating in Russia in 1995.[19] Bureaucratic corruption is equally pervasive. For example, *The Washington Times* reported in 1995 that Russian officials routinely receive a "fee" of $100,000 to permit the establishment of new banks and 15 per cent of the total amount of transactions in order to issue oil and weapon export licenses.[20]

Internationally-connected crime syndicates are involved in weapons trading, drug-smuggling, prostitution, extortion and other forms of racketeering. Their activities are not confined to the former Soviet Union, but include the US and Europe as well as other parts of the world. For instance, the US Federal Bureau of Investigations (FBI) has identified as many as 220 "Eurasian," mainly Russian-speaking, criminals operating in many parts of the US. In 1995 alone, the FBI investigated 35 cases connected with Russian criminal structures in the 14 different states, including the notorious case involving Vyacheslav Ivankov (Yaponchik).[21] Alarmed by these developments, FBI Director Louis Freeh stated in 1994 that "the whole nature, scope, and dimensions of transnational crime have changed so rapidly that we really have a new menu before us in terms of what is required and how we must react." An effective response to this menace, in Freeh's mind, would require "all of the former Cold War adversaries to consider reprogramming personnel and technologies to the fight of criminals and terrorists. Without new enhanced levels of international law enforcement cooperation, each country will pay a terrible price if it tries to fight crime largely by itself."[22]

Freeh's assessments corresponded with Moscow's thinking on these issues. The Russian Ministry of Internal Affairs, whose own military units are responsible for internal security, has sought cooperation with the FBI and other American law enforcement agencies to combat corruption, racketeering, and other terrorist activities. In fact, some cooperation efforts in these areas began even before Freeh's statement. In February 1993, Jim Moody, chief of the Organized Crime Section of the FBI, and

First Deputy Interior Minister Yegorov concluded a crime-fighting cooperation agreement. This agreement featured several areas for expanding cooperation including sharing intelligence information on criminal groups; assisting Russia in creating a modern anti-organized crime criminal code and other relevant legislation; identifying Russian criminals and other fugitives entering the US; and establishing a cooperation unit to combat organized crime.[23] Ivankov's arrest by the FBI on racketeering charges was the result of combined efforts by Russian and American law enforcement agencies. Russian-American cooperation in the fight against organized crime was strengthened with the establishment of a small FBI office in Moscow and the signing of a 1996 memorandum. In this agreement, the two countries pledge bilateral cooperation and action in crisis situations caused by terrorist acts on civilians, including airline passengers.

## THE RELATIONSHIP IS TESTED:   BOSNIA AND IRAQ

Although the United States and Russia made impressive strides toward initiating military cooperation in only a few short years, the Washington-Moscow post-Cold War strategic relationship has been tested since its inception. Two regional flashpoints, the war in Bosnia, and the issues of weapons inspections in Iraq, generated sharp differences.

### *Bosnia*

The conflict in Bosnia in August and September 1995 strained the US-Russian post-Cold War relationship. At first glance, the situation in Bosnia seemed to provide possibilities for joint strategic action between Washington and Moscow; it even offered the hope of diplomatic and military cooperation.

Over a considerable period of time, the United States and Russia had declared a readiness to act in concert to resolve the Bosnian crisis. They worked together within the framework of the Contact Group and the UN Security Council. Moscow supported joint decisions on Bosnia aimed toward containing and resolving the conflict. Even though some friction appeared from time to time, cooperation continued up to the eve of the NATO bombardment in Bosnia in August 1995. The two countries had generally acted in concert and showed a willingness to coordinate future activities. On 25 August, less than a week before NATO's bombing began in Bosnia, a representative from the Russian Foreign Ministry stated a belief in Washington's commitment to work with Russia in order to achieve a solution in Bosnia. As proof, he pointed to the sharing of information between the two governments.[24]

However, the 28 August 1995 shelling of Sarajevo's marketplace by Bosnian Serbs served as a provocation for retaliation, and the situation changed radically. NATO retaliated with Operation Deliberate Force, bombing numerous Bosnian Serb targets. Moscow's reaction to NATO's bombardment was sharply negative and emotional. The former Russian Deputy Foreign Minister, F. Shelov-Kovediaiev, described the environment in Moscow as "an insane asylum."[25] Moscow's strong reaction was connected to Russia's historic and cultural ties with Serbia, Russia's resistance to US/NATO assertion of dominance, and the fact that the West had appeared to ignore Moscow's call that diplomacy, rather than military force, should serve as the preferred tool for conflict resolution. The Sarajevo incident served as a litmus test for the relationship between Russia and the United States, and it raised fears that a new edition of the Cold War was about to begin. Such a possibility was openly suggested by President Yeltsin, who threatened that NATO's expansion "could lead to a 'conflagration of war' across the continent."[26]

Developments in the Bosnian conflict affected the entire US-Russian relationship, but were most pronounced in the sphere of military cooperation. Russian leaders raised the possibility of reconsidering Moscow's participation in NATO's Partnership for Peace (PfP) program. They spoke about the possibility of creating a military-political alliance of the former Soviet republics. The Yeltsin government also declared its unwillingness to place Russian military forces in former Yugoslavia under NATO command.

Despite these public pronouncements, Russian military leaders were not inclined to break completely with the United States. Rather, they took some steps to maintain US-Russian military relations. Grachev urged William Perry to stop the NATO operation in Bosnia, warning that possible escalation could lead to the broadening of the conflict in the Balkans. In a telephone conversation, Grachev offered to meet Perry in former Yugoslavia to discuss the possibility of formulating plans for joint action. Other Russian political and military officials also expressed their willingness to create a Russian and NATO force in Bosnia under a joint NATO-Russian command.

Washington's reaction was quite different. It soon became clear that the Clinton Administration was trying to reach a decisive result in Bosnia by taking strong action. Russia was not perceived as a supporter of Washington's new approach at that stage of the conflict. It was not surprising then that the result of the contacts between Grachev and Perry was, as *Rossiskaya Gazeta* stated, "zero."[27] Although the political and military leadership in Washington did not want to miss the opening in Bosnia, it also wished to avoid confrontation with Russia.

The opportunity came when a set of international and domestic factors coalesced, forcing the Clinton Administration to take an active role in the Bosnian conflict. The Dayton Accords, hammered out under principle American negotiator, Richard Holbrooke, required the stationing on the ground of a US-dominated NATO force. In order to strengthen support for its Bosnian policy, the Clinton Administration decided to include Russia in the peace-enforcement operation.[28]

Despite the fact that Moscow's role in the Dayton negotiation was marginal and "the Russian delegation was constantly knocking on the American door to get necessary information and documents,"[29] the Yeltsin Administration ultimately agreed to send a brigade to help enforce the Dayton Accords. General Grachev and Defense Secretary Perry worked out an agreement that placed Russian troops under the command of a Russian general who holds the title of deputy to the American commander of the NATO forces in Bosnia. Ironically, even though Moscow opposes NATO expansion, Russian troops would serve in the NATO-led peacekeeping force in Bosnia, IFOR (International Implementation Force). In the view of some Russian political analysts, Moscow entrapped itself: on the one hand, Russia objects to NATO's eastern expansion; on the other, the Russian military contingent participates in a NATO-organized operation.[30]

From an operational military perspective, it is important to note that the US-Russian joint engagement in Bosnia is viewed as a success. Officers who served in IFOR indicate that Russian and American peacekeepers managed to establish a positive working relationship. For example, Colonel-General G. Shpak, commander of Russia's Airborne troops, while having some concerns regarding the terms under which Russian troops would participate in former Yugoslavia, praised the tactical aspects of US-Russian peacekeeping cooperation.[31] US Army Colonel Michael W. Alvis, among the first combat commanders into Bosnia, and a Senior Fellow at the US Institute of Peace, offered the following observation concerning US military cooperation with Russian forces in Bosnia:

> Although the Russian Brigade was located in the US-led NATO sector, it was not subordinate to the local American commander there, as would normally be the case in traditional military operations. In this instance, the brigade was formally subordinate to the Russian general in Brussels. Despite this challenge, operations went remarkably well, on the ground. I attribute this success to a series of initiatives since the Cold War to foster cooperation between the two former enemies, most importantly the Partnership for Peace program, that was executed to prepare both military superpowers for exactly this type of situation. In fact, relations were so good, that the units even engaged in joint patrolling, a complex task that required careful coordination, even in traditional command and control relationships. The first joint patrol consisted of two Russian reconnaissance vehicles and 10 Russian soldiers combined with two Bradley fighting vehicles and 17 US soldiers and airmen plus a support vehicle. Because the mission was conducted in the Russian sector, the Russians were in charge. The mission went remarkably well and additional patrols were conducted, using the same units. Each patrol improved on the previous one as habitual relationships were optimized and face-to-face coordination encouraged.[32]

Thus, despite political tensions, clearly this did not affect the capacity of US and Russian military forces to perform quite well.

### *Iraq*

The crisis over weapons-inspections in Iraq is a second and ongoing issue that has tested the Washington-Moscow strategic relationship; and because it is connected to the volatile Middle East, it has the potential of inflicting more lasting damage in the relations between the two countries. The issue dates back to the 1991 Gulf War when the American-led coalition reversed Saddam Hussein's occupation of Kuwait and imposed a United Nations-supervised embargo on Iraq aimed at curtailing Baghdad's ability to rebuild its armed forces and acquire weapons of mass destruction. Faced with an increasingly deteriorating domestic situation, Soviet leader Mikhail Gorbachev begrudgingly blessed these restrictions despite the fact that Moscow enjoyed a close relationship with the Saddam Hussein's regime and the Soviet Union was Iraq's main weapons supplier.

The Iraqi strongman has repeatedly sought ways to challenge the UN restrictions, rebuild his military capabilities, and expand his authority over parts of his country declared as "no-fly zones" by the world body. The situation flared up in late 1997 when Saddam Hussein sought to restrict, and eventually expelled, the UN inspection team (UNSCOM). The Clinton Administration stated its intention to use military force to punish Saddam Hussein's violations of UN resolutions. As a result of a last-ditch diplomatic effort by Russian Foreign Minister Yevgeny Primakov, the use of force was temporarily averted. But the crisis was reignited a few weeks later when Saddam Hussein challenged the credentials of an American member of the inspection team.

Although Washington and Moscow share the view that the Iraqi regime must comply with UN resolutions, the crisis found the two capitals in disagreement concerning strategies for managing the problem. Washington held that if Saddam's challenges went unchecked, he could become a threat to his neighbors and eventually to world peace. The Clinton Administration was willing to discuss the possibility of eventually relaxing the oil embargo to allow Baghdad to purchase food and medical supplies. However, Washington's bottom line was firm: Saddam must allow UN inspectors "free and unfettered access to all sites" suspected of storing or producing weapons of mass destruction. To ensure compliance, Clinton was prepared to use force (and go it alone, if necessary) in the event that diplomatic efforts were unsuccessful.

In contrast, Moscow was equally emphatic in its position that diplomatic means should be used to solve the crisis. President Yeltsin declared on 17 February 1998 that "It is necessary to use all diplomatic possibilities. The use of force is the last and the most dangerous way and could lead to a world war."[33] Defense Minister General Igor Sergeyev echoed Yeltsin's remarks, telling his visiting American counterpart William Cohen that for "a military man, it is the worst thing to be late, but it's also bad to hurry too much while assessing the situation." Quoting Abraham Lincoln's statement that "force can conquer all, but its victory is short-lived," Sergeyev expressed doubts whether America's "uncompromising and tough stand over the situation in Iraq will help to strengthen stability in the world." Sergeyev also warned that the use of force may hamper "prospects for US relations in the military field."[34] In a rare display of unity, the government's position is supported by Russia's entire political spectrum. For example, ultra-nationalist leader Vladimir Zhirinovsky, no friend of Yeltsin's, implored the Russian president to use his "moral weight to prevent a war. Only you can stop it. Otherwise it will start."[35]

The crisis over Iraq may also have put some strain on crime and corruption fighting cooperation efforts between the United States and Russia. According to the 12 February 1998 edition of *The Washington Post*, UNSCOM inspectors recently discovered evidence of a 1995 agreement in which Moscow agreed to sell Baghdad "sophisticated equipment that could be used to develop biological weapons." The same source reported that "US intelligence agencies had privately warned UN officials that Russian intelligence operatives were spying on the United Nations Special Commission on Iraq and its personnel in New York and overseas." Moreover, the source indicated that "the Russian spy agency may have passed some of the information directly to Iraq," and added that "several US officials confirmed that the FBI was aware of the Russian intelligence operation." The Russian government spokesman categorically denied these reports as "crude invention," adding: "Russia has never made any deals with Iraq that would violate international sanctions."[36] US officials have adopted a "wait and see attitude," but regardless, whatever turn the story takes, it is likely to have some negative effect on the level of trust between American and Russian law enforcement agencies, at least temporarily.

## THE UNITED STATES AND RUSSIA AFTER THE COLD WAR: DISCORD OR COOPERATION?

Was the post-Cold War US-Russian military strategic partnership an unholy alliance doomed to fail as the pessimists from both sides believed all along? The answer to this question lies in the meaning of the concept of cooperation.

In his seminal work *After Hegemony: Cooperation and Discord in the World Political Economy*, Robert Keohane makes a clear distinction between harmony, discord and cooperation. He defines harmony as "a situation in which actors' policies (pursued in their own self-interests without regard for others) automatically facilitate the attainment of others' objectives." By his own admission, harmony can exist only in an "idealized, unreal world, where no one's actions damage anyone else."[37]

In contrast, cooperation "occurs when actors adjust their behavior to the actual or anticipated preferences of others, through a process of policy coordination." If actors refuse "to adjust their policies to each others' objectives," the result is discord. Keohane defines discord as "a situation in which governments regard each others' policies as hindering the attainment of their goals, and hold each other responsible for these constraints." Conflict ensues when one actor attempts but fails to convince the other to change its policies. Unlike in harmony, where there is no conflict, cooperation "does not imply an absence of conflict. On the contrary, it is typically mixed with conflict and reflects partially successful efforts to overcome conflict, real or potential." Keohane emphasized that "where harmony reigns, cooperation is unnecessary," and concludes that "without the specter of conflict, there is no need to cooperate."[38]

Keohane's theory both exemplifies and explains the nature and trajectory of post-Cold War US-Russian relations. The antagonism, discord, and conflict that dominated the Cold War period gave way to a relationship which displays the characteristics of cooperation. The end of the Cold War, along with the dissolution of the Soviet Union and the democratization process that got under way in Russia, did not and could not bring about a complete identity on the cultural orientation and strategic and national interests of the United States and Russia. At the same time, despite the fact that Washington and Moscow disagreed on a number of issues, they managed to find ways to coordinate and adjust their policies in order to avoid adverse consequences for each other. Quoting Charles Lindbloom, Keohane refers to this type of behavior as "adaptive coordination" and credits it for leading to cooperation.

Analysis of the trends in US-Russian relations over the past few years leads to the conclusion that the difficulties over Bosnia and Iraq were not coincidental. In fact, they were the next logical step in the development of US-Russian relations. The disagreements over these issues are part of the uncertainties in dealing with the geopolitical changes following the dissolution of the Soviet Union. The United States was left to adjust to its role as the sole remaining superpower in the world community. Russia, for its part, had to adjust to its reduced economic and military potential and to the new geopolitical situation.

For the opponents of US-Russian cooperation, the strain in relations between the two countries over the use of force in Bosnia was a gift from heaven. In the United States, it supported the arguments of those who continued to view Russia with suspicion. Communists and ultranationalists in Russia who opposed cooperation with the United States used this instance to support their claim that the unchecked pursuit of American interests would weaken Russia and guarantee US world dominance.

The Yeltsin government may have tried to use the situation in Bosnia to reinforce its image as an actor that still played an important role on the international stage. Moscow policy makers operated under the impression that Russia's influence with the Serbs could not be overlooked by Western diplomats and that this would give the Russian Federation leverage in its dealings with the United States and the NATO allies. Benjamin Lambeth is correct in his assessment of the motives of the Russian military leadership when he notes that "the Russian high command has not sought to go head-to-head with the United States and NATO. Nor has it viewed Western military involvement in the Yugoslav tragedy as a threat to Russian security. Rather, it has mainly sought respect for Russia as a power with legitimate interests in the region."[39]

The use of military force in Bosnia was supported by the relationship between the United States and its allies in NATO. Domestic politics also forced the Clinton Administration's hand to do something about Bosnia. The side effect of this decision and the steps taken to implement it strained Washington's relationship with Russia. At the same time, the crisis showed that Russia was incapable of taking any substantive counter measures that would have blocked Western actions on Bosnia. The logic of events eventually forced Moscow to abandon its initial emotional attitude and to follow the lead of the United States. While the Bosnian conflict may have engendered a certain reluctance toward continued participation in joint military efforts with the United States, Russia's political leadership emerged from the situation still committed to work with the United States in matters of international security and military cooperation.

With regard to differences over the potentially explosive issue of UN weapons-inspection in Iraq, Moscow and Washington agree that Saddam Hussein must comply with relevant UN resolution. However, the two countries differ in their approach to the crisis as well as the usefulness of sanctions. The differences have both strategic and economic components. US relations in the Middle East have been and continue to remain strong. Russia's have experienced a significant decline in recent years, and the Moscow leadership is interested in reestablishing that relationship and improving its standing in the Middle East.

Until the Gulf War, Moscow was the main supplier of military hardware and credits to the Iraqi regime. The UN sanctions that followed the war have deprived Baghdad of funds to pay an $8 billion debt which the cash-strapped Russian economy badly needs. Moreover, Russian oil barons are eager to see the economic sanctions lifted so they can do business in Iraq. Lukoil has a 23 year contract with Baghdad to develop Iraqi oil fields, and is eager to get started once economic sanctions are removed. Gennady Seleznyov, the communist speaker of the Russian Duma, summed up Moscow's attitude saying that "Russia has an economic interest in restoring ties with Iraq."[40] Although the outcome of the crisis has yet to play out, and despite some bombastic public statements, the two sides appear determined not to allow their differences over Iraq to damage their long-term military cooperation.

How have Russian and American military organizations responded to efforts to forge and maintain a cooperative relationship in the post-Cold War era? Despite hard feelings on the part of certain elements, the suffering and demoralized Russian military view military cooperation with the US as a vehicle which would enable it to reform and modernize its structure, and professionalize, depoliticize and democratize its values.[41] The willingness to cooperate is demonstrated by the fact that while disapproving of US intention to use force against Iraq, the Russian military is unlikely to withdraw its support for the Strategic Arms Reduction II (START II) Treaty.[42] At the same time, while there is bound to be a bit of reticence about working with the former adversary, US military forces have generally been open to cooperation and building contacts with Russia's armed forces. The success of US and Russian troops working together in Bosnia coupled with the positive accounts concerning their post-Cold War military-to-military contact suggests that considerable promise exists for future cooperation on the part of the US and Russian armed forces.

In terms of the relationship between the two countries' law enforcement agencies, while the US side has provided valuable intelligence information to Russian law enforcement agencies, Washington has been reluctant to "intervene in the internal affairs of Russia."[43] Policy makers seem to feel that a strong presence could prove counter-productive. It would give ammunition to communists and ultranationalists making the claim that Yeltsin, serving the interests of the West, is enabling Russia's transformation into a banana republic.

The post-Cold War US-Russian strategic relationship has not brought about a state of complete harmony, but neither has it reverted to the antagonism and discord of the Cold War period, as the pessimists anticipated. Instead, relations between the two former mortal enemies in the last seven to eight years have been and continue to be characterized by a mixture of conflict and partially successful efforts to overcome conflict. Defense Secretary Cohen recently captured the essence of the strategic relationship when, in the presence of his Russian counterpart, he stated: "Obviously, there will always be differences that we will have in the future, but the strength of the relationship is paramount. Where we have differences, we will work out our differences, but essentially, we intend to forge a strong partnership with Russia."[44]

The fact that these former mortal enemies were able to initiate cooperation in military and internal security matters in the immediate aftermath of the Cold War is not insignificant. Only a few years ago, the thought of US and Russian forces engaging in joint exercises on American and Russian soil or successfully cooperating in a regional peacekeeping operation would have been unimaginable. Political officials in both countries might look to the successful military engagement in Bosnia as evidence of exactly what potential exists as a result of concerted action on the part of both countries.

Of course, many obstacles remain in the area of US-Russian military-to-military cooperation. Much will hinge upon the terms of NATO's enlargement and the future development of Russia's relationship with the Western security alliance. Despite Russia's current economic difficulties, any arrangements whereby Russia is dealt with as a second rank power risks reversing recent progress in US-Russian relations and resurrecting the barricades between East and West. Mutual respect will be critical in developing long-term US-Russian cooperation. As the Bosnian and Iraqi cases illustrate, the two countries will not always be in complete agreement in managing international security issues. However, it is also possible that the two countries could utilize their influence in various regions of the world, capitalizing on their respective strengths, to work toward resolution of problem areas within the international community. The institutionalization of US-Russian military-to-military ties will constitute a core element in the development of the overall US-Russian bilateral relationship of the twenty-first century. Though Russia's society is likely to undergo periodic setbacks and upheavals in the reform process, still, one would hope that the shared interests of both the United

States and Russia in preservation of world security will lead to continued positive momentum in the development of bilateral military-to-military cooperation into the twenty-first century.

---

Anna Bukharova wishes to state that the views expressed here are those of the author and her co-authors and do not necessarily reflect the position of the Russian government or the Ministry of Defense of the Russian Federation. Anna Bukharova also wishes to acknowledge the valuable contributions to her work in this article by Dr. Nikita A. Chaldimov, Professor and Maj. Gen. (ret.), Member of the Commission on Human Rights under the President of the Russian Federation and Dr. A. Alexsandrov, Professor, Military Sciences Academy.

## NOTES

1.   Robert O. Keohane, "Cooperation and International Regimes," in Marc A. Genest ed., *Conflict and Cooperation: Evolving Theories of International Relations* (Fort Worth: Harcourt, Brace College Publishers, 1996), pp. 199-210.

2.   This chapter incorporates portions of unpublished papers by Anna S. Bukharova, "US-Russian Military-Military Cooperation:  Prospects for the Future" and Vagan M. Gevorgian, "International Crime and Terrorism," prepared for the conference of contributors in this project held at the Institute of USA and Canada Studies of the Russian Academy of Sciences, Moscow, Russia (July 1997). Also, the chapter draws upon Sergei A. Baburkin's earlier article "The Bosnian Crisis and the Problem of US-Russian Military Cooperation," *Mediterranean Quarterly*, Vol. 7, No. 4 (Fall 1996).

3.   *Kommersant* (15 May 1997).

4.   Les Aspin, *Annual Report to the President and Congress*, Washington DC  (January 1994).

5.   Ibid.

6.   Public Affairs News Release, Office of the Assistant Secretary of Defense, Washington DC (30 September 1993), p. A1.

7.   Major General Victor Mironov, "Russia's National Security Military Doctrine and the Outlook for Russian-US Cooperation in the Modern World," *Comparative Strategy*, Vol. 13, No. 1 (January-March 1994), p. 51.

8.   Ibid.

9.   Ibid., p. 52.

10. Office of the Assistant Secretary of Defense, Public Affairs, "Memorandum of Understanding Signed Between US Department of Defense and the Russian Federation Ministry of Defense," Washington DC (8 September 1993).

11. *Asia-Pacific Defense Forum*, Special Supplement, Issues #2-4 (Spring 1996), pp. 15,17,19-21.

12. "East Meets West in Cooperation from the Sea" and "31st MEU Works with Russian Marines in Cooperation at Sea," *31st Marine Expeditionary Unit Public Affairs Announcement* (14 August 1996).

13. Ibid.

14. "In the Spirit of Cooperation: Russian-US Joint Military Training in Ft. Riley," *Collegian,* Kansas State University Publications (27 October 1995).

15. Peacekeeper 94, Report on United States and Russian Combined Peacekeeping Training, The Third Infantry Division (US) and the 27th Guard Motorized Rifle Division (RF), Totskoye Training Areas, Russia (2-10 September), pp. 3-9.

16. *Kommersant* (15 May 1997).

17. Ibid.

18. *Nezavisimaya gazeta* (16 November 1994).

19. *Rossiskaya gazeta* (4 June 1995).

20. *The Washington Times* (1 September 1995).

21. Ibid.

22. Linnea P. Raine and Frank J. Cilluffo, eds., *Global Organized Crime: The New Empire of Evil* (Washington DC: Center for Strategic and International Studies, 1994).

23. "Russian Organized Crime and American Business Responses," *Russian Commerce News/Russian American Chamber of Commerce* (Fall/Winter 1994), pp. 15-16.

24. "Moscow, Washington Cooperate on Balkan Settlement," *FBIS-SOV* (28 August 1995), p. 15.

25. *Literaturnaya gazeta* (13 September 1995).

26. Alexei K. Pushkov, "Russia and NATO: On the Watershed," *Mediterranean Quarterly*, Vol. 7, No. 2 (Spring 1996), p. 18.

27. *Rossiskaya gazeta* (13 September 1995).

28. Pushkov, "Russia and NATO," p. 20.

29. Ibid. p. 23.

30. *Nezavisimoye voennoye obozreniye* (7 November 1997).

31. *Nezavisimaya gazeta* (16 April 1997).

32. Statement provided by Colonel Michael W. Alvis to Igor A. Zevelev, US Institute of Peace (February 1998).

33. Gareth Jones, "Yeltsin Lauds Russian Diplomacy, Tough On Iraq," *Reuters* (17 February 1998).

34. Susanne M. Schafer, "Russian Official Rebukes US," Associated Press (12 February 1998).

35. Jones, "Yeltsin Lauds Russian Diplomacy."

36. *The Washington Post* (12 February 1998), p. 1.

37. Keohane, "Cooperation and International Regimes," pp. 200-203.

38. Ibid.

39. Benjamin Lambeth, "Russia's Wounded Military," *Foreign Affairs*, Vol. 74, No. 2 (March-April 1995), p. 94.

40. *The New York Times* (14 February 1998), p. 3.

41. See Constantine P. Danopoulos, "Conclusions on Post-Totalitarian Civil-Military Relations," in Constantine P. Danopoulos and Daniel Zirker, eds., *Civil-Military Relations in the Soviet and Yugoslav Successor States* (Boulder: Westview/Harper Collins, 1996), p. 257-268.

42. *The New York Times* (14 February 1998), p. 3.

43. See Seymour M. Hersh, "The Wild East," *The Atlantic Monthly* (June 1994), p. 84. For details on American and Russian intelligence see Mikhail A. Alexsev, *Without Warning: Threat Assessment, Intelligence and Global Struggle* (New York: St. Martin's Press, 1997).

44. Susanne M. Schafer, "Cohen Casts Doubts on Russia's Efforts," *The Associated Press* (12 February 1998).

# 4

# Information Technology: US/ Russian Perspectives and Potential for Military-Political Cooperation

*Timothy L. Thomas*

Advanced information technology (IT)[1] systems and weaponry have caused significant changes in the international security environment. The changes are monumental, and not all are positive. Non-state sponsored groups with access to advanced IT can present dangers nearly on a par with nations. A threat could originate from a drug cartel, warlord, or mafia group's attack on an IT such as a nuclear power plant, or from the chaos generated by a computer virus inserted into a country's defense (air defense, nuclear, and so forth) computer system prompted by a variety of agendas.

At the same time, situational awareness in nations with access to high technology is more complete than ever before. The ability to monitor conversations and movements is extraordinary and affects the character, speed and precision of diplomatic and military responses against all types of threats. Realizing the impact of rapid new developments in

This article is dedicated to the memory of Boris Grigorivich Shumeyev, a friend and former administrator of the Institute of USA and Canada Studies, who worked diligently to improve US-Russian cooperation.

information technology on the emerging twenty-first century security environment, security officials in both the United States and Russia are trying to monitor and coordinate defenses and active measures. In the end, this will require closer coordination between the United States and Russia to ensure that one side does not misinterpret an event and send the world to the brink of an information war (IW).[2]

Following reconsideration of military priorities and national security interests as a result of rapid technological advances, both the United States and Russia elevated the protection of information assets to a strategic level. They also recognized the compelling need to master the speed of change in IT and to monitor its spread to rogue nations. IT change is reflected in restructured defense budgets, infrastructure reorganizations, and the security policies of these nations. Policy must address not only high technology threats from other nations but also the ability of terrorists to affect national interests as national armies once did. Further, IT has upset traditional military considerations such as the employment of military art.

This chapter will discuss three IT related topics: Russian and US views of the impact of IT on military-political considerations; how both countries are managing IT concerns, to include civilian restructuring; and opportunities and challenges for US and Russian cooperation in IT. The discussion is important in that IT offers a threat similar to what Herman Kahn termed "spasm war" in *On Escalation*, an irrational, spasmodic response to an attack (whether nuclear or IT) on a power's C3I (command, control, communication and intelligence) before or during crisis.[3]

## THE IMPACT OF INFORMATION TECHNOLOGY ON MILITARY CONSIDERATIONS

### *Russian Views*

For Russia, the initial concern regarding IT was its impact on society, and on the strategy and tactics of the armed forces. Over the past three years, Russia has actively pursued a methodology for the use of IT as well to ensure military-political stability. The conditions (to a Russian, contradictions) that IT methodologies must address are the same as in the past: social, political, economic, territorial, religious, nationalist, and ethnic, among others. Security analysts recognize, however, that the form or manifestation of these conditions has changed, as each now relies heavily on IT. Thus, as Russia develops policy to protect its national interests, preserve its territorial integrity, maintain its national sovereignty, and protect its population, information security and IT sit at or near the top of its priorities. Real military power, for example, will not only be determined by the quantity of forces but by the qualitative parameters of the force, allowing for the implementation of IT to achieve interoperability in planning; to integrate technical systems that support command and control and logistics functions; and to successfully utilize indirect actions (economic sanctions, communications blockades, demonstrations of force, use of peacekeeping forces, and so forth) to supplement direct deployments and strategies.

The impact of IT (from a Russian viewpoint) on military-political considerations affecting national security takes many forms. First, information resources require effective state policies that monitor information security, especially since the use of IT may not involve physical damage or loss of life, making it more acceptable (no ecological fallout) than nuclear weapons.[4] Attempts to disrupt information exchanges or flows, the illegal use and collection of information, unsanctioned access to information resources, the manipulation of information, the illegal copying of data from information systems, or the unauthorized theft of information from data bases and banks are all threats that can disrupt economic or military relations between nations and require a serious response.[5]

Second, parity in nuclear forces now can only be achieved through parity in IT. Information warfare systems (including intelligence and information collection) have upset norms of parity based primarily on numbers and quality.[6] Intelligence, command and control, early warning, communications, electronic warfare, "special software engineering effects," and disinformation are issues that upset the traditional correlation of forces, and appear as a hidden form of military-political pressure.[7] Superiority in IT, for example, could debilitate a nuclear coding or launch command procedure, making them unreliable or useless.

Third, Russia cannot allow a PSYWAR-IT (psychological warfare-information technology) campaign to destroy the Russian economy. According to some Russian analysts, the US Strategic Defense Initiative (SDI) was an attempt to economically exhaust the Soviet Union by causing it to spend money it did not have on systems it could not use. Some Russian analysts view current United States interest in "information warfare" as another such attempt.[8] Russian analysts advise not to enter an arms race such as IW that is planned by other countries, but to devise military-technical priorities that are suited to the economic opportunities and strategic goals of the country. An IT strike against the Russian market is another threat in this category.

Fourth, Russia cannot allow IT and information operations to debilitate the nation's psychological stability, or to cause leaders to make incorrect judgments and decisions. Information currently presents a threat to society, the individual, and state institutions in Russia since the population is in a transition period and many citizens are psychologically vulnerable (that is, without a firm ideological basis). Control of the mass media is one manifestation of this threat.[9] The Internet is also a concern to some Russian officials, since it potentially can be used to commit crimes or unite political parties and groups against the government. Finally, if a country's decision-making cycle is damaged through computer network penetration and insertion of disinformation, governments or agencies may reach incorrect conclusions and decisions.[10] This is particularly dangerous in crisis situations when nations are working under extreme time constraints.

Fifth, and perhaps most important, IT's use in information operations blurs the Russian concept of the initial period of war. Since information attacks may be silent and capable of hiding their source or origin, planning for or responding to an initial period of war becomes treacherously complicated. What constitutes and differentiates the start of a crisis period, period of imminent war, and an offensive information operation, and how would one determine when or how an operation started? How does one determine with accuracy who delivered the attack? Should one respond with information actions against all probable enemies or only the most likely? How long can one delay a response before the entire information infrastructure of a country is under attack and a response is no longer possible?

Sixth, IT greatly enhances the military effectiveness of weapons systems and exploits point targets. Qualitative and quantitative indicators of weapon effectiveness have been replaced by the amount of informatization (digitalization, miniaturization, computer coding, and so forth) that a weapon contains, allowing huge amounts of information to be processed. IT raises the combat potential of precision weapons, and affects correlation of forces calculations since the ability exists, theoretically, to hit strategic point targets (nuclear weapons, command and control nodes, centers of political and economic significance) anywhere via cruise missiles. Computer viruses are another concern generated by IT.

Many viruses and counter virus agents have been developed,[11] including a stealth virus.[12] By the year 2000, Russian scientists also expect to confront distance virus weapons, computer viruses introduced through radio channels or laser lines of communications directly into computers of strategic significance.[13]

Finally, IT has had a significant impact on military art. The space-air-ground character of contemporary war includes satellites that process information and offer navigation assistance, and airborne sensors that detect movement and coordinate fires on ground targets. The center of gravity for military confrontations has changed from land and sea theaters of military action to the air-space theater. Warfare has a real-time aspect, requiring forces to acquire/engage/move. Formerly cyclical military operations (periods of intense conflict followed by periods of standown) will be replaced by operations that are less cyclical and more linear. Winners will acquire/shoot/move faster than their opponents for longer periods of time. IT also assists in overcoming uncertainty in war, producing streams of information allowing for accurate situational awareness, limiting surprise in the traditional sense, and offering IT landlords the perspective of a chess player peering five or six moves into the future. Most significantly, Russian theorists realize that military art must be designed not only for opponents who are equal in the use of information technology, but also for those adversaries who are superior or inferior to friendly forces in this respect.[14] IT and the infosphere, defined as a body of general and specialized programs for creating, processing, and storing computerized data, will be likely targets if war occurs.

## US Views

For the United States, initial concern centered on how to employ or use IT, since America was dealt a superior IT hand from the beginning. Only later did the impact of IT on society and the nation's infrastructure become an issue. For example, the *1997 United States National Military Strategy* refers to information warfare as an asymmetric challenge that could circumvent US strengths, exploit US vulnerabilities, or confront the nation in ways that could not be matched in kind.[15] This also prompted the creation of a presidential commission to study the problem. The response of the US military to this challenge was a conceptual warfighting template entitled *Joint Vision 2010*, which rested on information superiority and technological innovation, and strived to implement new operational concepts of dominant maneuver, precision engagement, focused logistics, and full-dimensional protection.[16]

The impact of IT (from a US viewpoint) on military-political considerations affecting national security are, first, that the security link between the commercial and military sectors has grown much closer. In order to enable IT strategies, the military had to link itself closely with civilian technology. The military-technical revolution and revolution in military affairs (RMA) actually started in the civilian sector, led by computer chip and optical fiber technology. Military applications soon followed. It became apparent, however, that since the military sector continued to rely heavily on commercial technologies and enterprises (such as phone systems), it was as prone to criminal attack as the commercial systems. This has forced both sectors to share more ideas on joint commissions, and to develop joint visions for information security systems to protect IT.

Second, an extended reliance on IT may invoke an asymmetric attack from a weak IT opponent. America was confronted by this eventuality during the Gulf War. Saddam Hussein, unable to counter the coalition's high-tech force, resorted to SCUD, chemical, and ecological terror as counters. A better equipped and prepared force than Iraq could inflict serious damage on an IT force, as the Gulf War demonstrated. IT weaponry is a technique but not an end-all. One Russian has warned that an information attack against it will result in a nuclear strike against the source of the attack and the country that authorized the attack.[17]

Third, IT can contribute to maintaining an overseas presence with fewer forces. IT can provide a virtual presence almost anywhere in the world and monitor early indications and warnings of potential conflict areas or of treaty or international law violations. Overseas presence is provided by IT-equipped UAVs (unmanned aerial vehicles) and satellite surveillance. IT in a virtual presence role is supported by the worldwide presence of the US Navy, whose IT ability to affect ground operations has improved significantly, especially through the increased role of sensors and ships armed with cruise missiles. IT also supports the thinking of General Dennis Reimer, Chief of Staff of the US Army, who believes in strategic pre-emption, the ability to halt or prevent a conflict or crisis before it becomes debilitating or protracted — before it spreads out of control.[18] Pre-emption can contribute to shaping the environment diplomatically and economically, and can compel compliance with specific IT measures. The US learned prior to its intervention in Bosnia that modeling conflicts with superior computer graphics and virtual reality helped to compel compliance among the parties at the Dayton Accord negotiations. A three-dimensional computer model of Bosnia's terrain was developed and used by negotiators to show the presidents where the zone of separation must be located, and where their boundaries would be, with mapping provided by using real-time satellite images from flyovers of Bosnia.[19]

Fourth, IT allows for communications directly from the Pentagon to the foxhole, blurring the distinction between levels of action and complicating command issues. IT has produced communications achievements that are staggering. Senior officials in the Pentagon can now literally sit in on operations conducted by their forces or by others.

Fifth, IT is assisting in the discovery of new non-lethal weapons based on physical principles. The US military is working on the development of acoustic, vortex and microwave weapons.[20] Computers and recent advancements in miniaturized electronics, power generation, and beam aiming may finally have put pulse, electromagnetic radiation, and beam weapons on the cusp of practicality, according to some experts.

Sixth, IT has brought changes in several issues of military art. According to one analyst, some of the most significant are 1) an increase in the tempo of operations, which limits time for planning and decision-making, requiring organizational, doctrinal, force structure, and technological changes, and adaptations to both regular and irregular operations to compel or enforce norms of behavior; 2) the extended use of robotic reconnaissance mechanisms (such as UAVs, Joint Surveillance, Targeting and Radar Systems - JSTARS) and precision munitions, which allow tanks and artillery to discard range and other targeting essentials (terrain, multiple shots for bracketing, and so forth) and makes battlefield awareness and management easier; 3) increased rates of movement with precision, allowing units to outpace an adversary's ability to react; 4) use of sensors on vehicles, which allows reporting to be instantaneous, and provides situational updates at the flick of a switch at higher headquarters; and 5) the ability of small units to employ the former combat power of a division, affecting the balance between combat power and manpower, the nature of command and control, and distinctions of strategic and tactical levels of war.[21]

Another analyst has noted that complexity, a spontaneous consequence of imposing regulation and control on a chaotic state, is the defining characteristic of modern military organizations and operations, and is controlled by the cohesion and integrating ability of information. Military art is affected in that the military uses information to describe itself and an adversary, to organize itself, to offer visual or situational awareness through extracting, processing, and distribution of data, to execute a mosaic of deep and protracted operations (operational art), and to offer the grammar, language, syntax, and logic of complex systems, making them not only understandable but showing their evolutionary qualities. Armies are complex systems that flow in a sea of information, and only the use of cybershock can stop the flow via operations security, deception, psychological operations, electronic warfare, reconnaissance and counter reconnaissance, and tempo and surprise.[22] IT can also be useful to train the force via computer simulations and virtual reality scenarios. Also, IT can be used in training the force en route to a crisis by offering computer-generated problems in accordance with the situation on the ground.

Seventh, centers of gravity in warfare have changed. Past strategies involved the concentration of one's forces at a particular time and place to win a decisive battle. Information centers of gravity focus on weaknesses in information infrastructures and equipment. IT's disabling capabilities prohibit forces from massing, planes from finding targets in a quick and accurate manner, strategies from developing, and decisive points from being located, calculated and attacked. These operations could occur in peacetime as well as wartime, according to some. The main point to recognize is that the greatest challenge for the policy maker will be to manage a national intelligence architecture, which can rapidly identify the information center of gravity, prepare the information battlefield, and deliver the appropriate (non-lethal) information munitions to carry the day.[23]

Finally, IT can affect the weakest link on the battlefield: the individual soldier's mind. The mind is not protected by a firewall as is the computer, and the ultimate operator of equipment, the soldier/leader, is offered little protection in the IT environment. There are two forms of protection required: one from physical attacks (electromagnetic pulses, acoustic weapons, voice synthesis, and so forth) and one from attacks on the perception capabilities of the mind. This is especially true due to the quick pace of development in the production of holograms. These can be used to make an army look larger than it is, or to make life-sized tank and soldier holograms appear to move and thereby confuse or intimidate soldiers. Hologram technology "uses a laser to illuminate an object and write its image into a photo-refractive crystal, while another laser projects that image into a liquid scattering material."[24] Holograms are also being considered for their value in propaganda productions, such as morphing images of political leaders. Soldiers require training to recognize misleading information produced from holograms, voice synthesis or other psychological tricks.

Other reports indicate that the computer-operator interface will be a crucial area requiring attention. Progress in neuro-muscular control, mind control and connectivity developments suggest additional areas of focus. The point to underscore is that the mind is vulnerable and, therefore, it is necessary to devote greater attention to the potential use of non-lethal or other information-based technologies.

## MANAGING INFORMATION TECHNOLOGY

### *Russia's Responses*

In September 1997, Russia's Security Council discussed the draft version of the country's information security policy. It consisted of five parts: general principles (legal basis and role of information in society); threats to the Russian Federation's information security (to the country's information infrastructure and information resources, especially technical and constitutional ones); methods of ensuring Russia's information security (legal, organizational, economic); government policy foundations for ensuring information security (openness, ownership, legal equality); and the organizational structure and principles for designing the system (an aggregate of federal government agencies and organizations to coordinate activities) to ensure the country's information security (strategy, evaluations, coordination, certification, licensing, and implementing a unified technical policy). This policy is the strongest element of Russia's response to its concerns over the use of IT by foreign countries.[25]

To combat information threats to Russia, primary responsibility lies in the hands of the Federal Agency for Government Communications and Information (FAPSI). This agency combats hackers, foreign special services, and domestic criminals who aim to gain unsanctioned access to information and to disable electronic management.[26] FAPSI's deputy director, Colonel-General Vladimir Markomenko, is the only official voice to define Russian IW to date.[27] His definition suggests that IW is the use of IT against the state in the form of special electronic and communication devices, hardware and software attacks, and other technical means.

The Russian armed forces are working on combining IT with older psychological concepts such as reflexive control (a means or method used to convey specially prepared information to a person, organization or country to influence the adoption of a predetermined decision desired by the initiator of the action). Some Russian analysts believe that a combination of information warfare and reflexive control offers a greater danger than the direct use of military power:

> The most dangerous manifestation of the tendency to rely on military power relates not so much to the direct use of the means of armed combat as to the possible results of the use of reflexive control by the opposing side via developments in the theory and practice of information war.[28]

The Russian military is proceeding to develop IT even in the current military and economic crisis. Some of the effort involves skipping over several generations of weapons. Russian military officers write about using IT to develop virtual realities and synthetic environments in military affairs. Virtual reality to one Russian officer is a complex set of artificial images of an environment (situations) that take place in a real time or close to real time scale, replicating processes that are created in the human mind by software and hardware means.[29] Current uses for virtual reality training include creating systems to synthesize routine, crisis and battle situations at various levels; creating means to generate models (for preparing information for decision-makers) to help forecast political and military-political situations in regions and different countries; developing forms and methods of conducting the armed struggle; creating systems to train officers individually or in groups; and creating means of psychological influence for individuals and the mass consciousness of people.[30] It is believed that from the use of virtual reality systems, one will look at a battlefield from a bird's eye view and from the enemy side, providing an opportunity for preparing and running operations repeatedly in selected ways. Also, one can test weapon systems through virtual reality means before acquiring them. Virtual reality will also be used by the military leadership to improve doctrine and test personnel and equipment loss-free under varying climatic conditions, times of day, and levels of readiness.[31]

Russia's computer research and development process, which continues unabated, has produced some unexpected results unique to the Russian experience. One result is the neuron computer which, according to one expert, is expected to replace the pentium chip for speed and effectiveness in Russia. They are reportedly 1000 times faster than traditional computers. Military uses include the development of state-of-the-art high-precision weapons, optic devices to detect missiles, and use in anti-ballistic missile (ABM) programs and dual technologies. In financial markets, the computers could make highly accurate forecasts (reported 90 per cent accuracy) of currency and futures rates, stocks and other securities.[32]

In other fields, the government's science and technology committee approved the following information-related fields as priority directions in the area of critical federal-level technologies:

- multi processor parallel-structure computers
- computer systems based on neuronet computers, transputers, and optical computers
- speech, text, and image recognition and synthesis systems
- artificial intelligence and virtual reality systems
- information and telecommunication systems
- mathematical modeling systems
- microsystem technology and mircosensors
- superlarge integrated circuits and nanoelectronics
- optical and acoustic electronics
- cryoelectronics production technologies
- laser technologies
- precision and mechatronic technologies
- robotic systems and micromachines
- electronic-ion-plasma technologies
- intellectual systems for automated design and control[33]

## *US Responses*

President Clinton signed Presidential Decision Directive 39 (late 1995) and Executive Order 13010 (15 July 1996) to establish a President's Commission on Critical Infrastructure Protection. The commission was to develop a national policy and implementation strategy to protect critical infrastructures from cyber or physical threats. The commission received the report of the Defense Science Board for its consideration as well. By November 1997, the commission had written its report, distributed it, and disbanded. How the President will use the report remains to be seen. Critical infrastructures identified were: telecommunications, electrical power systems, gas and oil storage and transportation, banking and finance, transportation, water supply systems, emergency services, and continuity of government services.

High technology responsibility for protecting critical infrastructures and combating information threats to US society lies with the US National Security Agency (NSA), especially the relay of indications and warnings information to command authorities. NSA warns decision-makers of potential threats. This responsibility differs from the period of the Cold War when one department focused signals intelligence (SIGINT) specifically on the former Soviet Union, and another focused on Asia. These missions are gone, and the new missions of these two departments are to combat criminals involved 1) in transnational issues, irrespective of geography, and 2) in attacks on the commercial sector's information resources. A new threat matrix uses IT as one of its principal combatants and operators. NSA is also responsible for identifying and combating threats to and vulnerabilities of technologies and infrastructures (such as telecommunications). The focus for NSA has slipped to the infrastructure of an adversarial force's operating capability instead of planes, tanks, and ships. Regarding the protection of commercial projects, NSA is to provide technical expertise on encryption standards for commercial firms and on systems for recovering data in secure environments.[34] Many of NSA's responsibilities correspond with those of FAPSI, noted above, to include the close relationship with IW. In 1996, John Deutsch, then director of the Central Intelligence Agency, announced his intention to create a cyber warfare center at NSA.

The US armed forces' major contribution to its information security was a report issued in 1996 by the Defense Science Task Board entitled the Defense Science Board Task Force on Information Warfare (IW-D). The board made 13 recommendations to the Chairman of the Defense Science Board.[35] The board members did not prioritize the key recommendations, deciding that all should be implemented immediately. The board recommended establishing a center to provide strategic indications and warning, current intelligence, and threat assessments. They also recommended developing a process and metrics for assessing infrastructure dependency.

The US armed forces' focus on the development of a high-technology fighting force, known as Force XXI for the army and listed under varying names for the other services. Army testing at the National Training Center in the Spring of 1997 yielded significant results that appear to have placed the development and fielding of IT systems ahead of schedule. The only criticism to direct against the army's approach is that it has somewhat neglected the psychological impact of IT on the soldier.

The US military, like Russia, is also pursuing the use of virtual reality mechanisms to create artificial battlefields and work on potential problems in advance. Known as the Joint Training Confederation (JTC), 12 interacting systems (such as the Air Warfare Simulation [AWSIM]; the Corps Battle Simulation [(CBS]; and the Navy's Research, Evaluation and System Analysis Simulation [RESA]) were developed to train military forces of the US all over the world.

US research and development in the field of IT is focused on many items. Dr. Alvin H. Bernstein of the National Defense University divided technologies into pop-up (those that can distinguish threatening objects from decoys and then hide in their own signature) and fire-ant (the fiercely stinging, omnivorous side of technology). He listed "pop-up" as signatures, platforms, stealth, drones, loitering missiles, autonomous land crawlers, and submersibles, and "fire-ant" as sensors, emitters, microbots, mini-projectiles, miniaturization, and integrated software.[36] Thus, the implication is that core research and development strategies must focus on electronics, nanotechnologies, energy, software that emphasizes integration, and manufacturing technology to produce counter-stealth technology, automatic target recognition capabilities, robotics, non-lethal weapons, and rapid power projection capabilities.

## OPPORTUNITIES AND CHALLENGES FOR US-RUSSIAN COOPERATION IN INFORMATION TECHNOLOGIES

The Russian Draft Doctrine on Information Security indicated great interest in developing cooperation with other nations in the area of information security and technology. The doctrine notes that

> ...international cooperation on questions of ensuring information security is an indispensable component of the political, military, economic, cultural, and other forms of interaction of countries participating in the world community. Such cooperation should promote an increase in the information security of all members of the world community, including the Russian Federation.[37]

While it is unknown if the President's Commission on Critical Infrastructure Protection suggests cooperation or not, the US Defense Science Board report did not mention it. Cooperation is significant on a non-governmental level, however. For example, when Bill Gates, founder and President of Microsoft, visited Moscow in 1997, he discussed several cooperative ventures with his Russian hosts. His agenda included intellectual property rights and copyrights, and the use of Microsoft products in the Russian space agency, Central Bank, and various industrial companies. In an agreement with LUKOIL, a Russian oil conglomerate, it was decided to sign a general agreement defining a strategy for mutual cooperation.[38]

Governmental cooperation between the US and Russia in IT has moved more slowly. While there have been limited meetings at the highest levels to discuss some of these problems, there has been a heavy reluctance by the Pentagon and others to provide momentum to the process. Perhaps the Pentagon is in no hurry to share IW information because they are uncertain of tomorrow's geo-strategic arrangement. The fall of the USSR appeared to happen overnight, after all. On the other hand, any risk of giving away valuable information nearly has dissipated due to the vast amount of IW-related information available to the public. To date, well over 500 articles have been written by US analysts and scientists about US information systems and operations. Russians have been escorted to demonstrations of US advanced information-based and -supported artillery systems and even been briefed on information operations plans for a US theater.

While a variety of options exist, limited discussions do deserve to be explored in more detail, perhaps in a conference setting. Nuclear age discussions that proved so beneficial underscore the necessity of changing this reluctance. If computer viruses attack critical systems in the future, and appear to come from a state, when in reality an individual has sent the virus, will Russia and America launch nuclear weapons, as one Russian indicated their side would, because the sides didn't talk to one another? Without dialogue, the potential for improving global security is undermined. By failing to work together in the management of IT, misunderstanding and fear are encouraged.

Opportunities now exist for dialogue, but such operations may become even more limited over time if suspicion builds. Russia's willingness to discuss these issues is tied to its domestic and economic situation. There are many conservatives in Russia, as in the US government, who still see a US footprint (and vice versa, Russian) on every issue under discussion today. Some believe that a massive information operation has already been conducted against Russia. On the other hand, there currently are scores of well-informed Russian leaders, academicians and analysts who do not see an American conspiracy everywhere they look, want to exchange opinions, and can offer a tremendous representative sampling of expertise on all areas of information technology and theory.

Yet another reason for dialogue is the number of ties that Russia maintains with so-called rogue states (Iran, Iraq, Yemen, Libya, and so forth). Russia may be best positioned to help control non-state sponsored sources of information terrorism. This could only help America, which is the number one enemy of most of these states. On the other hand, some fear that Russia would share US conversations on these topics with these states. Another fear is that rogue members of Russian society (willing to sell secrets to the highest bidder) may be an even greater threat. However, this may be a moot point if 90 per cent of this information is already available for public consumption.

Neither side can afford to wait much longer. New technologies are continually appearing that may make the future even more difficult to manage and unstable. The US is awaiting the arrival of asynchronous transfer mode (ATM) systems, which will revolutionize the way soldiers communicate. As one recent discussion concluded:

> What will technology provide during the next century? Is it quantum computing? Is it molecular or DNA computing?...The key question is: what technologies, if any, will complement and/or replace the predictable silicon technology?[39]

Quantum computing uses the principle of superconductivity to increase the speed of computing and to reduce the heat that arises from millions of processing procedures (even small amounts of heat affect chips where size is measured in fractions of a micron). One Russian scientist working in America and sharing his discoveries in the field of quantum computing with his Russian colleagues estimated that by the year 2010 it will be possible to pack 64 trillion transistors on a chip instead of the 1995 figure of 64 million.[40] Clearly, this spiral will continue unchecked. It would only be prudent for both sides to establish a dialogue as soon as possible.

The use of IT has caused significant changes in the armed forces of both countries. General William Hartzog, commanding general of the US Army Training and Doctrine Command (TRADOC), reflecting on these changes, commented during the Task Force XXI Advanced Warfighting Experiment exercises at the National Training Center that:

> I don't think I've been involved in 34 years in anything even closely approaching this...I don't think we have ever had as large, complex or holistic a look at things. There are lessons that we will pick out from this that we would have never seen in any other kind of exercise or experiment...[41]

The armed forces of both Russia and the US have weighed carefully the impact of IT on their operations, as the discussion above indicates. They are also monitoring the impact of IT on the security interests of their respective states, and adjusting policy and organizational arrangements accordingly. However, keeping pace with rapid advancements in IT will be a continuous and difficult proposition.

One of the ways to bring about an understanding of IT's impact on the civilian and military components of both countries, and at the same time lower the fears associated with technological advancements, is to develop an agenda for cooperation. The discussion above suggests several areas that require immediate attention.

First, both sides need to develop a common terminology in order to discuss with both precision and understanding the meaning and impact of IT on military-political affairs. This should be the simplest phase for cooperation but, as peace operations have shown, it may be one of the most difficult. It took over three years for the two countries to develop a set of definitions to explain Russian and US concepts of peacekeeping, peace enforcement, and peace making. Today, these definitions are continuing to undergo change and modification, and there is no coordinating mechanism to update them. This only encourages misunderstanding. Without a doubt, Russian and US policy makers need to come to a common understanding of IT and IW terms. Otherwise, how will the sides be able to cooperate on, say, computer crime without unwittingly violating a legal issue for the other side?

Second, there must be an agenda to institutionalize the legal norms for not just Russia and the US but for all nations regarding IT and IW. What would constitute an information attack? What are the cyberspace borders that a country can consider as violations of sovereignty? What is considered to be IT theft in cyberspace? Are there IT developments that should be curbed or limited, and included in an IT non-proliferation agreement? There are literally hundreds of such questions to answer.

Third, an IT/information operations hot line should be established. The need for such a line was evident a few years ago when a student in St. Petersburg broke into the computer data base of Citicorps Bank and stole millions of dollars. As is well known, many such attacks go unreported today because banks do not want their clientele to know that their system is not 100 per cent safe. If this hacking occurs in the nuclear codes of either side, then the scale and consequence of the problem increases substantially. An information hot line would allow immediate notification between the two countries of a serious problem.

Fourth, discussions on the impact of IT on the military art of Russia and the US, especially in the areas of greatest concern (for example, the Russian understanding of the boundaries of the initial period of war), would be an invaluable undertaking. A good place to start work on this issue would be private military-political discussions or even a conference at the highest levels. Both sides could express their concerns and fears to sensitize one another to the impact of new IT developments on their national security policies. Such cooperation can only help reduce the likelihood of misunderstanding and can quickly move important concerns to the top of the agenda. It will no longer be an excuse to admit if only I had known what my action meant to you.

Fifth, it is important to recognize that soon both sides will have the ability to use holograms and other IT manifestations that will offer the opportunity to completely fool one another both on the battlefield and through the airwaves, whether it be TV or radio, and the press. Both sides should begin initial discussions on these issues before they are overtaken by rapidly changing technological developments. A hacker simulating an incoming ICBM nuclear attack on the radar screens of the military of either Russia or the United States is but one manifestation of this threat.

Finally, both Russia and the United States should have advisors sit together and discuss two documents: the Russian Federation Draft Doctrine on Information Security and the President's Commission on Critical Infrastructure Protection. The sides could discuss areas of concern and potential cooperation. Both nations should learn a great deal from such a process.

This chapter has focused on US-Russian bilateral relations. Certainly, US-Russian decisions concerning IT will influence other nations and vice-versa. These suggestions for expanding US-Russian bilateral cooperation in IT could easily be extended to include other nations. This is not only advisable, but necessary, as nations approach the interdependent security environment of the twenty-first century.

---

The views expressed in this article are those of the author and do not necessarily represent the official policy or position of the Department of the Army, Department of Defense, or the US government.

## NOTES

1.   Information technology (IT) is defined as all aspects of managing and processing information, and is characterized by the domain and tools of its usage. Two major components of IT remain hardware and software but IT's tasks, constantly being redefined, include processing, operating systems, network operating systems, data communication standards, high-speed communications, networking applications, the Internet, object-oriented technologies, and database technologies.   This definition is provided by The Center for Research in Electronic Commerce (CREC), University of Texas at Austin (1998) (http://cism.bus.utexas.edu/ram/collab/it.html).

2.   Some of the more important US works on information war include George Stein, "Information Warfare," *Airpower Journal* (Spring 1995), pp. 31-39; John Arquilla and David Ronfeldt, "Cyberwar is Coming," *Comparative Strategy*, No. 12 (1993), pp. 141-65; and Martin C. Libicki, *What is Information Warfare?* (Washington DC: Center for Advanced Concepts and Technology, Institute for National Strategic Studies, National Defense University, 1995).   Important Russian works on information warfare include Vladimir S. Pirumov, "Several Aspects of Information Warfare," paper presented at InfoWarCon 1996 entitled "Defining the European Perspective" (23-24 May 1996), Brussels, Belgium; V. I. Tsymbal, "Concept of Information Warfare," Academy of State Management, Moscow, Russia (14 September 1995); and A. A. Prokhozhev and N. I. Turko, "The Basics of Information Warfare," report presented at the conference entitled "Systems Analysis on the Threshold of the 21st Century: Theory and Practice," Moscow, Russia (27-29 February 1996).

3.   See Lawrence Freedman, "The First Two Generations of Nuclear Strategists," in Peter Paret, ed., *Makers of Modern Strategy* (Princeton: Princeton University Press, 1986), p. 762.

4. Unless, of course, the information strike is against a nuclear plant, causing a melt down and greater damage than a nuclear blast.

5.   "New Trends in Power Deterrence," *Armeyskiy sbornik*, No. 9 (September 1995), pp. 12-19 in *FBIS-UMA* (17 January 1996), p. 11.

6. Ibid., p. 12.

7. I. Panarin, "Troyanskiy kon XXI veka" (Trojan Horse of the 21st century), *Krasnaya zvesda* (8 December 1995), p. 3.

8. Georgiy Smolyan, Vitaliy Tsygichko and Dmitriy Chereshkin, "A Weapon That May be More Dangerous Than a Nuclear Weapon: The Realities of Information Warfare," *Nezavisimoye voyennoye obozreniye* (Supplement to *Nezavisimaya gazeta*), No. 3 (18 November 1995), pp. 1-2 in *FBIS-UMA* (6 December 1995), pp. 31-35.

9. Aleksandr Pozdnyakov, interviewed by Vladimir Davydov, "Information Security," *Granitsa Rossii*, No. 33 (September 1995), pp. 6-7 in *FBIS-UMA* (13 December 1995), pp. 41-44.

10. M. Boytsov, "Informatsionnaya voyna" (Information Warfare), *Morskoy sbornik*, No. 10 (1995), p. 70.

11. Pozdnyakov, "Information Security," p. 43. These viruses are Trojan horse, forced quarantine, sensor, and overload, and are described in the article.

12. B.P. Pal'chun and R.M. Yusupov, "Obespecheniye bezopasnosti komp'yutorynoy infosfery" (Providing Security in the Computer Infosphere), *Vooruzheniye, politika, konversiya (Armaments, Policy, Conversion)*, No. 3 (1993), p. 23.

13. See Timothy L. Thomas, "The Threat of Information Operations: A Russian Perspective," in Robert L. Pfaltzgraff, Jr. and Richard H. Shultz, Jr., eds., *War in the Information Age* (Washington/London: Brassey's, 1997), pp. 69-73. For further discussion concerning these military considerations (initial period of war, and so forth) see pp. 61-80.

14. Grigoriy S. Utkin, "Synthetic Environments and Virtual Reality: The Russian View," paper presented at the seminar entitled "Military Applications of Synthetic Environments and Virtual Reality" (16-18 September 1997), Stockholm, Sweden.

15. John M. Shalikashvili, *National Military Strategy of the United States of America: Shape, Respond, Prepare Now: A Military Strategy for a New Era* (Washington DC: Government Printing Office, 1997), p. 9.

16. Ibid., p. 17.

17. Tsymbal, "Concept of Information Warfare."

18. General Dennis J. Reimer, "The Army and the Cyberspace Cross-roads," *Defense Issues*, Vol. 12, No. 33 (http://www.dtic.mil/defe...nk/pubs/di97/di1233.html).

19. "Powerscene: An Overview," Cambridge Research Associates, Inc., McLean, Virginia (November 1995). Also see Timothy L. Thomas, "Virtual Peacemaking: Conflict Prevention Through the Use of Information Technology" (September 1997), paper under consideration for publication in *Parameters*.

20. Douglas Pasternak, "Wonder Weapons," *U.S. News and World Report* (7 July 1997), pp. 38-46.

21. James K. Morningstar, "Technologies, Doctrine and Organization for the RMA," *Joint Force Quarterly* (Spring 1997), pp. 37-43.

22. James Schneider, "Black Lights: Chaos, Complexity, and the Promise of Information Warfare," *Joint Force Quarterly* (Spring 1997), pp. 26-28.

23. Robert Steele, "Virtual Intelligence:  Conflict Avoidance and Resolution through Information Peacekeeping," distributed at conference entitled "Virtual Diplomacy," US Institute of Peace, Washington DC (2 April 1997).

24. Andrew Gilligan, "Army goes to war with platoons of holograms," *The Sunday Telegraph*, London (11 May 1997), p. 5.

25. *Russian Federation Draft Doctrine on Information Security* (13 August 1997) in *FBIS-SOV* (3 September 1997).

26. Aleksey Okhskiy, "FAPSI: Only Powerful Organizations are Capable of the Comprehensive Protection of Information," *Sevodnya* (8 September 1995), p. 3 in *FBIS-SOV* (28 September 1995), p. 20.

27. Vladimir Markomenko, "Invisible, Drawn-Out War," *Nezavisimoye voyennoye obozreniye* (16-21 August 1997), p. 1.  Markomenko lists the functions of Russian IW (electronic warfare, electronic surveillance, hacker warfare and psychological warfare) and describes them in this article.

28. A. A. Prokhozhev and N. I. Turko, "The Basics of Information Warfare," report at the conference enitled "Systems Analysis on the Threshold of the 21st Century: Theory and Practice," Moscow (February 1996), p. 251.

29. Utkin, "Synthetic Environments and Virtual Reality: The Russian View," p. 11.

30. Ibid.

31. Ibid., p. 12.

32. INTERFAX (14 February 1996) in *FBIS-UMA* (28 February 1996), p. 64.

33. Andrey Fonotov, "Science and Technology Policy," *Rossiyskaya gazeta* (8 August 1996), p. 6 in *FBIS-UST* (8 August 1996).

34. Barbara Starr, "U.S. Puzzle Palace Seeks New Clues to Combat Old Threats," *Jane's Defense Weekly* (3 September 1997), pp. 35-36.

35. "Report of the Defense Science Board Task Force on Information Warfare-Defense, Office of the Under Secretary of Defense for Acquisition and Technology," Washington DC (November 1996).

36. Alvin H. Bernstein, "Conflict and Technology: The Next Generation," National Defense University, unpublished paper.

37. *Russian Federation Draft Doctrine on Information Security.*

38. Stanislav Leonidov and Denis Kirillov, "Microsoft Increases Pressure on Russian Market," *Moskovskiye Finansovyye Izvestiya* (14 October 1997), p. 1 in *FBIS-SOV* (9 January 1998).

39. Juris Hartmanis, "Roundtable: The Future of Computing and Telecommunications," *Issues in Science and Technology* (Spring 1997), p. 72.

40. Vladimir Pokrovskiy, "A Russian Scientist is Making a Quantum Computer but No One Knows in America or Here," *Obshchaya gazeta* (30 October-5 November 1997), No. 43, p. 14 in *FBIS-SOV* (9 January 1998).

41. Dennis Steele, "AWE: Testing Soldiers and Equipment," *Army* (June 1997), p. 28.

# 5

## Proliferation Challenges and Nonproliferation Opportunities in the Post-Cold War Era

*William C. Potter*

To paraphrase Charles Dickens, the post-Cold War era has the potential to be both the best of times and the worst of times for nuclear nonproliferation. This chapter identifies some of the major nonproliferation opportunities that have arisen as we approach the next millennium, as well as a number of the new threats that have emerged. An effort is made to compare US and Russian perspectives on these issues and to suggest a number of concrete steps that can be taken to reduce the threats.

### NEW OPPORTUNITIES

Shortly after midnight on the morning of 13 May, the 1995 Nuclear Nonproliferation Treaty (NPT) Review and Extension Conference concluded after one month of prolonged and often heated discussion. The meeting, attended by delegates from 175 countries, agreed without a vote or formal objection, to indefinite extension of the NPT.

The treaty extension was a truly historic accomplishment and provided an indication of what might be possible in the post-Cold War environment. The Conference demonstrated that an extraordinarily large number of states — from North and South, rich and poor, nuclear and non-nuclear — agreed that international security and their own security was best served by halting the spread of nuclear weapons. Consistent with their long tradition of cooperation for nonproliferation, the United States and Russia worked together very closely to help secure the indefinite extension of the NPT.[1] This cooperation was apparent in the group of 25 principal players who met regularly with Conference President Jayantha Dhanapala as "Friends of the President." It also generally was manifest at the meetings of the three Main Committees, and especially in Main Committee I, which addressed issues relating to nuclear disarmament. Both countries, along with France and the United Kingdom, routinely took a stance that emphasized the significant progress that had been made in reducing the nuclear arsenals of the superpowers. They also strongly resisted all attempts to achieve anything less than indefinite extension of the NPT.[2]

As the first major, multinational, post-Cold War nuclear disarmament conference, the 1995 NPT Review and Extension Conference also clearly demonstrated that the community of nations was interested in so-called vertical, as well as horizontal, proliferation. This concern with reducing the arsenals of the nuclear weapons states was most apparent in the two resolutions adopted at the Conference on "Strengthening the Review Process for the Treaty" and on "Principles and Objectives for Nonproliferation and Disarmament." The latter resolution, also adopted by consensus, committed the nuclear weapons state parties to the treaty to conclude a Comprehensive Test Ban Treaty (CTBT) no later than 1996, a date that they actually met. Although both the United States and Russia are among the 148 states that have signed the CTBT, neither has yet ratified the treaty.

In the past few years, one also can point to significant progress in moving toward universalizing membership in the NPT. Important recent NPT adherents that supported the extension decision were China, Argentina, South Africa, Ukraine, as well as all of the other Soviet successor states. Today only a small number of states — most notably India, Pakistan, and Israel — stand outside of the NPT. The United States and Russia share the conviction that a universal NPT regime is highly desirable, but differ in the risks they attach to the nuclear capabilities of Israel, Pakistan, and India and the political and economic capital they are prepared to expend in seeking to reverse the proliferation decisions of these states. These differences are reflected in Moscow's efforts to export nuclear reactors to New Delhi despite the absence of international safeguards on all of India's nuclear facilities and US reluctance to pursue a forceful nonproliferation policy toward its long-time ally in the Middle East. Notwithstanding these differences, Russia and the United States agree that the spread of nuclear weapons to any additional states would be very destabilizing.

One of the most promising recent nonproliferation developments is the growth of nuclear-weapon-free zones (NWFZs). Unlike most other nuclear arms control negotiations that are dominated by the nuclear weapon states, NWFZ proposals typically have been initiated by the non-nuclear weapon states of the region concerned. Although NWFZs vary from region to region, they generally share a prohibition on the development, manufacture, production, and stationing of nuclear weapons in the zone, as well as guarantees by the nuclear weapon states not to use, or threaten to use, nuclear weapons against the nations within the zone. In recent years, support for NWFZs has grown dramatically, and NWFZs have entered into force in Latin America, the South Pacific, and Southeast Asia, and have been opened for signature in Africa.[3] In November 1997, the First Committee of the UN General Assembly also endorsed the creation of a NWFZ in Central Asia — a resolution sponsored by Kazakhstan, Kyrgyzstan, Tajikistan, Turkmenistan, and Uzbeskistan. Significantly, for the first time, the United States and Russia both formally endorsed the zone's creation. This resolution is important because although the United States and Russia traditionally have supported the principle of NWFZs on the basis of arrangements freely arrived at among the states in the region, in practice their support has been difficult to obtain and has been contingent upon the NWFZ meeting a number of criteria.[4]

Since the end of the Cold War and in the aftermath of the Gulf War, one can discern a growing assertiveness on the part of international organizations with nonproliferation responsibilities. Illustrative of this development is the 31 January 1992 statement of the UN Security Council that "the proliferation of weapons of mass destruction constitutes a threat to international peace and security." This language, endorsed by both Russia and the United States, is significant since it provides the legal basis under Chapter 7 of the UN Charter for the use of force against perpetrators of weapons of mass destruction proliferation. One also can point to the very effective work of the UN Special Commission on Iraq (UNSCOM), the strengthened international safeguards regime known as "93 & 2," and enhanced Nuclear Supplier Group (NSG) guidelines. Although differences between the United States and Russia over

UNSCOM activities in Iraq became more pronounced in Fall 1997, representatives of the two states have nevertheless worked together well for much of UNSCOM's history. The United States and Russia also both supported the granting of new authority to the International Atomic Energy Agency (IAEA), which includes the use of "no notice" inspections, IAEA access to any place on the site of nuclear facilities, and the use of environmental sampling as part of the IAEA's safeguards regime.[5] Consistent with their positions of generally supporting the strengthening of international nonproliferation activities, the United States and Russia were among the 27 states that endorsed the April 1992 Nuclear Supplies Group guidelines which set forth full-scope safeguards as a condition for exports.[6]

In summary, if one were inclined to make the case that these are the best of times for nonproliferation, one could point to a number of important developments which include:

1. The indefinite extension of the NPT;
2. The negotiation of the CTBT;
3. The near-universal scope of the NPT;
4. Evidence that proliferation is not a one-way street;
5. The growth of NWFZs;
6. New assertiveness on the part of international organizations after the Gulf War.

## NEW THREATS

Despite these major nonproliferation achievements, it is evident that many of the old divisions between the nuclear weapon states and the non-nuclear weapon states remain. There also are new divisions among the nuclear weapon states on proliferation issues which threaten to impede progress in arms control and disarmament. Although the list of challenges to the current nuclear nonproliferation regime is very long, the discussion in this chapter is confined to five items: 1) The rise in the threat of nuclear terrorism; 2) the risk of illicit nuclear trafficking; 3) the danger of a new tactical nuclear arms race; 4) the potential breakdown in US-Russian cooperation for nonproliferation; and 5) ignorance and complacency on the part of the public at large and elected officials.

### Nuclear Terrorism

Nuclear terrorism subsumes a variety of threats. The ones most often discussed in the Western press involve the seizure of nuclear weapons by renegade military factions or the use of diverted fissile material to fashion a nuclear device. A much more likely scenario, however, is an attack on or sabotage of civilian nuclear power installations or spent fuel storage sites. These are not hypothetical threats. There are at least four episodes since 1992 in which nuclear power plants in the post-Soviet states were the targets of terrorist actions.

*February 1992*: Oleg Savchuk, a computer programmer at the Ignalina Nuclear Power Plant in Lithuania was arrested for trying to sabotage a reactor at the plant by introducing a virus into the computer system. The alleged sabotage coincided with a breakdown in the cooling system of the first reactor, although there was no confirmed link between the two incidents. Savchuk may have introduced the virus and then called it to the attention of the plant management in order to receive a bonus for meritorious service.

*4 November 1994*: Kestutis Mazuika, a 42-year-old Lithuanian national in Sweden threatened the destruction of the Ignalina Nuclear Power Plant unless a payment of $8 million were made to a secret organization (NUC-41 "W") which he claimed to represent. Mazuika made the demand in a four-page hand-written letter in Russian he presented to a secretary in the office of the Swedish Prime Minister in Stockholm. The letter specified that $1 million was to be handed over to Mazuika on 7 November and the remainder was to be deposited in a Swedish bank. The letter claimed that the secret organization had well-trained representatives at the Ignalina facility and was prepared to blow up the plant.

Mazuika was arrested when he returned to the Prime Minister's office on 7 November. During the investigation of the case he was examined by a psychiatrist and judged to be mentally sound. He claimed that the organization NUC-41 "W" forced him to commit the act. Legal action was taken against Mazuika in both Sweden and Lithuania. He was sentenced to four years of imprisonment in Sweden, but was released after one year and returned to Lithuania. Although he was initially charged under Article 96 of the Lithuania Criminal Code — "Extortion of State property" — he was not sentenced in Lithuania due to this conviction in Sweden. According to the Lithuanian Nuclear Safety Inspectorate (VATESI), security at Ignalina was bolstered after the case.

*9 November 1994*: A terrorist threat that was taken very seriously occurred shortly after Mazuika's arrest and also involved the Ignalina facility. In the early morning of 9 November 1994, VATESI received information from the German Federal Ministry for Environment, Nature Conservation, and Nuclear Safety about an alleged plan to sabotage the Ignalina Nuclear Power Plant. According to the information, a local organized crime boss (Georgy Dekanidze) threatened to blow up the Ignalina plant in case his son Boris, who was on trial for a contract murder, were sentenced to death. On 20 November other Lithuanian authorities received an additional communication from the same German ministry indicating that preparations for the act of sabotage were completed and would be carried out by several employees of the nuclear plant on 15 November 1994 in the event of a death verdict.

Based upon this information, the Lithuanian Prime Minister Adolfas Slezevicus sought the assistance of the Swedish government, which agreed to provide a team of bomb experts and trained search dogs. The team arrived on 14 November and a search was conducted between the 14th and 16th, during which time units One and Two of the nuclear plan were shut down. Physical protection of the site also was increased and access to the plant was very restricted. No sign of sabotage, however, was uncovered. The shutdown cost the plant $10 million.

Despite the terrorist threat, Boris Dekanidze was sentenced to death on 10 November for masterminding the murder of Lithuanian journalist Vitas Lingys, who had written articles exposing extortion rackets run by the "Vilnius Brigade."

*Spring (Probably March) 1997*: Five men were caught after penetrating the Kursk Nuclear Power Station, which houses four RBMK-1000 reactors. The men had reached the plant generator and reportedly had plans to try to disable the reactor and seize the control room. Although Russian authorities initially believed that the men were associated with a "green" group, the intruders appear to have hatched the attack plan for extortionist purposes. Russian authorities, who have made only vague public references to a terrorist incident at a civilian nuclear power station in early 1997, have not treated the Kursk attack as a serious incident because the perpetrators did not have the capability to implement their plan and were not linked to a larger, politically motivated group.

In addition to the forementioned four cases involving sabotage, attacks, threats, or perceived threats against civilian nuclear power stations in Russia and Lithuania, there are at least two other nuclear terrorist episodes in the past two years in Russia. One occurred in 1995 at the Severodvinsk submarine production facility, where an employee who had not been paid for several months posted a warning that the shop containing two reactors would be blown up.[7] The second, widely reported episode, involved the recovery of a small quantity of Cesium-137 on the grounds of Izmailovsky Park in Moscow in late 1995. The radioactive material was found by a Russian television crew at the location reportedly provided to it by Chechen leader Shamil Basayev. Russian Interior Ministry officials indicated that the material might have been obtained from an inventory of nuclear waste or an isotope storage facility in the Chechen capital. Russian authorities reportedly had previously received threats from Chechen separatists against a number of nuclear facilities, including the first breeder reactor at Beloyarsk. Russian intelligence sources also report that US officials had warned the Russian government earlier that Chechnya might mount some form of nuclear-related terrorism and suggested that Russia enhance security (including air defenses) at its nuclear power sites.

Although Russian authorities, in response to the Chechen conflict, have taken some steps to heighten security at civilian nuclear power plants, most civilian nuclear facilities are deficient in such basic defensive elements as intact perimeter fences, more than token armed guards, vehicle barriers, surveillance cameras, metal detectors at entrances, and control cages. Unfortunately, these gaps in perimeter defense are compounded by an approach to the terrorist threat that is fixated on Chechens. As the assistant director of one major Russian nuclear research center told me not long ago, there is little concern about perimeter defense against terrorists since "Chechens look different than us" and would be recognized before they could get close to the site. Also contributing to the vulnerability of most nuclear power facilities in the former Soviet Union to terrorist attack is the failure of security at these sites to take account of the changed nature of the terrorist threat. In the Soviet period, the primary risk was perceived to be an external one; today most experts are more concerned about the "insider" threat. Unfortunately, these new threats are not reflected in the designs of most Russian nuclear power plants. Moreover, little US nonproliferation assistance to Russia has been directed specifically to mitigating the threat of radiological sabotage because that danger — unlike the diversion of fissile material — is not regarded as impacting directly on US national security.

## Nuclear Diversion

According to conventional wisdom, since the collapse of the Soviet Union there have been only four confirmed cases in which more than minuscule quantities of HEU or plutonium have been exported from the post-Soviet states, and another three cases in which HEU or plutonium were diverted from Russian nuclear facilities, but were seized prior to export. An additional four cases of diversion and/or export are sometimes included in the list of cases of proliferation concern, but do not clearly meet the standard of unambiguous sources to corroborate the diversion, or the size of enrichment level of the material.[8] The conventional wisdom further holds that there has been no proliferation significant diversion or export seizure since the confiscation of 2.72 kg. of HEU on 14 December 1994 in Prague. This alleged lull in illicit nuclear trafficking has led some analysts to conclude that the risk of nuclear diversion and export has diminished significantly.

Although this interpretation may be correct, it also is likely that Western observers of the nuclear trafficking scene have missed significant instances of diversion and/or export. Despite the pledges at the April 1996 Moscow Nuclear Safety and Security Summit to enhance US-Russian intelligence cooperation regarding nuclear smuggling, it is doubtful if Moscow has provided Washington with any meaningful, new information on nuclear diversions. Besides the six cases of theft or loss of nuclear materials in Russia reported by the Russian nuclear regulatory body Gosatomnadzor in 1996, there are credible reports of other instances of proliferation-significant nuclear trafficking since December 1994 involving the non-Russian successor states.

Potentially the most serious and sensitive case involves the possible seizure this past year in Belarus of individuals possessing HEU which Russian and Georgian officials believe came from Sukhumi, Georgia. Identification of the source reportedly was derived from the background of the individuals possessing the material and the enrichment level and characteristics of the HEU.

Although rarely identified as a site of nuclear activity, Sukhumi has long been a nuclear research center, and in 1992 possessed an inventory of approximately 2 kg of weapons-usable HEU. Because Sukhumi currently is under Abkhaz control, with no IAEA safeguards in place, neither Moscow nor Tbilisi knows how much HEU remains on site. Authorities at Sukhumi also appear to be without reliable information, and recently requested assistance from Minatom to determine the stock of fissile material at the research facility. The most current information available to Minatom is based upon an inventory taken in 1992. Although Minatom sought to send a team to Sukhumi in the Summer of 1997 for the purposes of taking a physical inventory there, it was stopped at the Ahkhaz border by Russian border guards who said they could not enter without Georgian permission. No such permission was obtained, the Russian nuclear specialists returned to their home sites, and no further information on the amount of HEU that remains at Sukhumi is known.

In addition to the Sukhumi-Belarus case, Gosatomnadzor reported the loss in mid-1996 of approximately one kg of HEU enriched to 90 per cent U-235 at the Tomsk Polytechnical University. The material was in a fresh fuel bundle for the university's research reactor. After an investigation by two teams from Gosatomnadzor and the facility, it was concluded that the bundle probably had been included inadvertently in a batch of spent fuel sent to Tomsk-7 in 1994. That date was derived from a comparison of physical inventories taken at the university. The material was never recovered. Tomsk-7 officials said it was impossible to try and find the material, and the case was closed.

The other cases of nuclear diversion reported by Gosatomnadzor appear to involve primarily low-enriched uranium (LEU) and spent fuel. Sites at which losses have been reported include the A.A. Bochvar All-Russian Institute for Inorganic Materials (VNIINM) in Moscow, which conducts research on MOX fuel and spent fuel reprocessing and waste treatment technology;[9] the Electrostal Machine Building Plant, which fabricates both HEU fuel for naval propulsion and fast-breeder reactors and LEU fuel for VVER and RMBK reactors; and the metallurgical plant in Glazov, which is engaged in the purification of uranium and its conversion to metal. At least one case at Glazov involved the loss of hundreds of kilograms of LEU, only a portion of which was recovered.

### *Tactical Nuclear Arms Race*

Tactical nuclear weapons have not figured prominently in the arms control and disarmament agenda since the Bush and Gorbachev initiatives in the Fall of 1991. They constitute a growing proliferation threat, however, and unless creative steps are undertaken, one may soon witness new deployments of and increased reliance upon sub-strategic nuclear arms. The danger stems from a number of technical, economic, and political factors including the weapon size, basing, changes in military doctrine and NATO enlargement.

Because they are relatively small and widely dispersed, and because older weapons lack electronic locks, tactical nuclear weapons are more vulnerable to unauthorized use or theft than are strategic weapons. An additional danger is that, in anticipation of interruptions in communications, field commanders may be given launch authority in times of crisis.

The Bush and Gorbachev declarations of 1991 significantly reduced the risk that these substrategic weapons might be used. Many of the US warheads were dismantled or destroyed, with the remainder secured in domestic storage.

The Russian government, for its part, reaffirmed the Soviet commitment to eliminate all nuclear warheads on land-based tactical missiles as well as nuclear artillery munitions and mines. It also proceeded to withdraw nuclear warheads, remove all tactical weapons from Russian surface ships, submarines, and land-based naval aviation; and to secure all tactical nuclear weapons that were not eliminated at Russian bases.

Russia's unilateral steps to eliminate or secure categories of substrategic weapons coincided with Moscow's efforts to remove all tactical nuclear weapons from the territories of the non-Russian republics and redeploy them in Russia. That redeployment was accomplished by the Spring of 1992.

Unfortunately, one need not believe General Lebed's charges about nuclear suitcase bombs in order to be concerned about the security of relatively small tactical nuclear weapons — especially those for aircraft which are not kept at central storage sites — and the danger of unauthorized or imprudent use. Economic hardship, political uncertainty, and the general malaise in the armed forces has put the security of these weapons in doubt. As former Russian Defense Minister Igor Rodionov said in February 1997, cash shortages and warped morale may make Moscow's nuclear arsenal "uncontrollable."

The problem of tactical nuclear weapons in Russia is magnified by Russia's growing reliance on nuclear arms as its conventional forces deteriorate. This dependency is reflected in Russia's abandonment in 1993 of its no-first use policy, and in the open discussion among prominent Russian military and defense industry figures of the need to develop a new generation of nuclear munitions for tactical and battlefield use. Some advocates of tactical nuclear weapons go so far as to contemplate Russian abrogation of the 1987 Intermediate Nuclear Force (INF) Treaty.[10] The dangers in this shift of emphasis are compounded because of Moscow's reliance on a "launch-on-warning" nuclear strategy and by the deterioration of Russia's early warning system.

This very destabilizing trend in Russian policy will almost certainly be reinforced and accelerated should the United States depart from the 1972 Anti-Ballistic Missile (ABM) Treaty and seek to achieve a national missile defense capability. Even more certain to exacerbate Russia's dependence on nuclear weapons and to prompt a reversal in the 1991 initiatives is NATO expansion. Indeed, it is hard to imagine a Western initiative better conceived to encourage the redeployment of Russian tactical nuclear weapons on ships at sea and on tactical aircraft. Under such circumstances, Europe could experience a new arms race involving those nuclear weapons most susceptible to unauthorized use, theft, and accident.

### Strains in the US-Russian Nonproliferation Relations

One of the less well known but important stories of the Cold War is the parallelism and often close consultation and cooperation between the US and USSR on nuclear nonproliferation issues.[11] Indeed, this cooperation generally persisted across Democratic and Republican administrations and during even the hottest points of the Cold War.

Ironically, today, after the end of the Cold War, there are indications of major new strains in the US-Russian nonproliferation partnership. These strains are evident in the current stalemate in strategic arms control negotiations, major disputes over Russian nuclear exports to Iran and India, the lack of meaningful progress in intelligence sharing regarding illicit nuclear trafficking, the lack of cooperation on important regional security issues (in the Middle East), and domestic political pressures in both countries to emphasize short-term, economic and military considerations to the neglect of longer term international security and nonproliferation objectives.

In the United States, these tendencies are reflected in the push for NATO enlargement, congressional pressure to abrogate the ABM Treaty, powerful opposition to the Cooperative Threat Reduction Program and the Comprehensive Test Ban Treaty, and a tendency to emphasize trade sanctions rather than economic incentives in dealings with Iran.

The tendency to emphasize economic over nonproliferation considerations is equally, if not more, pronounced in Russia. Among the examples in which nonproliferation considerations have been subordinated to economic objectives are Russian efforts to ease sanctions against Iraq and trade initiatives toward Iran, China, and India. The latter case is particularly telling since it prompted Russia in 1996 to amend a domestic export control regulation that was at odds with the government's interpretation of the April 1992 Nuclear Supplier Group guidelines. According to this interpretation, the guidelines were only applicable to contracts initiated after April 1992. The inconvenient regulation that might have legally precluded Russian nuclear exports to India was Government Regulation No. 1005 (21 December 1992), which specified that nuclear exports to non-nuclear states could only be made if all of the recipient country's nuclear activity were under IAEA safeguards.[12] In contrast, Government Regulation No. 574 (8 May 1996) conveniently amends Government Resolution No. 1005 and stipulates that full-scope IAEA safeguards were only required under contracts concluded before 4 April 1992. Under this "grandfather clause," Russia has sought to argue that since an initial agreement to provide India with two VVER-1000 reactors was concluded in 1987, a successor agreement in 1996 was not subject to the 1992 full-scope safeguards requirement.[13]

Sadly, one of the unanticipated consequences of the growth of pluralism and democracy in Russia is the difficult task of marshaling and maintaining support for arms control and disarmament measures, including those in the sphere of nonproliferation. This dilemma is apparent not only in parliamentary opposition to the Strategic Arms Reduction II (START II) Treaty and the Comprehensive Test Ban Treaty (CTBT), but in the government's failure to prosecute known cases of nuclear diversion and missile technology export violations (most glaringly the export of strategic gyroscopes to Iraq in 1995).

## *Complacency and Ignorance*

Although not generally thought of as proliferation threats, one might argue that the greatest challenges to nuclear nonproliferation at the end of the millenium are complacency and ignorance. These tendencies find expression in the US Congress, the Russian Duma, and in most national parliaments which remain woefully uneducated about nonproliferation issues and generally are unprepared to allocate the resources commensurate to the threat. More often than not, parliamentaries today are preoccupied with pressing domestic issues, and display scant interest in and even less knowledge of international issues, especially those which are not directly related to economics. For many this disposition is reinforced by the mistaken perception that with the end of the Cold War and the diminution of the traditional danger of superpower nuclear conflict, there are no longer any real nuclear dangers. From such a perspective — all too prevalent today in both the United States and Russia — there is little incentive to invest in such vital but esoteric nonproliferation programs as IAEA safeguards, export control assistance, tracking and interdicting illicit nuclear trade, and training the next generation of nonproliferation specialists.

One consequence of nonproliferation and arms control illiteracy on the part of the legislative branch of government in the United States and Russia is that in the absence of a remarkable arms control renaissance in the US Congress and the Russian Duma, it is hard to imagine much progress in gaining ratification of already concluded arms control and nonproliferation treaties such as the CTBT (in the United States) and the CTBT and START II (in Russia), not to mention more ambitious disarmament and nonproliferation measures. One possible lesson from this current stalemate associated with the domestic politics of arms control, may be the need to focus on nonproliferation measures that do not require ratification.

In some respects even more disturbing than the ignorance about nonproliferation issues on the part of national representatives is the state of knowledge by otherwise well educated citizens. Although this low knowledge base is deplorable, it also is understandable given the general absence of opportunities for study of the subject. Few if any high schools have curricula that expose students to issues of weapons proliferation or strategies for their control, and the possibility for university training is not much better. Remarkably, the Monterey Institute of International Studies is the only graduate school in the United States that offers a formal concentration in Nonproliferation Studies — an unfortunate situation if we take seriously the claim by US Secretary of Defense William Cohen that the threat of weapons of mass destruction proliferation is the paramount national security threat to the United States. No university offers such a concentration in Russia.

## WHAT IS TO BE DONE?

There is no shortage of good recommendations about what needs to be done to address these pressing proliferation problems. Some actually have been adopted as US and Russian policy. Rather than reiterate these points, the remainder of this chapter identifies some additional steps that might usefully be taken.

*1. Expand CTR Cooperation in the Area of Reactor Security*

Nuclear power plants in the Soviet Union were not designed to confront current terrorist threats which could lead to catastrophic accidents with global consequences. More attention should be given under the Nunn-Lugar Cooperative Threat Reduction program to enhance reactor security as part of the larger effort to strengthen the national nuclear safeguards system. At a minimum, current physical protection efforts need to be coordinated with work to upgrade the safety and security of the four dozen nuclear power reactors currently operating in five post-Soviet states. The threat of radiological sabotage and nuclear extortion, however, is by no means confined to the post-Soviet states, and requires much more attention from the world community than has been given to date.

*2. Purchase all HEU from Non-Russian Successor States*

The United States and Russia should seek to reduce the quantity of fissile material which must be protected and the number of sites where fissile material is stored. As part of a program of consolidation and elimination, the United States should undertake to negotiate the purchase of all highly enriched uranium (HEU) known to reside at research facilities in the non-Russian successor states. Given the relatively small, but nevertheless significant, quantities of weapons-usable material at sites in Belarus, Georgia, Kazakhstan, Latvia, Ukraine, and Uzbekistan, a uranium "buy-up" approach to the non-Russian republics represents a low cost, high return nonproliferation strategy.

A similar HEU purchase plan might usefully be applied to other sites outside of the former Soviet Union where fissile material is stored under inadequate safeguards and is vulnerable to theft.

To the extent that HEU actually is being used by research facilities (as is the case at Institute of Nuclear Physics in Uzbekistan), the United States also should provide the small amount of money needed to convert the research reactor to run on low-enriched uranium. Plans for such conversion already have been drawn up by Russian engineers and could be implemented at some sites in three-four months at about $1 million per reactor. The principal obstacle to the HEU purchase plan is the difficulty of gaining interagency agreement in the United States. This difficulty is a product of the interagency battles that were waged during the ultimately successful operation of "Project Sapphire," which resulted in the removal by the United States, of 600 kilograms of HEU from the Ulba Metallurgy Plant in Ust-Kamenogorsk, Kazakhstan.

*3. Negotiate Constraints on Sub-Strategic Nuclear Weapons*[14]

One approach to forestalling a tactical nuclear arms race that deserves consideration is a negotiated freeze on both the number and location of tactical deployments. Jonathan Dean, an advocate of this approach, has proposed that a freeze could apply initially to the area covered by the Conventional Forces in Europe (CFE) Treaty — from the Atlantic to the Urals.[15] A freeze would not reduce the number of NATO's nuclear arms, but it would preclude their eastward deployment, as well as the redeployment of Russian tactical weapons to areas west of the Urals.

A negotiated freeze — with provisions for verification — would be preferable to another round of unilateral declarations. The Russian government has already indicated that it does not put much stock in statements of intent, such as NATO's "three no's" statement in December 1996 that it had "no intention, no plan, and no need" to station nuclear weapons on the territory of new members. But a freeze that contained a provision of reciprocal on-site inspections could provide the basis for reductions in, and eventually the elimination of, tactical nuclear weapons in the region covered by the freeze.

Another important disarmament measure would be the codification in a legally binding treaty of the 1991 Bush-Gorbachev declarations on the withdrawal of substrategic weapons. This is important because the declarations contain no verification provisions. Although the withdrawals appear to have been implemented, the weapons could be redeployed at any time — a policy that some Russian officials have advocated as the appropriate response to NATO expansion.

In February 1996, Swedish Foreign Minister Lena Hjelm-Wallen said that many small states are even more concerned with the reduction of substrategic nuclear weapons than they are with strategic arms reductions. She urged that the 1991 unilateral declaration be codified to guard against "fluctuating international or domestic developments."

Only Norway has responded positively to Hjelm-Wallen's proposal. Although the lack of Russian enthusiasm is understandable, it is more difficult to explain the silence of the United States and the other Western states. It will be difficult to engage Russia in any negotiation until the issue of NATO enlargement is resolved, but it would be prudent to begin studying what a verification regime might look like for a treaty that incorporated the elements of the 1991 declarations.

Given Russian concerns, the impetus for eliminating tactical nuclear weapons will have to come from the United States. As a first step, the United States could declare that it will unilaterally bring home all air-based tactical nuclear weapons currently deployed in Europe. That policy could go a long way toward dispelling Russian fears about NATO, and it would help to revive the spirit of 1991.

Although the Clinton Administration has shown no inclination that it is prepared to take such a bold step, the pro-NATO credentials of Secretary of State Madeleine Albright would make the move politically feasible. An emerging but powerful advocate for the move is the US Air Force, which regards its nuclear mission in Europe as a serious drain on its conventional preparedness.

### 4. *Utilize Education As a Nonproliferation Tool*

Neither the US nor Russian government has appreciated how education might be used as a nonproliferation tool. As a consequence, there is a tremendous gap between government statements about the danger of weapons of mass destruction proliferation and the absence of funds allocated to train the next generation of nonproliferation specialists.

One reason for the failure of national governments to provide funds for education in the proliferation sphere is the tendency of the national security communities in most states to conceptualize proliferation decisions primarily in terms of technological-and security-driven causes with corresponding technical and international security fixes. Instead, it is desirable to focus more on the domestic political context in which proliferation decisions are made, and to devise an educational strategy that reinforces proliferation restraint by fostering the development of nonproliferation cultures, norms, and political constituencies.

Although this nonproliferation community - and capacity - building effort is critically needed in a number of so-called "problem countries," a multi-tiered and sustained educational effort that targets students in high schools and universities also is necessary in the United States, Russia and the other nuclear weapon states. One useful step that could be taken in the United States would be passage of legislation to create a National Nonproliferation Education Act. Such legislation, perhaps modeled after the National Defense Education Act would, among other things, provide fellowship support to US and selected foreign graduate students for advanced multidisciplinary training in nonproliferation.

## CONCLUSION

The end of the Cold War has greatly reduced the threat of thermonuclear war and has provided important, new nonproliferation opportunities. Especially promising are strides in the direction of the near-universal scope of the NPT, the rapid growth of NWFZs, and greater assertiveness on the part of international organizations with nonproliferation responsibilities. These very positive developments, however, should not obscure the existence of very real, and in some instances new, threats involving the spread and use of nuclear weapons. They include a rise in the risk of nuclear terrorism, the significant potential for illicit nuclear trafficking, and the danger of a new, tactical nuclear arms race.

Although the indefinite extension of the NPT represented a major step forward in international efforts to strengthen the nuclear nonproliferation regime, severe problems remain due to financial, political, and technical obstacles, as well as to widespread ignorance and complacency regarding proliferation threats on the part of both citizens and their elected representatives. In addition, significant differences continue to exist among states about the importance of nonproliferation objectives relative to other domestic and foreign policy goals. These differences are notable even between states such as the United States and Russia, which have an unusual history of cooperation for nonproliferation. Ironically, the end of the Cold War, the collapse of the Soviet empire, and the dismantling of much of the Soviet military industrial complex have contributed to a number of new proliferation problems, and have exposed strains in US-Russian nonproliferation cooperation. Although the similarities in US and Russian perspectives on proliferation are likely to continue to overshadow the differences, one can also expect disagreements to persist into the next millennium as both Russia and the United States struggle to reconcile "old thinking" with new political and economic realities.

## NOTES

1. For a discussion of this history see William C. Potter, "US-Russian Cooperation for Nonproliferation," in Sharyl Cross and Marina A. Oborotova,

eds., *The New Chapter in United States-Russian Relations* (Westport: Praeger, 1994), pp. 39-56.

2. See "Delegate Perspectives on the 1995 NPT Review and Extension Conference: A Series of Interviews Conducted by Susan Welsh," *The Nonproliferation Review* (Spring-Summer 1995), pp. 1-24 and Tariq Rauf and Rebecca Johnson, "After the NPT's Indefinite Extension: The Future of the Global Nonproliferation Regime," *The Nonproliferation Review* (Fall 1995), pp. 28-42. Although the official Russian position was supportive of the consensus in Main Committee III that peaceful nuclear explosions (PNEs) have no economic value, there were indications that the Russian delegation was not united in this perspective.

3. See Jozef Goldblat, "Nuclear-Weapon Free Zones: A History and Assessment," *The Nonproliferation Review* (Spring/Summer 1997), pp. 18-32.

4. The United States has been most explicit among the nuclear weapon states in setting forth these criteria: 1) The initiative for the creation of the zone should come from the states in the region concerned; 2) All states whose participation is deemed important should participate in the zone; 3) The zone arrangement should provide for adequate verification of compliance with its provisions; 4) The establishment of the zone should not disturb existing security arrangements to the detriment of regional and international security or otherwise abridge the inherent right of individual or collective self-defense guaranteed in the UN charter; 5) The zone arrangement should effectively prohibit its parties from developing or otherwise possessing any nuclear device for whatever purpose; 6) The establishment of the zone should not affect the existing right of its parties under international law to grant or deny other states transit privileges within their respective land territory, internal waters and airspace to nuclear powered and nuclear capable ships and aircraft of non-party nations, including port calls and overflights; and 7) The zone arrangement should not seek to impose restrictions on the exercise of rights recognized under international law, particularly the high seas freedoms of navigation and overflight, the right of innocent passage of territorial and archipelagic seas, the right of transit passage of international straits, and the right of archipelagic sea lanes passage of archipelagic waters. See Tariq Rauf, *Nuclear-Weapon-Free Zones (NWFZs): Questions & Answers* (Monterey: Center for Nonproliferation Studies, Monterey Institute of International Studies, May 1997), pp. 6-7.

During the Cold War, the Soviet Union identified two criteria for supporting a NWFZ: 1) The readiness of other nuclear powers to accept and honor the denuclearized status of the area; and 2) The completeness of obligations of the contracting powers and the extent to which they ensure the zone's denuclearized status.

More recently, Russian foreign policy has promoted the idea that nuclear weapons only be deployed on the national territories of the nuclear-weapon states, and has taken measures to accomplish this objective to its own nuclear arsenal. (See Rauf, p.7.)

5. The new safeguards arrangements consist of two parts, the first of which was approved by the IAEA Board of Governors in June 1995 and now is being implemented, and the second of which was approved by the IAEA Board in May 1997. See "International Nuclear Safeguards Strengthened," Fact Sheet, The White House (16 May 1997).

6. See Tadeuz Strulak, "The Nuclear Supplies Group," *The Nonproliferation Review* (Fall 1993), pp. 2-10. As will be discussed below, Russia has taken a very broad interpretation of the guidelines to permit the export of nuclear plants to India on the grounds that the export contract was initiated prior to the adoption of the NSG restrictions.

7. See Oleg Bukharin, "Upgrading Security at Nuclear Power Plants in the Newly Independent States," *The Nonproliferation Review* (Winter 1997), p. 32.

8. These cases are summarized in William C. Potter, "The Post-Soviet Nuclear Proliferation Challenge," Testimony to the Senate Governmental Affairs Subcommittee on International Security, Proliferation, and Federal Service (5 June 1997). See also Potter, "Before the Deluge? Assessing the Threat of Nuclear Leakage from the Post-Soviet States," *Arms Control Today* (October 1995), pp. 9-16.

9. Gosatomnadzor ordered certain activities at the Bochvar Institute shut down for six months in 1994 because of lax arrangements for handling plutonium at the site.

10. See, for example, Viktor Mikhailov, "NATO's Expansion and Russian Security," *Vek* (20 September 1996). For a useful review of Russian thinking about tactical nuclear arms see Nikolai Sokov, "Tactical Nuclear Weapons Elimination: Next Step for Arms Control," *The Nonproliferation Review* (Winter 1997), pp. 17-27.

11. See Potter, "US-Russian Cooperation for Non-Proliferation."

12. The title of the regulation was "On Approval of the Statute Regulating Exports and Imports of Nuclear Materials, Technology, Equipment, Installations, Special Non-Nuclear Materials, Radioactive Sources of Ionizing Radiation and Isotopes." See in particular Article V.b.

13. The earlier 1992 agreement was never implemented due to problems of financing.

14. A more detailed set of policy recommendations related to reducing the threat of a tactical nuclear arms race is provided in William C. Potter, "Unsafe at Any Size," *The Bulletin of Atomic Scientists* (May/June 1997), pp. 25-27, 61.

15. Jonathan Dean, "Using the NPT Review Process to Advance Nuclear Disarmament: What Steps Beyond the Fissile Cutoff?" Paper presented at the Seminar on Nuclear Disarmament After the Extension of the NPT, Kyoto, Japan (2-5 December 1996), pp. 3-4.

# 6

---

# The Russian Quest for a New Identity: Implications for Security in Eurasia

*Igor A. Zevelev*

Dramatic changes have taken place in Russia during the past seven years. From an international perspective, the most significant transformations have occurred in Russia's geopolitical situation, its role in global affairs, and its military might. Russia's territory has reverted to that of the seventeenth century, and it has lost its most prized territorial possessions in Europe. Russia has lost all of its Soviet-era allies, and its military is in dismal condition. As a result, Russia is now geographically more detached from Western and Central Europe than in any period since Peter the Great.

Nevertheless, many still view Russia with suspicion, perceiving it as a potential threat. According to popular views, pre-revolutionary Russian imperialism persisted throughout the communist period, and remains at the heart of Russian foreign policy even after the Soviet collapse. This is the view of Henry Kissinger, Zbigniew Brzezinski, and many other scholars and politicians in the United States; it is largely shared by the eminent Russian historian Yuri Afanasiev.[1] Steven Sestanovich refers to this school of thought as "geotherapy."[2] Why does this perspective remain so strong despite dramatic changes in Russia? The issue seems to be even more interesting if one compares the views of "geotherapists" with the position of those who can be called "geomourners."

"Geomourners" may be easily found among Russian communists or members of Vladimir Zhirinovsky's Liberal Democratic Party. Many liberals believe that Russia is about to disappear from the global arena as well. Vladimir Lukin, the Chairman of the Russian State Duma's Committee on Foreign Relations, former Ambassador to the United States, and one of the leaders of "Yabloko," the liberal faction in the Duma, argued that "the main Russian strategic interest in the coming two decades will be extremely simple: to survive."[3] Lukin singles out the "civilizational" factor as the major threat to Russia and fears that the country's disintegration as a distinct community will result from the gradual disappearance of common ideas, laws and values uniting the country's population. Under such circumstances, any external threat to security, even a small one, might become fatal.

Why are there such differences in perceptions of Russia in the context of international security? On the one hand, there is an image of an aggressive, scheming, conspiring imperialistic state. On the other hand, there are concerns for an endangered nation struggling to survive. In attempting to answer this question, one should examine the problem not only from traditional perspectives concerning security, but also by incorporating non-traditional perspectives. This article will attempt to establish the relevance of Russian identity and its transformations for assessing regional security in Eurasia. This approach yields some useful insights for understanding new challenges to global security emerging from this part of the world.

Both geotherapists and geomourners paradoxically rely on the same assumption that Russia has lost its old imperial identity and has not found a new one. Geotherapists fear that Russia will fail to find such a new role and will revert back to the old role by attempting to create a new empire. Geomourners are also afraid that Russia will not find a new role, but unlike geotherapists, they are more concerned about the possibility of chaos, disintegration, and Russia's gradual fading away. Viewed in such a light, the two seemingly opposite perspectives are not so different. Both adumbrate post-imperial transformations of Russia and the loss of its previous identity, though they do not always use exactly this term. The major difference is in the perception of threat: imperial restoration versus chaos and disintegration. The positive alternative seems to be the same for both geotherapists and for some Russian liberal geomourners. They claim that Russia will cease to be a threat to the world and to itself when

it becomes a "normal" European nation-state, abandoning its imperial
ambitions.

## NATION-BUILDING AS A POTENTIAL SECURITY THREAT

If the term "nation-state" is intended to define a situation in which the
borders of a nation approximate those of the state, Russians had spent
several centuries building an empire, not a nation-state.  The British
historian Geoffrey Hosking recently reinterpreted Russian history of the
1552-1917 period, attempting to demonstrate how and why the Russians
failed to develop a strong sense of a nation.  Hosking argued that the
process of  empire-building obstructed nation-building in Russia.[4]
Relying on his earlier work and on Hosking's ideas, Richard Pipes
proclaimed that building a nation-state in Russia was an immediate
political task[5] and even came up with a formula, assuming that history
develops in a clear "progressive" direction towards some well-known and
well-defined goal:

> The Russians of today would be well advised to give up fantasies of re-
> conquering their lost empire — fantasies common to both conservatives
> and democrats — and concentrate on building a genuine nation-state.
> Nationalism, defined as 'a feeling of community and solidarity,' which
> the West has put behind itself and which it has turned into a reactionary
> doctrine, is distinctly progressive at the stage of history at which Russia
> happens to find itself.[6]

Foreign policy and security deliberations of geotherapists have finally
been placed into a seemingly solid theoretical framework with a deep
historical perspective.  Partly reflecting this view, US policy in Eurasia
has been based on the assumption that Russian neo-imperialism is the
major obstacle to a positive and progressive process of nation-building on
the territory of the former Soviet empire.

Indeed, both common sense and political theory (and the two so rarely
concur!) suggest that people need a bond of collective identity, especially
after the collapse of despotic regimes that ruled over them.  The process of
democratization makes the search for a new bond even more urgent, since
it is no longer provided by old authoritarian structures.  Respect for basic
human rights and the establishment of democratic institutions are possible
only when there exists some kind of integrated community, usually in the

form of a nation-state, to which individuals are loyal. Out of such a collection of individuals, a "people" is created. Therefore, cultivating a devoted political community is essential for Russia's survival as a meaningful polity, which presently cannot be taken for granted. A nation-state provides the best possible framework for creating such a community.

Yet, the idea of instantaneously constructing a nation-state in today's Russia might be seriously flawed not only theoretically and historically, but also in terms of consequences for security. It is a problematic and dangerous political goal for the Russian elite to undertake and for American political strategists to encourage.

The nation-state is not a uniform condition. It is, in fact, a highly specific historical phenomenon that does not (and most probably never will) exist in most of the world. Is it possible that Russia (or any other modern state) will simply retrace, step by step, the path of Western European countries a couple of centuries later? Does the process of accelerated globalization have any impact on today's nation-building? It is important to realize that the stage of history at which Russia happens to find itself now is not the eighteenth century, but the nuclear age. On the more concrete level of national security, the question is whether it is possible to risk the tumultuous perils of building a genuine nation-state in a country with nuclear weapons? Western European nation-states emerged out of centuries of wars and oppression. Michael Howard, an eminent scholar of the history of war, has argued: "From the very beginning the principle of nationalism was almost indissolubly linked, both in theory and practice, with the idea of war... In nation-building as in revolution, force was the midwife of the historical process."[7] Too often, the "feeling of community and solidarity" has been founded on hostility toward others.

In the process of building a nation, the crucial questions are who should belong to the nation and what should be its boundaries.[8] The most destructive feature of any nation-building process has been the amalgamation of smaller political entities (ethnic, religious minorities) or the breaking-up of bigger ones (typically multiethnic states). The boundaries of any Western European state, and corresponding nations, were usually defined by numerous wars, internal violence, or by combination of the two.[9] In today's Russia, such a definition is more complex, and seems to determine so much more. The issue of the Russian people's boundaries determines their attitudes toward the non-Russians within Russia, Russia's relations with neighboring newly independent states, and the international security of Eurasia.[10] For Russia, constructing a nation-state on the rubble of the empire would inevitably challenge its federative structure, which contains a number of ethno-territorial units, and jeopardize the issue of external borders that are still based on artificial administrative boundaries, drawn by the Bolsheviks, effectively excluding 23 million ethnic Russians from their presumed homeland. Indeed, such a nation-state building effort could easily undermine the entire system of regional and global security.

Hosking wrote that "Britain *had* an empire, but Russia *was* an empire – and perhaps still is."[11] The collapse of the Soviet Union meant much more for Russia than just the loss of colonies. It was a loss of identity. Political, historical, cultural, ethnic boundaries, as well as a subjective mental map held by most Russians share no congruence. There has been no clear and historically consistent criteria for distinguishing "we" from "they" in the Russian consciousness. Confusion over the boundaries of the Russian people has been the major factor of Eurasia's historical development for at least three hundred years. This phenomenon has enormous and contradictory implications for current issues of stability, security, and peace in the region. Unfortunately, this issue has not been adequately incorporated into international relations, foreign policy, and security studies. Such a lacuna can be explained to a great extent by the fact that during the Soviet period there was practically no connection between identity issues and foreign and security policy. The existence of artificial distinctions between these two disciplines has hindered the examination of the newly emerging link between them after the end of the Cold War. In the years following the breakup of the Soviet Union, there has been a comfortable blanket of silence over the issues of Russian identity, its boundaries, and the fate of Russian nationhood. Yeltsin, the driving force of the empire's dissolution, went out of his way to downplay the "national" themes, emphasizing instead the conflict in socialism versus capitalism, communists versus democrats, and slow versus rapid reform.

However, without addressing the issues bound up with the Russian identity, it is impossible to understand, for example, why Yeltsin unleashed a full-scale war to keep culturally and politically alien Chechens within Russia, while at the same time ignoring the strong desire of six million Russians living compactly in adjacent northern Kazakhstan to be a part of Russia.[12] Does it mean that Russia's major challenges to peace and security in Eurasia will come from within, or is there a possibility for interstate conflicts? The war in Chechnya demonstrated that Yeltsin was ready to resort to extreme measures to achieve his goals of building the Russian state within current borders. Notably, the United States has shown an unusual tolerance in this situation. However, one may only speculate on what America's reaction would be if Yeltsin decided to encourage and support irredentism among ethnic Russians in neighboring states. Since firm and unconditional support of the Soviet successor states' sovereignty is a pillar of US policy in the region, aimed at curbing Russian neo-imperial ambitions, the US response probably would have been incomparably stronger, especially if Ukraine or the countries adjoining the Caspian Sea were involved.[13]

A "national" redefinition of identities always contains a significant destabilizing component and, as such, might be considered a security threat. The war in Chechnya proved that any solution of the "Russian question," understood as the unfinished quest for identity, might have serious consequences. Even the seemingly peaceful and democratic idea of preserving the sovereignty and territorial integrity of the post-Soviet states within their current borders might end up giving their rulers a free hand within those borders. It might also freeze in place frontiers that are not viable in the long term and stimulate the growth of tensions between the governments trying to build sovereign nation-states and millions of people attaching their loyalties to another territory.

Forcing the construction of a nation-state in Russia may place the painful and explosive issues concerning the frontiers of the Russian people onto the country's political agenda. It is probably better to keep these issues behind the lines of Russian politics and foreign relations. This argument can be supported by analyzing two major problems. First, the reasons for the low level of national consciousness among Russians and the historical ambiguity over the borders of "the Russian people" will be discussed. Second, the issues of nation-building in Russian intellectual history, again from the perspective of defining Russia's boundaries, will be examined. This analysis will be followed by an attempt to outline implications of the transformations of Russian identity for Eurasian security.

## INARTICULATED NATIONHOOD

Because of many historical factors, Russians have emerged from the USSR as an incomplete nation, with a surprisingly low level of national consciousness and the absence of a mass-based national movement. This fundamentally differentiates them from other former Soviet republics, particularly the Baltics, Georgia, and Armenia.

The Russian Empire and its successor, the Soviet Union, were contiguous empires, like those of the Hapsburgs or the Ottomans; there were no natural boundaries between the center and the periphery. In fact, in the Russian and Soviet cases, the center was represented by the capital city — St. Petersburg and, later, Moscow — not by some well-defined, core territory. It was geography that played an important role in the formation of Russian national consciousness, a fundamental characteristic of which is the combination of somewhat intertwined ethnic and imperial components. Richard Pipes, Roman Szporluk, and Richard Sakwa contend that the Russian Empire has been formed before the modern national identity of Russians emerged.[14] Further, Geoffrey Hosking showed that the Russian elite was more interested in expanding the boundaries of the empire than in promoting the belief in nationhood. Unlike Pipes, Hosking attributes the non-emergence of the Russian nation not to the backwardness of the country, but to specific geographical, historical, and political circumstances.[15]

Various authors also point to different periods of history when trying to identify a boundary between supranational and ethnonational orientations of the Russian Empire. Russian historian Nikolai Tsymbayev found that the shift to ethnonational policy occurred at the turn of the eighteenth century.[16] Richard Sakwa suggests the 1880s as a watershed.[17] Both orientations have existed throughout Russian history, including during the Soviet period. One or the other may have prevailed at different times, but the Soviet era encompassed periods of stronger internationalism in the 1920s and stronger Russian ethnonationalism from the 1930s through the early 1950s.

The absence of clear boundaries between the empire and its Russian core led some analysts to conclude that there was no dominant ethnic group: all groups, including Russians, were subjects of an imperial center.[18] This thesis, though seemingly serving self-justification of Russians, plays an extremely important role in their post-Soviet psyche. There is practically no significant theory or political force in present-day

Russia that views the empire as a vehicle for Russian interests at the expense of other peoples. That remains in sharp contrast to emerging ideology and official historiography in the Newly Independent States. More important, it reflects a deep-rooted belief in the Russian consciousness that the empire did not serve Russians' interests and was instead a burden (Alexander Solzhenitsyn); or beneficial for all peoples, not only Russians (Gennady Zyuganov); or detrimental to everyone because of its communist nature during the Soviet period (liberals).

One more inhibiting factor for the development of mass-based Russian nationalism is the overlap of cultural, linguistic, and historical distinctions between Russia, Belarus, and Ukraine, leading to a confused boundary between Russians and other Eastern Slavs.[19] For centuries, it made the Russian elite "soft-pedal" their nationalism, much like the existence of the "home empire" of Scotland, Wales, and Northern Ireland in the United Kingdom suppressed English nationalism.

An important factor contributing to the weakening of Russian national consciousness was the concept of the "Soviet people" and the reality that supported it. People from mixed marriages, those living outside their "homelands," and Russians from large urban (and more cosmopolitan) centers were the most responsive to this concept. Russians accepted it more readily than other ethnic groups, because to be "Soviet" implicitly meant being a Russian-speaker and acknowledging the "civilizing" mission of the Russian culture and its extraterritorial nature throughout the entire Soviet Union. In theory, there was much in common between the "melting pot" paradigm in the US and the "Soviet people" concept in the USSR. (The notions of multiculturalism and diversity in the American experience also had an ideological cousin in the USSR: the "free union of flourishing nations"). The first attempts to develop a theory of the "Soviet people" can be traced back to Nikolai Bukharin.[20] Nikita Khrushchev revisited this theme, emphasizing the fusion of nations under communism, and promising its attainment in the near future. In the 1970s, this idea was revived, when it was solemnly pronounced that the "Soviet people" became a "new historical entity," not just a concept.

Some Russian nationalists claimed that the imperial role deprived Russians of their ethnic identity. Slavophile writers grouped around the magazine *Nash Sovremennik* worried that "Soviet patriotism" was undermining Russian national consciousness, fretting that Russian city dwellers frequently referred to themselves as "Soviet people." It is fashionable but unwise to easily discard any reality that stood behind the concept of the "Soviet people." The concept adequately reflected some trends (intermingling of peoples into a new entity), while ignoring others (national awakening).

Throughout the entirety of Soviet history – from Vladimir Lenin to Mikhail Gorbachev — there was one common policy denominator that could not but greatly weaken the formation of the Russian national consciousness, further blurring its distinction from an imperial consciousness and simultaneously contributing to a possible nationalistic revival in the future: the struggle, though not aways consistent, by successive Soviet regimes against Russian nationalism. Lenin developed the concept of two nationalisms – one of an oppressive nation and one of the oppressed; the former was dubbed as reactionary, triggering his theoretical and political crusade against "Great Russian chauvinism." The struggle against Russian nationalism was continued by Nikolai Bukharin and, later, by Joseph Stalin.[21] The most inconsistent warrior against Russian nationalism, Stalin, initially upheld Lenin's perspective on Great Russian chauvinism as the major threat and local nationalism as a justified response to it in his *Report on National Factors in Party and State Development*, published in 1923. After the Sixteenth Party Congress (1934) until his death in 1953, Stalin's rhetoric and deeds amounted to a complete departure from Lenin's ideas and his own earlier views; Stalin's actions in that period were also characterized by a vigorous policy aimed at promoting Russian achievements rather than Soviet internationalism. This shift was reflected, among other policies, in the promotion of the Russian language in the USSR's non-Russian republics. (Russian Communist leader Gennady Zyuganov currently glorifies this stage in Soviet nationality policy).

Decades later, Alexander Yakovlev, then acting head of the Department for Propaganda of the CPSU, made a name for himself by denouncing Russian nationalism. Yuri Andropov, then head of the KGB, reportedly considered Russian nationalism, not liberal dissidents, as a major threat to Soviet state security.[22] According to very revealing memoirs by Gorbachev's assistant A. S. Chernyaev, the first and the last president of the USSR opposed the idea of creating a Russian *(Russkaya)* republic in the Soviet Union because it could have led to the "end of the empire."[23] "The systematic constraint of Russian nationalism"[24] was the price the Soviet leadership was ready to pay for the preservation of the multinational state. Stalin, with his instruments of terror, was probably the only Soviet leader confident enough in his strength to allow Russian nationalism to develop, since he was not afraid of the expected reaction from non-Russian nationalities. Yet in this regard, Hugh Seton-Watson may be correct when he concluded that "in the Soviet period there has been more Russification than Russian nationalism. The Russification has been less a conscious policy than an unintended consequence of the political and economic centralization of the Soviet empire. The Soviet leadership, from 1917 to the present day, has not been inspired by Russian nationalism."[25]

State institutions facilitate nation-building. In the twentieth century, states have more often created nations than the reverse. The entire Soviet Union was a homeland for Russians, in sharp contrast with other ethnic groups inclined to refer only to their titular republic as their homeland. The Russian Socialist Federated Soviet Republic, which was supposed to be a republic for Russians (and not only Russians, but also many nationalities of its autonomous republics, okrugs, and oblasts) within the framework of the USSR, lacked many of the attributes of other republics. The imperial center had merged with the ethnic Russian center; the RSFSR had neither a separate capital city, nor (until 1990) its own Communist Party, nor (unlike Ukraine and Belarus) its own seat in the United Nations. In short, the institutional weakness of the RSFSR contributed a great deal to the underdevelopment of Russian national consciousness and confusion over the boundaries of the Russian people.

Rogers Brubaker suggests a provocative parallel between Russians in the USSR and whites in the United States.[26] Both groups served as an "invisible core," a zero-value for their countries. While other communities could afford to emphasize their distinct cultural heritage, Russians in the USSR and whites in the US, while actually shaping their respective countries' dominant cultures, downplayed their ethnic distinctiveness vis-a-vis smaller ethnic groups. Not surprisingly, this particular status gave rise to grievances among politically marginal and potentially violent groups of Russian nationalists or militant white separatists in the United States. Vladimir Bondarenko, a leading publicist of the Russian nationalist newspaper *Zavtra*, has frequently published apologetic commentaries on what he calls the "right-wing patriotic movement" waging a "holy war" of "white resistance" in the US. He has predicted the failure of the "American multicultural experiment," the disintegration of the US, and mass suffering of American whites. One of the common denominators among Russian nationalists and right-wing

American patriots is an extreme suspicion of globalization and a deep-seated mistrust of multinational institutions.[27] It should come as no surprise then, that extreme nationalists have so far been the most vocal advocates of building a Russian nation-state.

## NATION-BUILDING IN RUSSIAN INTELLECTUAL HISTORY

Mass-based nationalism often follows the nationalization of the elite. Many factors have blocked the emergence of Russians as a strong ethnopolitical community with well-defined boundaries. But what about the intellectuals? Have they tried hard enough to "awaken" the Russians nationally? Have they developed any concept of Russians as a distinct nation with established frontiers?

For a century and a half, the debate over the Russian identity, nation formation, and Russia's future has focused primarily on Russia's relation to and interaction with the West.[28] However, another aspect is of equal importance: interactions with the neighboring peoples of Eurasia and the boundaries of the Russian people in this context. At the end of the twentieth century, this second aspect is becoming even more important in the search for a new Russian identity. Nevertheless, this dimension of the problem, while having its own history of intellectual reflection in Russia, has often been missing from the discourse or played a secondary role.

The roots of the current discussion on Russian identity can be traced back to the nineteenth century debates between Slavophiles and Westernizers. Slavophiles emphasized the unique character of the Russian civilization, based on Slavic Orthodox communitarian traditions. It was opposed to alien Western civilization, with its alleged rationalism and faceless codified law. In contrast, the Westernizers argued that Russia should emulate and learn from the rationalism of the West. The problems of the Russian Empire's multiethnicity, interactions between Russians and other peoples, and the frontiers of the Russian people played no significant role in these debates, establishing a tradition for many Russian intellectuals. Characteristically, the specific problems of Russia's national minorities were first raised in a relatively consistent theoretical manner not in the intellectual salons of St. Petersburg or Moscow, but in Kiev, by the Brotherhood of Saints Cyril and Methodius. Led by a Ukrainian poet and public figure, Taras Shevchenko, and a Russian student of Ukrainian history, Nicholas Kostomarov in 1846, these debates could hardly countenance the separation of Slavs. In fact, Shevchenko and Kostomarov elaborated the idea of a pan-Slavic federation of liberal states, including Russia, Ukraine, Poland, Bohemia, Serbia, and Bulgaria. (Nobody defined present-day Belarus as something distinct in those days).

In 1869, Nicholas Danilevsky, in his *Russia and Europe*, tried to fuse Slavophilism, pan-Slavism, and a policy of imperialism.[29] Essentially, Danilevsky recast the liberal pan-Slavic idea in conservative imperialist thought. Slavic culture, in Danilevsky's view, could serve as a basis for Russian leadership of a newly created federation of Slavic peoples whose capital would be in Constantinople.

There was one more significant intellectual development in the nineteenth century that left an important imprint on later discussions: the idea of the "universal" character of the Russian identity. Started by Slavophiles, this idea was developed by Dostoevsky, who wrote in his famous 1880 sketch on Pushkin: "For what else is the strength of the Russian national spirit than the aspiration, in its ultimate goal, for universality and all-embracing humanitarianism?"[30] In his deliberations, Dostoevsky, like both Slavophiles and Westerners, referred only to Europe: "Yes, the Russian's destiny is incontestably all-European and universal. To become a genuine and all-around Russian means, perhaps (and this you should remember), to become brother of all men, *a universal man*, if you please."[31]

It could be argued that Dostoevsky expressed with remarkable passion some very important features of Russian national consciousness: its openness, inclusiveness, and messianism. While Danilevsky drew boundaries, though very broad ones, Dostoevsky went beyond them; Dostoevsky admired Pushkin for his ability to understand and include the entire European culture into the Russian soul.

Russian policy in the nineteenth century, however, was driven not so much by these ideas, but by the doctrine of "official nationalism," formulated by Count Sergei Uvarov. Orthodoxy, autocracy, and "nationality" were proclaimed the pillars of the empire. The third principle, "nationality," (*narodnost'*) was the most ambiguous, especially after the Polish revolt of 1830 and the nationalization of ethnic groups in the second half of the century. This was a subject for very different theoretical and political interpretations. Yet the central question remained unresolved: Was the Russian Empire a state of and for ethnic Russians, or was it a multiethnic entity that somehow required loyalty to the monarchy?

The Russian intellectual elite, while responding to the nationalization process, usually lagged behind the developments among the non-Russians, who had already constructed collective mental boundaries between themselves and Russians in the second half of the nineteenth century. Slavophiles and Westerners, Danilevsky, Dostoevsky, Uvarov, and others, were concerned with the Russians' relation to Europe, Slavic unity, and the universe, but not to other peoples within the empire. In their minds, the "Little Russians" (Ukrainians), the "White Russians" (Byelorussians), and the "Great Russians" (ethnic Russians) comprised one Russian people, while all others (*inorodtsy*) were practically excluded from the theoretical discourse. This occurred because ethnic or national consciousness among both the elite and the masses was still relatively weak in this premodern empire. Evidently, it was a mistake to ignore the developments in the empire's Western part, most of all in Poland, where national consciousness was becoming stronger.

As the nationalization process gained momentum in the second half of the nineteenth century, the policy of Russification started to take shape in the Russian Empire, especially under Alexander III. There was an evident shift from the de-ethnicized mindset of the imperial court, which was mostly concerned with the loyalty of the subjects to the czar, to more ethnically articulated attempts to make Russians out of the non-Russians in some cases, and to secure Russian dominance over other "awakening" peoples in other cases. This shift established a background for defining Russians as a separate nation.

By 1917, when loyalty to the czar had thoroughly eroded among Russians, they did not yet constitute a modern cohesive nation. There is no consistent evidence in the history of Russian society or intellectual thought or social history to support the assumption of Jeff Chinn and Robert Kaiser that "nation and homeland" – rather than czar and religion — became the focus of Russians' loyalty."[32] In fact, most Russian thinkers stressed the opposite. Petr Struve wrote: "The collapse of the monarchy, after a brief period of general shock, showed *the extreme weakness of national consciousness in the very core of the Russian state, among masses of the Russian people* [emphasis added]."[33] Struve argued that in pre-revolutionary Russia, the nation was opposed to, and in disagreement with the state; hence he favored a reunion between them. Amazingly, like the Slavophiles of seventy years earlier, he did not address the problem of multiethnicity in the Russian "nation" and the place of ethnic Russians in the state as something of crucial significance.

In that regard, he was much in line with other liberal thinkers and politicians.  Pavel Milyukov, the leader of the Constitutional Democratic Party of Russia, wrote about the formation of a Russia's new supra-ethnic nation, which had begun to develop well before 1917.[34]

An important contribution to the debate on Russian identity was made by the Eurasians, a group of young intellectual-emigres (Pyotr Savitsky, Nikolai Trubetskoy, Georgi Frolovsky, Pyotr Suvchinsky, and others) in the 1920s.  Unlike the Slavophiles, they went beyond their Slavic roots in search of the basis for the Russian nation.  Arguing that Turkic and Finn-Ugric elements played a key role as well, they were the first to incorporate non-Slavic peoples into the discourse on the identity of Russians.  According to them, Eurasia was cemented by a common geographic space and self-consciousness; it was neither European nor Asian, it was Eurasian.  Though the Eurasians differed significantly from other thinkers in many respects, they continued the tradition of a non-ethnic definition of Russianness.

The Bolsheviks seemed to be the party that devoted the greatest attention to the "nationality question."[35]  The most important features of their view was the declaration of the Russian empire as a "prison of the peoples," the denunciation of "Great Russian chauvinism," and a proclamation of the right for self-determination for all the peoples of the country.  Contrary to these principles, Bolsheviks gradually re-created the highly-centralized state within borders similar to those of the empire.  The price they paid was the suppression of Russian ethnic nationalism and the creation of ethno-territorial units of different levels of autonomy for the non-Russians.

The Soviet theory of a "nationality question," as well as actual policy in this realm, were far from being consistent throughout more than seven decades.  Up to the early 1920s, the internationalist perspective dominated. Relying on Karl Marx, Russian revolutionaries Pyotr Lavrov, Pyotr Tkachev, Georgi Plekhanov, and Vladimir Lenin believed that the national question was subordinate to social class, and that nations would disappear, or "merge," in a future communist paradise.  A future Russian nation envisioned by Milyukov was transformed into a global communist nation by Lenin; both liberals and Marxists of that time did not see a future place for the nationality question.  There was an important difference, however. Bolsheviks were ready to make significant concessions to the non-Russians by giving them ethno-territorial homelands and the right to self-determination to gain allies in the struggle against the czarist empire.  The regime was sure that Russians, as a more "advanced" nation, did not require such blandishments, since they would be satisfied with the Bolshevik social ideal. For Lenin, the national interests of Russians did not exist separately from the interests of world proletariat. In this respect, Dostoevsky's "universality" of Russians took a new, Marxist form, while remaining practically the same in its essence: diluting their ethnic identity in broader humanitarian or social missions. One of the first Russian thinkers who pointed to this continuity was Nikolai Ustrialov. The questions of who should belong to the Russian nation and what its boundaries should be were irrelevant in this context.

When the goal of a world socialist revolution was postponed indefinitely, concessions to nationalities within the Soviet Union became lasting rather than temporary. Centralized party rule was a critical counterbalance to this ethnonational federal system. As the influence of the party began to diminish under Gorbachev, the state simultaneously began to collapse.

## THE UNFINISHED QUEST FOR IDENTITY: SECURITY IMPLICATIONS

A new Russia has begun to define its identity from the ground up; very little from its past can be applied to the present. Intellectual history has not provided contemporary thinkers and politicians with adequate tools for assessing how Russia's age-old quandary fits in a new geopolitical situation. Nevertheless, we can isolate three major options for the future development of a new Russian identity: neoimperial, ethnic, and civic.

Russian culture was formed throughout the past three centuries within an imperial framework. "Universalism" (*vselenskost'*) became the key feature of Russian "high culture." On the one hand, it helped the Russian culture to gain worldwide recognition. Far from being "provincial" or "narrow-minded," it easily absorbed the achievements of other, particularly European, cultures and made outstanding contributions to humankind. On the other hand, the attempts to include everyone culturally and otherwise into a limitless, "universal" Russia have been in constant conflict with particular aspirations of neighboring peoples, who largely did not want to become "universal," seeing Russification behind such "universalism" and perceiving it as a threat to their very existence. Historical and cultural messianic traditions stand in sharp contrast to the new geopolitical situation in which Russia finds itself today.

No longer hidden under imperial veil, ethnic identity has become more salient to Russians after the collapse of the Soviet Union. Although ethno-nationalism is not politically well organized in Russia, it might emerge ascendant, especially if a goal of nation-state building is introduced into contemporary political discourse, since the term "nation" has had a strong ethnic, not civic, connotation in Soviet and post-Soviet academia, public opinion, and politics. As has happened many times in the history of Europe, a well-articulated common culture may come to be defined as the ideal political boundary, leading to ardent claims that all Russians must be reunited under one political roof. As Anthony Smith notes, "Aggrandizing their homelands through the mobilization of ethnic sentiment among kinsmen outside the 'homeland' was the mark of many a European irredentism in the last century and later."[36]

The redefinition of Russia in more concrete ethnic terms, in line with those of all Soviet successor states may become the most dangerous undertaking in its history, primarily due to redrawing of Eurasia's borders which will inevitably accompany the implementation of an ethno-nationalist project. The essence of the ethno-nationalist program is to restore a geographical congruence between the state and the nation by building the Russian state within the area of settlement of the Russian people and other Eastern Slavs. Politically, this means the reunification of Russia, Belarus, Ukraine, and northern Kazakhstan, the last an area Alexander Solzhenitsyn, the contemporary intellectual force of ethnonationalism in modern Russia, identifies as "Southern Siberia and Southern (Trans)Urals."

If the experience of other countries is any guide, nation-building on the rubble of an empire is usually an endeavor of ethno-nationalists. Kemalist Turkey started its experiment with a nation-state by subjecting its Armenian, Greek, and Kurdish minorities to genocide and expulsion.[37] Austrians welcomed the Anschluss after twenty years of living in a small postimperial state. Serbia and Croatia became aggressively nationalistic and began to redraw the post-Yugoslavian political map through the use of brutal force. All the former Soviet republics have adopted ethno-political myths, identifying the state as a homeland of "indigenous" people. Intellectually, all these policies relied on the Romantic historicist tradition, claiming that humanity could be divided neatly into nations, and stipulating that culturally — or ethnically — defined nations possessed sacred rights; in such a way these nations' leaders could downplay the individual human rights and due respect for minorities.[38] The policy of ethnonationalism is especially dangerous when it is supported by powerful outside forces that prefer to see an anti-imperial struggle cast in rosy hues, ignoring the darker side.

The development of civic identity also de-legitimizes Russia's current boundaries by questioning the collapse of the Soviet Union: why was it impossible to build a de-ethnicized, democratized, state within the old borders? The "politically correct" answer is that this option would not have met the ethnonational aspirations of the non-Russians; they did not want to live in the old empire and thus created their own states. Russians have again found themselves in a multiethnic milieu within new borders, and 25 million of them were left outside. The "national question" for Russians was not resolved by the collapse of the Soviet Union. On the contrary, it was rather created. Russia within its current borders is "more a bleeding hulk of empire: what happened to be left over when the other republics broke away."[39]

The development of a civic identity hardly matches the other options in the sense of a quick mobilization potential; in fact, it might mean a rather weak state for a long period. In order to build a true civic identity, it is necessary to have or develop a common idea, history, heritage, traditions, legitimate boundaries accepted by all citizens, and strong and effective state institutions. Nothing in this list exists in Russia thus far. As a multiethnic political community within the boundaries of the modern Russian Federation, the Russian nation is new, unstable, and weak. Regular elections, political institutions, and common economic and social problems and policies might gradually serve as the integument for this new political nation, further separating it from the other Soviet successor states. However, internal divisions, first of all between ethno-territorial units and the center, are strong and are becoming even more important. Separatist Chechnya is an extreme example of the difficulties in building a common civic identity in Russia. It is an evident security concern not only for Russia, but for the rest of the world, which will be affected by the security and power vacuum in Eurasia.

Russia is not alone in confronting immense difficulties in building a civic identity. As Walker Connor observed, "Scholars associated with theories of 'nation-building' have tended either to ignore the question of ethnic diversity or to treat the matter of ethnic identity superficially as merely one of a number of minor impediments to effective state-integration."[40] States in many parts of the world have been unsuccessful nation-builders, and many governments have failed to induce their subjects to shift their primary loyalties from informal subdivisions (ethnic, religious groups) to formal, legalistic state structures.[41]

Many in Eurasia and the West view the vague boundaries of the Russian people as an unnerving and threatening phenomenon that could very well lead to imperial restoration. A Russian nation-state, on the contrary, is seen as a well-tested, familiar, and peaceful alternative. The crux of this article holds that the approach of nation-state builders overlooks many grave threats to international security that may evolve from an attempt to mechanically line up Russia with its neighbors. Inarticulated Russian nationhood is one of the key factors explaining why the Soviet Union's collapse occurred so peacefully, especially when compared to the violent disintegration of another communist federation – Yugoslavia, where most Serbs encountered no ambiguity concerning their nation or national identity. Russia without the clear-cut frontiers may be the only peaceful solution to the "Russian question" after the breakup of the Soviet empire. Paradoxically, inconsistent and messy relations between Moscow and ethnic republics within the Russian Federation, and moderate and sometimes tremendously ineffective policies toward the Russians in the "near abroad" might be a better solution for security in Eurasia than attempts to shape a clear-cut approach toward nation-state building and the inevitable redrawing of borders. The Russian government is pursuing such an ambiguous policy not because of its wisdom, but because of its weakness.

The blurred political map of Eurasia might be more in line with the coming process of globalization than the two-centuries-old system of nation-states emerging from bloody wars. Boundaries between nation-states are becoming increasingly less significant as a result of the globalization of the international community, and there is no reason for Russians and other Eurasian peoples to repeat all the steps and mistakes made by Western Europe. The "German question" has been finally resolved within the framework of European integration, when the borders that Germans had fought over for a century, became obsolete.

US foreign policy makers are so preoccupied with putative Russian imperial ambitions in Eurasia that they can easily fail to recognize other challenges to peace and security on the continent. Ethnonationalism is among the most significant challenges. At present, "integrationalism," or expanded economic integration of the former Soviet republics, leading to some sort of a voluntary political union, may be the only viable alternative to imperialist, ethno-nationalist, or isolationist programs, which are destabilizing and threatening to Eurasian peace.

Support for research for this article from the Woodrow Wilson International Center for Scholars and United States Institute of Peace is gratefully acknowledged. The author would also like to thank Peter Pavilionis for assisting with the final preparation of the manuscript.

## NOTES

1. See Yuri Afanasiev, "A New Russian Imperialism," *Perspective*, No. 3 (February - March 1994) and Yuri Afanasiev, "Seems Like the Old Times? Russia's Place in the World," *Current History*, No. 93 (October 1994).

2. See Stephen Sestanovich, "Geotherapy. Russia's Neuroses, and Ours," *National Interest*, No. 45 (Fall 1996).

3. *Nezavisimaya gazeta* (19 December 1996).

4. Geoffrey Hosking, *Russia: People and Empire* (Cambridge: Harvard University Press, 1997), pp. 478-81.

5. See Richard Pipes, "Introduction: The Nationality Problem," in Zev Katz, ed., *Handbook of Major Soviet Nationalities* (New York: Free Press, 1975), p. 1.

6. Richard Pipes, "Birth of an Empire," *New York Times Book Review* (25 May 1997), p. 13.

7. Michael Howard, *The Lessons of History* (New York: Oxford University Press, 1991), p. 39.

8. See Hosking, *Russia: People and Empire*, p. 486.

9. Ibid.

10. Concrete border disputes in the post-Soviet space were analyzed in Thomas Forsberg, ed., *Contested Territory: Border Disputes at the Edge of the Former Soviet Empire* (Brookfield: Edward Elgar, 1995). Broader questions of the links between geography and ideology in Russia were examined in Mark Basin, "Russia Between Europe and Asia: The Ideological Construction of Geographical Space," *Slavic Review*, Vol. 1, No. 50 (Spring 1991), pp. 1–17. Various cognitive maps of Russians in their relation to national identity were studied by Katheline Parthe, *Russia's "Unreal Estate": Cognitive Mapping and National Identity*, Occasional Paper No. 265 (Washington DC: Kennan Institute for Advanced Russian Studies, July 1997).

11. Geoffrey Hosking, "The Freudian Frontier," *Times Literary Supplement (London)* (10 March 1995), p. 27, as quoted by Roman Szporluk, "The Fall of the Tsarist Empire and the USSR: The Russian Question and the Imperial Overextension," in Karen Dawisha and Bruce Parrott, eds., *The End of*

*Empire? The Transformation of the USSR in Comparative Perspective* (Armonk: M. E. Sharpe, 1997), p. 70.

12. George Breslauer was the first to point out this striking contradiction.

13. Richard Pipes, "Is Russia Still an Enemy?" *Foreign Affairs*, Vol. 76, No. 5 (September/October 1997), p. 73.

14. Richard Pipes, "Introduction"; in Roman Szporluk, *Communism and Nationalism. Karl Marx versus Fiedrich List* (New York: Oxford University Press, 1988), p. 206; Richard Sakwa, *Russian Politics and Society* (New York: Routledge, 1993), p. 101; and Richard Pipes, "Is Russia Still an Enemy?" p. 68.

15. See Hosking, *Russia: People and Empire*.

16. Nikholai Tsymbayev, "Rossiya i russkie. Natsional'ny vopros v Rossiiskoi imperii" (Russia and Russians: National Question in the Russian Empire)" *Russkii narod: istoricheskaya sud'ba v XX veke* (Russian People: Historical Destiny in the Twentieth Century) (Moscow: ANKO, 1993), pp. 39–50.

17. Richard Sakwa, *Russian Politics and Society*, p. 101.

18. See Andrei Zubov, "Sovetsky Soyuz: iz imperii v nichto?" (The Soviet Union: From Empire into Nothing?) *Polis*, No. 1 (1992), pp. 56–75; Alexander Vdovin, *Rossiiskaya natsiya* (The Russian Nation) (Moscow: Libris, 1995), pp. 136–38; and Jeff Chinn and Robert Kaiser, *Russians as the New Minority* (Boulder: Westview Press, 1996), p. 65.

19. For the analysis of different trends in historiography on this issue see Hugh Seton-Watson, "Russian Nationalism in Historical Perspective," in Robert Conquest, ed., *The Last Empire: Nationality and the Soviet Future* (Stanford: Hoover Institution Press, 1986), pp. 15–17. See also Roman Szporluk, "The Fall of the Tsarist Empire and the USSR," pp. 70–71, where struggling with historical myths, he categorically creates a new "negative" myth concerning the non-existence of links between Muskovy and medieval Kiev.

20. See Vdovin, *Rossiiskaya natsiya,* p. 105.

21. See Yuri Slezkine, "The USSR as a Communal Apartment, or How a Socialist State Promoted Ethnic Particularism," *Slavic Review*, No. 2 (Autumn 1994), p. 425.

22. See Vdovin, *Rossiiskaya natsiya,* p. 184.

23. Anatoly Chrenyaev, *Shest' let s Gorbachevym* (Six years with Gorbachev) (Moscow: 1993), p. 279, as quoted in Vdovin, *Rossiiskaya natsiya,* p. 138.

24. Ronald Suny, "Russia, the Soviet Union, and Theories of Empire," Address delivered at the Center for International Security and Arms Control, Stanford University (14 March 1996), p. 19.

25. Hugh Seton-Watson, " Russian Nationalism," p. 28.

26. Rogers Brubaker, *Nationalism Reframed: Nationhood and the National Question in the New Europe* (New York: Cambridge University Press, 1996), p. 49.

27. See, for example, his account of a trip to the U.S. in *Zavtra*, No. 50 (December 1996).

28. See, for example, Liah Greenfeld, *Nationalism. Five Roads to Modernity* (Cambridge: Harvard University Press, 1992), pp. 261–74.

29. Nikolai Danilevskii, *Rossiya i Evropa* (St. Petersburg: "Glagol," 1995).

30. Feodor Dostoevsky, "Pushkin: A Sketch," in M. Raeff, ed., *Russian Intellectual History* (New York: Harcourt, Brace & World, 1966), p. 299.

31. Ibid., p. 31.

32. Chinn and Kaiser, *Russians as the New Minority*, p. 61.

33. Petr Struve, "Patrioticheskaya trevoga 'renegata,'" *Nezavisimaya gazeta* (7 February 1995), p. 3

34. See P. N. Milyukov, *Natsional'nyi vopros: Proiskhozhdenie natsional'nosty i natsional'nye voprosy v Rossii* (The Nationality Question: Origins of Nationality and Nationalities Questions in Russia) (Prague: Svobodnaya Rossiya, 1925).

35. For the analysis of the Bolsheviks' approach to the "nationalities question," see Alexander Vdovin, "Natsional'naya politica bol'shevikov i eyo al'ternativy," in *Russkii narod: istoricheskaya sud'ba v XX veke*, pp. 119–78 and Robert Kaiser, *The Geography of Nationalism in Russia and the USSR* (Princeton: Princeton University Press, 1994), pp. 96-150.

36. Anthony Smith, *The Ethnic Origin of Nations* (Oxford: Basil Blackwell, 1986), p. 222.

37. The perils of the Turkish example for Russia were highlighted by Anatol Lieven in his "Restraining NATO: Ukraine, Russia, and the West," *The Washington Quarterly* (Autumn 1997), pp. 73–74.

38. For more on the Romantic views of nationhood see Margaret Canovan, *Nationhood and Political Theory* (Cheltenham: Edward Elgar, 1996), pp. 6-9.

39. Hosking, *Russia: People and Empire*, p. 485.

40. Walker Connor, *Ethnonationalism: the Quest for Understanding* (Princeton: Princeton University Press, 1994), p. 29.

41. See Connor, *Ethnonationalism,* p. 90.

# 7

# Environmental Security: Challenges for the United States and Russia

*Barbara Jancar-Webster and Vassily I. Sokolov*

Prior to the end of the Cold War, the Soviet political leadership made an attempt to recast the international agenda within the framework of *New Thinking*. *New Thinking* was a comprehensive concept of international security whereby special attention was devoted to environmental security as a new dimension of international security along with armed aggression, nuclear proliferation and the spread of weapons of mass destruction, terrorism, organized crime, drug trafficking, ethnic and religious hatred. This idea was incorporated in the official documents adopted by the 26th Party Congress of the then ruling Soviet Communist Party and was featured in the political rhetoric of then General Secretary of the Communist Party Mikhail Gorbachev and Foreign Affairs Minister Eduard Shevarnadze.[1]

The initially reserved reaction of the West to the concept of environmental security has two probable explanations. In the first place, the West was reluctant to let the Soviet Union gain political advantage from an initiative that seemed derived from changes in international policy orientation rather than a demonstrated awareness or concern on the part of the Soviet leadership of the actual state of the global environment. The initiative clearly contradicted recent revelations regarding the failure of official Soviet efforts to protect the country's national environment.[2] The other reason may be attributed to the fact that at that time Western nations did not perceive environmental degradation as a security issue.

A decade later, the pendulum has swung the other way. In the United States, Vice President Albert Gore, former Secretary of State Warren Christopher, and Secretary of State Madeleine Albright have made strong statements in support of environmental security as an international issue.[3] On Earth Day 1997, the State Department issued its first annual report entitled *Environmental Diplomacy: the Environment and US Foreign Policy*. In the past ten years, there has been a proliferation of a large spectrum of academic publications on environmental security and several research centers, specializing in environmental security have emerged in the United States and other NATO countries.[4] In the late 1990's, no one believes any longer that the new post-Soviet states, including Russia, are in a position to take an active part in the construction of an international system of environmental security. Each confronts a deep economic crisis and radical changes in national and international priorities. While the environment is among these priorities, it has been relegated to the lowest place on the agenda. What the Commonwealth of Independent States (CIS) now seeks is the establishment of effective multilateral and/or bilateral cooperation based on accurate estimation of each country's existing priorities and needs.

This swing in political focus derives from the new realities of the post-Cold War world. The East-West security challenge that was the focus of the international agenda during the last half century is gone. Its disappearance has uncovered an entirely new panorama of existing risks and threats, most of them non-military in nature. Of all of these, environmental risks are probably the largest in scale, the most immediate (urgent) in their impact on human development, and most costly in required actions. These risks are national, transnational and global. The international community will need to develop means to manage environmental problems at every level of social organization if it intends to build a comprehensive security system and maintain global stability. Environmental problems are related to almost all aspects of human life; they permeate most activities in every state. Problem solving in this field will require an even greater effort to build mutual trust and confidence than was required in the disarmament process.

The purpose of this chapter is to try to elaborate a common approach to the environmental security issue that is suited to the realities of both the United States and Russia, as well as to the urgency of global needs, and to analyze West-East cooperation and assistance on environmental issues.

## THE ENVIRONMENT AS A SECURITY ISSUE

There are many linkages between environment and security. Throughout human history, most armed conflicts have been linked to the possession of land or other natural resources or survival in a specific natural environment. Today, as public policy makers in different countries delve more deeply into the causes and consequences of conflict and instability in the post-Cold War world, it is increasingly clear that non-military risks such as environmental degradation, resource depletion and scarcity, rapid population growth and refugee flows, play a key role in the evolution of national formulas for a comprehensive security system, with international and global implications. Most attempts to specify the linkages between the environment and security have focused on environmentally caused scarcities and conflicts, and on compelling evidence of the interrelationships between environmental problems, human health concerns, genetic integrity, and economic and political instability.

It is evident however that not all environmental problems are security problems. When each problem is assessed separately, most of them can hardly be considered as security problems, with such notable exceptions as Chernobyl or Bhopal that required immediate response actions. Environmental pollution can be treated as a security issue only on the basis of the potential or actual social degradation caused by pollution. Criteria for the inclusion of environmental pollution into a security formula would include the extent of damage to human health, the degree to which food production is disrupted, and the degree to which the pollution can be linked to out-migration from the polluted area. Understood in this context, the content of environmental security may vary among regions and may encompass a series of problems or stresses that stretch across time.

Environmental problems may only be considered real security issues where they cut across and/or intersect the spectrum of human security issues: economic security, food security, health security, personal security, community security and political security, depending on the scale of their impact. For example, the drying of the Aral Sea with its accompanying environmental degradation (loss of fresh water and arable lands, wind-blown distribution of sea-bed salts, radical changes in public health and life expectancy, and so forth) and associated economic collapse (total decline of fishery, restricted agriculture, and so forth) is a potential security challenge for the entire Central Asian region threatening the political stability of the Newly Independent States (NIS). The Aral Sea problem is also a security issue for Russia which no longer has a territorial linkage to the Aral Sea basin, but continues to share responsibility for the problem. In this sense, regional stability will be contingent upon the integration of environmental resource elements into regional national security formulas.

Failure to address existing environmental conditions is likely to result in economic and political instability, life-threatening health effects, and possible international conflict. Regional or civil conflicts, hastened or exacerbated by environmental stress, could involve the international community or specific countries in costly and hazardous military interventions, peacekeeping, or humanitarian operations. It is evident that some environmental security issues are of immediate concern (Chernobyl), while others are mid- or long-term in scope. The latter include the global environmental challenges with high potential to disrupt the global economic system and irreversible environmental effects for all humanity.

Environmental stress generated by the growing needs of the world population is one type of environmental damage with global effects. Rapid population growth, large-scale population migrations and differential demographic patterns may present challenges to environmental security. The world is projected to have nearly eight billion people by the year 2025, the majority of whom (85 per cent) are expected to live in the non-industrialized world.[5] Population pressure on ecological systems and resource overuse can lead to shortages of essential resources such as food, water, and fuel, resulting in possible conflicts of differing scale and level of intensity, and social degradation. The World Resources Institute estimates that today approximately 60 per cent of the less industrialized world's poorest people live in ecologically vulnerable areas.[6] In poorer countries, environmental scarcities set limits to agricultural options and force those already impoverished to seek their livelihood in ecologically endangered areas like cities, that are especially vulnerable to conflict. The plight of the large urban area is a good example of how environmental scarcities interact with political, economic, social, and cultural factors of instability.

Climate change brought about by the growing concentration of "greenhouse" gases in the atmosphere is a second type of environmental stress with large international implications, including potential conflicts, deterioration in public health, increased migration of refugees. The warming of the Earth could have serious negative consequences on all humankind, including a rise in sea levels, and changing climatic conditions and agricultural patterns. Global environmental stress is further manifested by chlorofluorocarbons (CFCs) depleting the Earth's ozone layer, thereby allowing a higher level of ultraviolet light to reach the earth's surface, causing direct harm to people and vegetation.

Deforestation, degradation of arable land and loss of biodiversity are a third set of contributing stress factors to global environmental instability. Experts differ as to the rate at which these processes are taking place. The rate of deforestation is critical because tropical forests, covering only six per cent of the earth's surface, not only process and store the carbon dioxide from the atmosphere, but also provide habitat for some 50-60 per cent of all wild species. A recent Worldwatch Institute estimate holds that the world is losing approximately seven per cent of all arable land every decade through land degradation. The consensus estimate for the per centage of at least moderately degraded lands is approximately 30 per cent of the world's arable land.[7] The continued increase in degraded agricultural land is a serious threat to food production and hence food security for the large majority of the populations in Africa and Asia.

Finally, conflicts can arise from environmental stress in neighboring states due to transboundary effects. The best known example is acid rain. "Diplomatic wars" over acid rain responsibility are familiar to both North America and the European continent.[8] Similar types of problems arise from the use of international waters. Access to fresh water and its resources, as well as the level of allowable polluting effluent that may be poured into a body of water traversing many countries are already sources of international tension in many parts of the world. Many argue that water shortage is the environmental problem most likely to lead to violent conflict, the situation in the Middle East being the most frequently cited possibility in the existing literature.[9]

Current environmental issues constitute a visible demonstration of global interdependence. Not all global concerns are necessarily national concerns; sometimes they are not even considered part of the national interest. The "proliferation" of global environmental concerns has been a long and contradictory process[10] where international discussion, cooperation (and probably pressure) played key roles. For example, Soviet government officials paid no attention to the risks of global warming or ozone depletion until these issues were raised abroad. Only under the influence of international discussions did the Soviet debate over global warming and ozone depletion move from the abstract theoretical plane to the consideration of practical policy responses. Similarly, a majority of the countries which began to grapple with global environmental risks, did so only after these issues had been placed on the international agenda.

Environmental mobilization and the consolidation of international community progress can provide a foundation for preventing environmental risks. According to M. Renner from Worldwatch Institute "Environmental security depends critically on international coordination and cooperation."[11] Environmental security issues force the evolution of the concept of national security from the simple defense of specific national interests towards cooperation and compromise.

Beginning with the Stockholm Conference on the Human Environment in 1972, tremendous efforts went into the formation of international environmental regimes. The regimes existing today are primarily based on conventions and other instruments of international law. Hundreds of environmental agreements are in force at bilateral, regional and international levels. A general strategy for environmentally sound, "sustainable" development as well as numerous specific environmental prescriptions were elaborated by the Brundland Commission on Environment and Development, discussed at the Earth Summit on Environment and Development in Rio de Janeiro in 1992 and recently by the UN Special General Assembly on Rio+5 process in 1997 June in New York. On the institutional side, the United Nations Environmental Programme (UNEP) and the UN Commission on Sustainable Development are assigned to facilitate national environmental programs and cooperation among nations. Environmental issues have become increasingly prominent in the activities of other international organizations. The establishment of the Global Environmental Facility (GEF) together with the World Bank, UNDP and UNEP created a financial mechanism for resource transfer from developed to developing countries to address global environmental challenges.

Some will argue that the majority of unresolved problems on the international agenda are those where basic concerns, like national sovereignty, national interest, and national security, play a key role. Nevertheless, to borrow the words of Prime Minister of Sweden Carlsson, the evidence suggests that "...the old pillars of sovereignty and non-interference in international affairs are slowly giving way to a more flexible system, based as much on concern for the security of people as for security of states."[12]   "National security" is evolving into "human security," a concept which better connotes the realities of the world at the close of the twentieth century.

Most of the major armed conflicts in the last decade are not directly connected to "the country-against-country" principle.[13]   This is yet another signal that the nation-state system is in the process of evolution. Global economic integration is its most visible manifestation, together with the gradual loss of governmental control of activities performed, at least in many developing countries, due to permanent budget shortfalls, growing external debt, and the inability to control transnationals.   In addition to these problems, these states must learn to manage environmental stresses.  The aggravating factor of growing environmental insecurity is that degradation is most evident in the areas that have the least economic and technological capacity to cope with change.  Facing global challenges,  state-centric international entities are losing more and more of their capabilities to solve current and future problems.

Environmental security is directly linked to military activities and security.  The best known and discussed view holds that the military sector represents a threat to environmental security.  The development, production and deployment of military weapons and weapons systems, and the maintenance of armed forces have destructive effects on the environment.  Most of the risk, however, is associated with warfare or armed conflicts and especially with the use of weapons of mass destruction.  The environment thus makes a cogent argument for dealing with the legacy of war.[14]   Moreover, it is well known that the military sector consumes a large amount of energy and natural resources, depriving society of financial resources urgently needed for social and economic development and environmental protection.

At the same time, as we consider the idea of a comprehensive, integrated security system, we must admit that military security (prevention of aggression) remains a part of this system in the foreseeable future.  Hence, it seems to be more practical to bridge the interests of environmental and military security by focusing the debate on such issues as optimal size of the military sector (including reductions and conversion issues), evolution to a more "environmentally sound" military sector and use of army scientific and technological capacities and experiences for environmental purposes.  In the military sector, there is growing understanding that it is much more difficult to maintain troops and conduct military operations in truly environmentally degraded places containing toxics, radionucleids or having undrinkable water, with no earthquake or flood controls.

## MILITARY INTERESTS AND THE GLOBAL ENVIRONMENT: THE SOVIET/RUSSIAN CASE

Although it might seem contradictory, in both the United States and Soviet/Russian societies, a certain learning about global environmental risks has come from military preparations and activities, or at least military preparations have had a catalytic effect on the learning process. For example, nuclear arms testing initiated research on the long range transport of dangerous pollutants. A considerable amount of learning concerning atmospheric risks was a consequence of developments in the aviation and space industry, important segments of the Soviet economy that were closely linked to the military sector. The most poignant case was that of ozone depletion. The first satellite fitted with an ozone measurement device was put in orbit as early as 1965. At that time, the primary concern was not the potential health effects of ozone depletion, but potential changes in air currents and atmospheric turbulence that might affect aviation and rocketry, as well as possible health risks for the crews of high-altitude aircraft. Research on this issue was later expanded in order to determine the atmospheric effects of the supersonic Tu-144 and of multiple launches of missiles and rockets.

The Soviet military's interest in the risk of anthropogenic climate change increased sharply in the early 1970s. During the war in Vietnam, the US use of environmental modification, such as cloud seeding to slow down adversary offensives, and the use of defoliants to deprive the adversary of food and ground cover, brought an increasing number of reports on US military climate research into the public focus, while debates in the US Congress raged over the morality of the military use of environmental modification. In 1973, the US Senate finally passed a resolution calling for the prohibition of such techniques. US actions prompted the Soviet military and government to pay closer attention to the prospect of what was termed "geophysical war."

The debate in the USSR over "geophysical war" raised the risk of ozone depletion long before it became an issue of broad international concern, as the launching of rockets and other weapons were explored with the objective of creating "windows" above certain locations in the enemy's territory to permit unlimited penetration of ultraviolet rays.[15]

The possibility of geophysical war marked a major turning point in the Soviet debate on these issues, for it was the first time that the prospect of climate manipulation had been cast wholly in a negative light.

Overburdened by high military expenditure imposed on the economy by the Cold War, the USSR launched an intensive international effort to secure a global ban on all activities aimed at modifying the environment for military purposes. In August 1974, the Soviet government placed on the agenda of the United Nations a draft treaty on prohibition of the military use of environmental modification. The United States responded positively to these efforts, and the result, after two years of negotiation, was the signing of the Convention on Prohibition of Military or Any Other Hostile Use of Environmental Modification Techniques.

A further connection between military issues and global climate change emerged in the early 1980s with the debate over "nuclear winter": the hypothesis that the large quantities of smoke and debris thrust into the atmosphere by a major nuclear exchange could block out solar radiation, with disastrous — and perhaps terminal — consequences for all life on Earth.[16] The publication of this hypothesis generated a number of major efforts to model the climatic consequences of nuclear war. These constituted a significant contribution to the debate over the prospects for global climate change — a contribution which survived the fall off in interest in the issue of nuclear winter itself. International efforts to evaluate the nuclear winter scenario were enthusiastically supported by the Soviet government, although in this case the primary impetus came not from the military but from the top political leadership, which sought to use the issue to stimulate popular opposition to the ongoing modernization of nuclear weapons by the US and NATO.

Although military concerns did play a crucial part in stimulating Soviet interest in global environmental risks, the role of the Soviet military cannot be said on balance to have been positive. Like any military community, it used its power to obstruct the collection or dissemination of any information that might conceivably be of interest to foreign intelligence agencies, including all data concerning emissions from military industrial facilities. This policy and appropriate restrictions were of course supported by many industrial ministries, that saw no reason to provide any additional ammunition to internal proponents of more aggressive environmental policies and sought to minimize monitoring expenses and mandated large-scale investments in pollution control.

After the demise of the Soviet Union, the Russian military confronted environmental questions of a new dimension involving Russia's legal liability for the environmental degradation caused by the Soviet military bases in Eastern Europe. The situation was similar to that discovered by the Germans after the closing of US bases in Germany. In both cases, a preliminary assessment of the negative environmental impact of the bases made it clear that in addition to environmental madness there were solid political and economic reasons, such as the property rights on the abandoned facilities, for the German and East European claims for reparation. However, unlike the US military, the Russian military had to learn about environmental management from the ground up. A special Environmental Department was created within the Ministry of Defense for this purpose. Thus, it was through the military sector that the new leaders of Russia came to learn in a practical way that environmental claims can be a serious subject of international relations.

## DIMENSIONS OF ENVIRONMENTAL SECURITY IN RUSSIA

The recent decades have seen environmental issues in both the international and social context become a focal point for the elaboration of national priorities mainly due to the enormous damage to the national economy brought about by environmental degradation, technological accidents such as Chernobyl, large oil spills in the Northern regions and radioactive contamination caused by the military industrial complex.

The disintegration of the USSR brought about a radical change in the framework for the implementation of international agreements. The administrative mechanisms originally in place to control the implementation of international obligations had disappeared or were abolished, and new ones had yet to be established or were ineffective.

The system of national priorities was changed in an historically short period of time. Environmental goals were pushed far down on the agenda of the Newly Independent States (NIS) facing seemingly more pressing problems of economic and social survival. As a result, there continues to be a large gap between declarations and legislation in the field of environmental protection and the implementation of an effective and efficient environmental management system.

The former republics are now reorganizing themselves as separate sovereign states. The ultimate implications of this process for the management of regional and global environmental risks are rather uncertain. Traditionally, the republics within the USSR did not pay any significant attention to global issues, since most of the scientific activity and all of the decision-making concerning these issues took place in Moscow. As of the present writing, it appears that the majority of the NIS are aware of developments in the field, but in most cases, the level of available national scientific expertise falls short of that necessary for independent action. As a result, most of the new states are not ready to participate actively in the management of global environmental risks.

What are the major challenges of environmental security facing Russia as the major inheritor of the legacy of the Soviet Union? First, there is the direct threat to human health and survival from increased environmental pollution leading to the exhaustion of human capital. Environmental pollution has been specifically listed among the primary factors for the unprecedented decrease in life expectancy in Russia to its lowest point for males in 40 years in 1994 to 57 years,[17] and the sharp increase in infant mortality. Current estimates indicate that from 20 per cent to 50 per cent of all foods are now contaminated by pesticides, nitrites and heavy metals in concentrations dangerous for human life.[18] Approximatly 30 million people inhabiting 15 per cent of Russian territory are living in conditions defined as "critical" from the point of view of environmental survival.[19]

Second, environmental degradation leads to the loss of natural resources critical to the growth of the national economy. It is hard to imagine that the country with such abundant water resources risks water shortages, at least on a regional basis. Nearly 75 per cent of surface water supplies can no longer be used for drinking purposes; approximately 30 per cent of ground water sources are now contaminated; 250,000 hectares of land are now suitable only for waste disposal, and approximately five billion tons of man-made industrial and municipal waste are being stored in these areas.[20]

Third, environmental degradation has clear international implications for Russia and its international trade. In particular, compliance with international conventions (such as on ozone depleting agents or on transboundary air pollution) poses serious domestic and international constraints. Environmental standards set by the international community or individual countries serve as non-tariff barriers for Russian commodities, while the bringing on line of production facilities to meet those standards requires investment in the appropriate technology that risks reducing the competitiveness of Russian goods in the world market.

In recent years, the substantial drop in production (more than 50 per cent in industry) has led to an overall decrease in environmental pollution in the Russian Federation. However, calculations of pollution production per unit of GDP show a trend towards increasing pollution.[21] If this trend continues, as economic growth picks up, the country could face the need for stronger and more strictly enforced measures of pollution control. The level of environmental protection funding is estimated for the year 1996 at 0.1 per cent of GNP. The government justifies such low financing of environmental activities by citing the urgent priority to find a way out of the current economic crisis and to level the economic and social disparities in the transition to the market economy. The government's critics argue that economic growth predicated on "pollute first, clean-up later" ends up in a much higher tab for end-of-pipe clean-up, risking future economic slow-down for immediate and short-term gains. A modern market economy, they urge, cannot function efficiently without an effective system of environmental protection.

Given the seeming chaos of the transition to a market economy, the devolution of central power to local institutions of government and administration, and the unstable political and economic situation, many enterprise managers and local government officials are making their own decisions on key economic issues related to the transition. The signing of a contract between local government and a wildcat logger can bring about irreparable harm to the environment, with unforeseen and unmanageable negative environmental consequences.

The low level of federal funding of environmental activities has sharply impacted the national resource base. The increased supply of raw materials and natural resources to the international market without adequate environmental protection is leading to the exhaustion of the resources base, new needs for foreign currency and a growing external debt.

Amid the pessimism, there are grounds for greater optimism. The integration of Russia into the world economy means that industrial enterprises must become more profitable in order to survive. One consequence of this development will be the more efficient use of natural resources. The collapse of the command economy has been accompanied by a sharp drop in industrial activity, and hence in the production of pollutants. A second source of hope is the new system of international cooperation that has been developed to deal with the troublesome effects of transition in the former socialist states.

## WEST-EAST ENVIRONMENTAL COOPERATION

The United States and the Soviet Union/Russia have a long history of environmental cooperation, dating back to the first cultural exchange agreements in the 1960s and gaining content and permanency in the 1970s, following the Stockholm Conference. In the late 1960s, US scientists were quick to take up the cause of Lake Baikal that their Soviet colleagues had managed to bring to their attention. International questioning of Soviet development of the world's deepest freshwater lake helped bring into being the first comprehensive development plan in the Soviet Union based on environmental indicators and with a strong environmental component.

During the 1970s, Soviet and United States environmental cooperation became institutionalized in an environmental exchange agreement signed in 1972, that provided a mechanism for the elaboration of long-term programs primarily in the field of conservation and wildlife protection. A major landmark was the signing of the international protocol on the protection of the polar bear. The present-day migratory bird program is an outgrowth of this early cooperation in conservation.[22]

With the collapse of the Soviet Union in 1991, the environmental exchange agreement lost its legitimacy as the two countries faced the potentially destabilizing aspects of the Soviet Union's legacy of environmental degradation to the successor states. Chernobyl and the Aral Sea were the popular international symbols of this degradation, but there was rising international concern regarding nuclear dump sites, the fate of nuclear waste in Siberia, nuclear contamination of the Arctic rivers that flowed into the Arctic Ocean, and sulfur dioxide pollution from the large nickel processing plants in the Kola Peninsula, and the gigantic nickel mine at Norilsk in Siberia. In 1993, the United States Congress enacted into law an aid package, about five per cent of whose funds were earmarked for environmental protection in Russia and the NIS, and about ten per cent went indirectly to environmental remediation through the promotion of greater energy efficiency. The purpose of this environmental aid was not to assist directly in the remediation of Russia's most salient environmental problems, as to develop the methodologies, infrastructure, institutions and legislative framework that would enable Russia to restructure its existing system of environmental protection into one better adapted to a market economy .

United States' aid did not take place in a vacuum. Rather it should be seen as one prong in a multipronged international initiative to help Russia resolve those environmental problems that contribute to stabilizing its emerging economic and political system. The World Bank, the Global Environmental Facility (GEF), and other international financial institutions provided the large scale funds for major clean-up or rebuilding projects, such as the sewer system in St. Petersburg. The European Union together with the individual EU member states provided funds for projects of interest to them. The Scandinavian countries were perhaps the most generous in their aid to environmental remediation in the Baltic Sea and in the Kola Peninsula.

The delivery of financial aid for all projects in the Russian Republic is coordinated through a committee of high level Russian officials, representatives from the US and other lending countries, and representatives from the major international financial institutions. Aid delivery further must go through an evaluation process mixed with lender nation political goals and objectives and insistence by the international lenders of Russia's implementation of their structural adjustment criteria. [23]

The record of US environmental aid to the Federation in the 90s is uneven, reflecting the ups and downs of US-Russian relations for the decade. The whole issue of aid fell into disrepute following the breaking of the news in June of 1997, of a large-scale financial scandal involving Harvard's Institute for International Development (HIID), the US Agency for International Development (USAID), and Russia's then first deputy Prime Minister Anatoly Chubais. The ripples of the scandal spread as far as Russia's Central Bank and Federal Securities Commission. When an USAID investigation concluded that two of the institute's leading employees had used their positions and USAID resources for personal gain, the US government canceled its $14 million contract with the Harvard Institute that underwrote a major program of economic and financial reform in the Russian Federation. The US Congress may also have lost its interest in aiding Russia. In 1994, Russia was receiving $1.6 billion in aid. In 1996, it received a tenth of that or $163 million, and many members of Congress wanted to reduce that to $150 million for 1997. [24] A large part of Congressional reluctance may be attributed to disillusionment over the level of crime and corruption, the reliability of safeguards protecting nuclear materials and stored nuclear warheads, and what Congress perceived was rising anti-Semitism and religious persecution. The passing of the law requiring official approval for permission to import a foreign religion further alienated members who already are unhappy about the Russian sale of nuclear technology to Iran, and fear that Russia is developing its own chemical and biological weapons arsenal.

On its side, Russia experienced a loss of face in being unable to stop the US from insisting on the enlargement of NATO. The staging of NATO war games on former Soviet territory, one in the Black Sea under the guns of the deteriorating Russian fleet at Sevastopol, and the other in Kazakhstan, seemed to be a sadistic twist of the NATO knife a little deeper into the Russian wound. The strain in US-Russian relations hampered US investment in Russia, although the United States continued to be the largest foreign investor in the country[25] and did little to encourage increasing financial assistance on the part of the US government. At the present writing, Ukraine receives the highest percentage of US aid of all the NIS with Russia as the second highest recipient.

On a more positive note, the US and Russia have continued their long-standing cooperation in the area of conservation, particularly in the Arctic. This cooperation is best exemplified by the US and Russian agreement to create an international transboundary park on the Bering Straits. Exxon and other US corporations are also contributing to biodiversity maintenance projects such as bringing back the Siberian tiger from near extinction. The Arctic was also the venue of a far-reaching and comprehensive US, Russian and Norwegian agreement in 1997 establishing an Arctic Military Environmental Regime. The agreement covers such important issues as the safe storage and transport of nuclear spent fuel, the treatment of low and high level radioactive waste, remediation of contamination sites and personnel training in the safe handling of radioactive materials.

Aid from the international financial institutions has been considerable, but does not begin to approximate the financial rescue packages assembled for the East Asian tigers to deal with their structural weaknesses. In 1996, the IMF approved a $10 billion loan, but delivery of loan tranches has been uneven, held up by Russian difficulty in reducing government spending and persistent problems in tax collection. Russia is no longer at the top of the list of IMF borrowers and at the beginning of 1998, Boris Yeltsin announced that he hoped to phase out all IMF loans by the year 2000.[26]

International global finance see in Russia's oil and gas industry the best investment opportunities and the key to the country's economic transformation. Since 1993, billions of dollars have been spent on modernizing and reconditioning abandoned wells in the Siberian oil fields. Estimates of upwards of $60 billion USD are projected by AMOCO for the planned development with the Russian oil company, Yugankneftegas, of the North Priobskoye field in Western Siberia. At risk is the fragile Siberian ecosystem and the social disintegration of the indigenous peoples living there. Russian and international environmental groups are questioning the project, demanding environmental rehabilitation of existing oil fields and a comprehensive study of the efficiency potential of Russia's oil industry before the project is given final approval.[27]

Russia has requested and obtained money from the international and national lending institutions to help restore its environment. As a rule, however, these monies frequently benefit the environment only indirectly and have been very small when compared to foreign investment in oil and gas. For example, of the $159 USD Russia received from the World Bank in 1996, $70 million was allocated for the purchase of energy-efficient gas equipment for ten Russian cities. Russia was further awarded two grants from the GEF. The first of these in the amount of $60 million is to help Russia phase out the consumption of ozone-depleting substances. The second of $20.1 million is to assist the Russian biodiversity program.[28]

The evidence suggests that while aid for environmental projects continues to be forthcoming, it does not begin to address the amounts needed to resolve the Russian environmental security problems identified above. Russians assert that most of the aid goes to benefit consultants from the major global corporations and little reaches the grass roots problem areas. International and Western agencies fault the absence of adequate legal and institutional infrastructure. At best, the financial aid offered for environmental remediation is a fraction of the funds from global corporations for oil and natural resource exploration and exploitation. Under these circumstances, it should come as no surprise that Gennady Zhuganov's rhetoric accusing Yeltsin of being bought by the US and the international community finds support among the Russian public. One understandable response to the political and economic constraints imposed on approval of relatively small loans by the international financial institutions to Russia is that the developed states actively seek the disintegration of the Russian Federation.

Until the ascendancy of Gorbachev, the Soviet Union was only a peripheral player in global environmental politics, although it was signer of all the major environmental agreements. With Gorbachev, the USSR began to assume a more proactive role, particularly in the Arctic area. Since the end of the eighties, Russia has signed some 63 international agreements. However, the deterioration of its economic position has virtually brought its ability to implement these agreements to a standstill. With the ascendancy of the US as the sole remaining superpower, the international community seemed to lose interest in the region. In international negotiations, Russia found itself ignored. Agreements were presented for its signature without prior consultation that took into consideration Russian interests.

At first, the UN had no official category for the former Communist countries that were trying to change to a democracy and a market economy. Within the UN, Russia found itself outside and indifferent to the special blocks of developing nations, such as the Group of 77, and could not be considered in the same category as the highly industrialized nations. It was not until the Rio Conference on the Environment and Development in 1992, that Russia was able to obtain for the first time, recognition of a special status for countries with a transitional economy. Russia's hard-line over the expansion of NATO helped persuade the US to offer the Federation a place at the G-7 and the Paris Club.

The strengthened Russian position was evident in the Climate Change negotiations. Russia strongly supported the principle of flexibility in meeting target emission reduction deadlines. Article 4.6 was included in the agreement at the insistence of the transition states with US support. In the final treaty document, the Russian Federation and Ukraine committed themselves to stabilization of emissions at their 1990 levels. By contrast, the East European countries anxious to enter the EU had to commit themselves to an eight per cent reduction of 1990 levels.[29]

## FUTURE US-RUSSIAN COOPERATION IN GLOBAL ENVIRONMENTAL POLITICS

Russia occupies 13 time zones and straddles the continents of Europe and Asia. The Russian land mass contains some of the most fragile ecosystems in the world and also large quantities of the world's most desirable natural resources. Russia, the United States and China have the world's largest deposits of coal. Russia is a major player in the oil and gas industry. Russia holds the largest stand of virgin northern forests stretching from the White Sea to the Pacific. An international environmental agreement that ignores the Russian Federation or seeks to isolate Russia must ultimately fail in its purpose.

There are three areas where the expansion of US-Russian cooperation can play a key role. The first is in the area of climate change, the second is in the area of biodiversity and the third is in the area of nuclear safety and security. It is interesting to note that in 1972, when the state agreement on environmental cooperation between USA and USSR was signed, the project on climate was included in the agenda under pressure of the American delegation. This project has now been assessed as one of most successful in the history of bilateral cooperation on environment. With such a strong foundation on which to build, a firm commitment from Russia and the United States on reducing emissions serves to contain the Chinese desire to industrialize first and clean-up later. The effects of climate change impact the two countries differently, and Russia may indeed find itself a beneficiary of that change. However, both countries share a common interest in limiting potential damage and hence destabilizing still weak political systems, including those in the countries in transition, and the Chinese system, now being undermined by a transfer of power struggle, the rising aspirations of the Chinese people, and vulnerabilities of the rapidly growing Chinese economy to world markets. The recent loan by the World Bank for the purchasing of energy-efficient gas equipment is an important step in shoring up damaged US credibility regarding its commitment to helping Russia cope with her pollution problems.

In the second area, biodiversity, Russia and the United States have a twenty-year history of cooperating to save endangered Arctic and Siberian species. With a more porous frontier and a weak economy, the flora and fauna of the great Eurasian plains are at greater risk than at any previous time. With the devolution of central power, many local and provincial administrators, searching to better the local economy and their own political fortunes, search out lucrative deals with unscrupulous foreign businessmen and entrepreneurs, particularly from Asia. A strong joint US-Russian commitment to the biodiversity treaty, including the rights of indigenous peoples, would shore up that treaty from being undercut by economically pressed governments of the developing world, and the predation of global corporations. Here too, a GEF grant to assist Russia in its promotion of biodiversity provides tangible confirmation of the international community's interest in the future of Russia's endangered species.

In the third and last area, nuclear safety and security, the US and Russia are the only two countries that can make the world safe from the dangers of nuclear power. Here Russia would need to be more forthright about the amount of nuclear waste poured into the Arctic Ocean and the Sea of Japan. It would also need to provide a more accurate accounting of nuclear contamination in its formerly closed cities in the Urals. Most important, Russia needs to calm Western fears of the risk of the management of nuclear weapons escaping Federal control. On its part, the United States would have to be more open about its nuclear tests during the fifties, particularly in the South Pacific. The United States and the NATO countries must demonstrate greater commitment to helping Russia deal with its nuclear legacy. Both countries would have to come to a firm agreement about the sale and proliferation of nuclear power plants. While the US and Russia are not the only countries that market nuclear power plants, as nuclear superpowers, they have the largest nuclear stockpiles and thus must take the lead in showing responsibility. Last but not least, Russia and the US must tackle together the difficult questions of pursuing an environmentally sound and sustainable military. As suggested in an earlier section of this chapter, sustainable development in the military sector of the national economy involves important common decisions, such as setting limits to the use and exploitation of the various kinds of weapons, setting limits on the size and disposition of armed forces, and limiting research and technical experimentation that have the potential to put the environment at risk. More international agreements along the lines of the Arctic Environmental Agreement confirm the world on this path.

Today, the United States may be tempted to put on Gorbachev's mantel and be the dominant arbiter of global environmental security. Despite the demands of the European Union for US leadership in the environmental area, this chapter has argued that the interdependent nature of environmental security precludes the US from being the sole guarantor of the global environment. The Russian political leadership may think it is not yet ready to play an active role. However, such thinking is short-term. The emergence of environmental risks as the number one global security problem at the end of the 90s automatically places Eurasian Russia at the center of the security issue. US-Russian cooperation is the cornerstone of any comprehensive global environmental security structure.

## NOTES

1. See, for example, M. Gorbachev, Speech in Murmansk, *Izvestia* (2 October 1987) and E. Shevarnadze, "Ecology and Diplomacy," *Literaturnaya gazeta* (22 November 1989).

2. M. Feshbach and A. Friendly, "Ekologicheskaya al'ternativa. Istoki body, Znaki body," *Ekologicheskaya al'ternativa* (Moscow: Progress Publishers, 1992) and A. Yablokov "Strana-mutant. Zakonnoe Dwight Boolean tsivilizatsii, " *EKES-Magazine*, Vol. 2 (1991), pp. 36-39, 64.

3. See "Official Statements," *Environmental Change and Security Project*, The Woodrow Wilson Center, Washington DC, No. 3 (Spring 1997), pp. 110-25.

4. Recently established research centers include The Woodrow Wilson Center's Environmental Change and Security Project, The Center for Environmental Security of the Pacific Northwest National Laboratory, The Cambridge Global Security Programme in UK, Ecological Center for International and European Environmental Research, The Nautilus Institute for Security and Sustainable Development, Environment and Security Study by NATO Committee on the Challenges of Modern Society and many others.

5. World Resources Institute, "Population and Health," *World Resources 1990-1991* (New York and Oxford: Oxford University Press, 1990), Table 4.1, p. 50 and US Bureau of the Census, International Data Base (October 1997), (http://www.census.gov/ipc/www.worldpop.html).

6. World Resources Institute, *World Resources, 1996-1997* (New York: Oxford University Press, 1996), p. 30.

7. Data for the two previous paragraphs are from: L. Brown et al. *Vital Signs 1997. The Environmental Trends That are Shaping our Future* (Washington DC: Worldwatch Institute, 1997), p. 41; Melissa Leach and Robin Mearns, eds., *The Lie of the Land* (London: James Currey/Heinemann, 1997); and Mohammed Kassas, "Desertification" in Robert Paehkle, ed., *Conservation and Environmentalism: An Encyclopedia* (New York and London: Garland Press, 1995), pp. 175-76.

8. See, for example, V. Sokolov, "Kislotnye dozhdi I mezhgosudarstvennye konflikty," *Nauka i zhizn*, Vol. 7 (1985), pp.35-37 and V. Sokolov, "SShA — Kanada: ekologicheskie konflikty," *Priroda I chelovek*, Vol. 1, 1985.

9. See, for example, M. Lowi, *Water and Power: The Politics of a Scarce Resource in the Jordan River Basin* (Cambridge: Cambridge University Press, 1993) and E. Kally, *Water and Peace: Water Resources and the Arab-Israeli Peace Process* (Westport: Praeger Publishers, 1993).

10. See, for example, R. Benedick, *Ozone Diplomacy: New Directions in Safeguarding the Planet* (Cambridge: Harvard University Press, 1991) and L.

Susskind, *Environmental Diplomacy: Negotiating More Effective Global Agreements* (New York: Oxford University Press, 1994).

11. M. Renner, "Enhancing Global Security," *State of the World - 1989: A Worldwatch Institute Report on Progress Towards Sustainable Society* (New York and London: Norton & Company, 1989), p.145.

12. Cited from Congressional Program, *The Convergence of US National Security and the Global Environment*, First Conference, Aspen Institute, Washington DC (2-16 November 1996), p.16.

13. M. Renner, "Transforming Security," *State of the World - 1997: A Worldwatch Institute Report on Progress Towards Sustainable Society* (New York and London: Norton & Company, 1997), p.116.

14. See, for example, A. Wesing, "Environmental Warfare: Manipulating the Environment for Hostile Purposes," *Environmental Change and Security Project*, The Woodrow Wilson Center, Washington DC, No. 3 (Spring 1997) and A. Vavilov, *Ekologicheskie posledstvia gonki vooruzhenii*, (Moscow: Mezhdunarodnye otnoshenia, 1984), pp. 145-49.

15. See, for example, G. Radchenko, "Geofizicheskaya voina", *Morskoi sbornik*, Vol. 9 (1973); V. Jarov "Geofizicheskaya voina i ee posledstvia," *Voennyi vestnik,* Vol. 1 (1976); and *Sovetskaya voennaya entsiklopedia*, Vol. 2 (Moscow: Voenizdat, 1976), p. 523.

16. For the details of exploring this hypothesis in the USSR see the article by V. Alexandrov and G. Stenchikov in *Zhurnal vychislitelnoi matematiki i matematicheskoi fiziki,* Vol. 24, No. 1 (1984), pp.140-44 and A. Kondrat'ev, *Nauchnaya i populyarnaya knigi* (Leningrad: Gidrometizdat, 1987).

17. Mark Glukhovsky, "Why do Russian People Die Early?" Summary of Moscow Carnegie Center report by A. Vishnevsky and V. Shkolnikov, "The Death Rate in Russia, Main Risk Groups and Priorities for Action," *Moscow News*, No. 5 (12-18 February 1998), p. 10.

18. Data from a study by the Research Institute of Geography, Russian Academy of Sciences, summarized in *Segodnya* (5 January 1994), p. 5.

19. USSR, Ministry of Natural Resource Use and Environmental Protection, *Natsional'nyi doklad CCCR k konferentsii OON 1992 goda po okruzhaiushchei crede I razbitiiu* (National Report of the USSR for the 1992 UN Conference on the Environment and Development), (Moscow: Ministry of Natural Resource Use and Environmental Protection, 1991), p. 224 and Interview with then Russian Minister of the Environment, Viktor Danilov-Danilyan, *Zelenyi mir* (Green World), No. 4 (1994), p. 3.

20. See Murray Feshbach, Editor-in-chief, *Environmental and Health Atlas of Russia* (Moscow: PAIMS Publishing House, 1995), Maps 2.88 and 2.89, n.p. In his introductory comments, Yu. Bobrow estimates that 20 per cent of the total volume of drinking water is not used for its designated purpose and that 50 per

cent of the population drinks water that does not meet hygenic standards. See Yu. A. Bobrow, "The Use and Contamination of Water," in Feshbach, pp. 2-18.

21. See Feshbach, *Environmental and Health Atlas of Russia*, Map 2.59, "Changes in the Total Volume of Pollutants per Unit of Output in 1992 Compared with 1991 (per cent)," and Map 2.85, "Change in the Volume of Polluted Sewage Dumped into Natural Water Sites per Unit of Output Produced in 1992 Compared with 1991 (per cent)," n. p.

22. For a review of Soviet Environmental Policy during the 70s, see Barbara Jancar, "Soviet Environmental Policy toward the Third World," in W. Raymond Duncan, ed., *Soviet Policy in the Third World* (New York: Pergamon Press, 1980), pp. 49-83.

23. Barbara Jancar-Webster, "New Directions in US Environmental Relations with Russia" Sharyl Cross and Martina A. Oborotova, eds., *The New Chapter in United States-Russian Relations: Opportunities and Challenges* (Westport: Praeger, 1994), pp. 113-36.

24. Floriana Fossato, "U.S./Rus: Is the Era of Western Aid to Russia Coming to an End?," Radio Free Europe/Radio Liberty (RFE/RL) Special Report No. 6 (11 June 1997), p. 2, (http://www.refrl.org.nca/features/1997/06).

25. According to James Collins, the current US Ambassador to the Russian Federation, the US share of all foreign investment in Russia is $5 billion, or about 25 per cent of total foreign investment. See Floriana Fossato, "Russia: The Amount of Change Has been Extraordinary," *RFE/RL Features*, Prague (12 December 1997), (http://www.rferl.org/nca/features/1997/12/ F.RU.971212144120.html).

26. Robert Lyle, "1997 in Review: IMF's Year Begins and Ends in Russia," *RFE/RL Features* 1997, Vol. 12 (1997), p. 1, (http://www.rferl.org/nca/featuresw/1997/12).

27. Ellen Smidt, "The World Bank and Russian Oil," *The Ecologist*, Vol. 27, No. 1 (January-February 1997), pp. 21-27.

28. Natalia Gurushina, "World Bank Gives Russia $80 Million Environmental Grant," *RFE/RL Newsline* (3 June 1996), p. 1, (http:solar.rtd.utk.edu/cgi-bin/friends/omri/select-rec.pl).

29. Kyoto Summit, "Global agreement to cut greenhouse gas emissions: Summary," p. 2. Data Source Provider: European Commission, Service du Porteparole Document Reference, Based on Commission Press Release IP/97/1106 of (11 December 1997), Subject Index Codes: Environmental Protection, Meteorology (http://www.rec.org/Mailing-List-Editor.html)

# 8

## New Directions in US Security Policy and Mexico After the Cold War: Democracy, Trade, Migrants and Drugs

*Edward J. Williams*

In the late 1990s, the United States and Mexico muddle toward a new relationship for the approaching millennium. US security considerations play a role in the evolving equation, but they differ from the security factors that dominated the bilateral relationship through the late 1980s. US policies for the coming millennium concentrate on North American economic integration and encourage Mexico's movement to political reform. US policy makers no longer fix solely on rigid political stability to frustrate the supposed designs of Soviet expansionism.

At the same time, US policy makers elaborate novel nuances and extrapolations of "security" policy, including the claim that drug trafficking and undocumented migration endanger US national security. In the process, policy makers confuse settled understandings of security and complicate an already complex bilateral relationship between Mexico and the United States.

This chapter describes and analyzes the Mexican component of contemporary US security policy. The discussion divides into four parts. A short description of traditional US security policy in Latin America and Mexico follows this introduction. It sets the scene for the central component of the chapter — an explication of contemporary and emerging policy. Three foci define the policy for the approaching millennium: 1) the move toward a new form of political stability evolving from the hesitant dawning of participatory democracy in Mexico; 2) Mexico's economic growth and stability within the context of the regional integration institutionalized by the North America Free Trade Agreement (NAFTA); and 3) novel extrapolations of traditional security policy defining drug consumption in the US, "narco–trafficking" originating from Mexico, and undocumented migration from Mexico as threats to US national security.

The analysis of drugs and migration forms a special contribution of this chapter to definitions of national security discussed in this book. While other chapters touch on components of those two themes, they are more fully developed in US–Mexican relations than in other areas discussed in this study.

The fourth and final section of the paper analyzes the complications and inconsistencies of the several components of US security policy in Mexico, developing once again the drugs and migration theses. The analysis highlights the intrinsic contradictions of US policy.

## US TRADITIONAL SECURITY POLICY IN LATIN AMERICA AND THE MEXICAN VARIANT

The principles of traditional US Latin American security policy were fairly straight forward, although the Mexican variant reflected minor complexity. The fundamental principle followed the Monroe Doctrine (1823) in defining extra–Hemispheric presence in the Western Hemisphere as a threat to US security. Especially early on, foreign military presence formed the crux of the defined threat. As time went on, extra–Hemispheric political and economic presence also disturbed the tranquility of US policy makers. In that sense, French troops in Mexico or German naval power in the Caribbean certainly transgressed US security, but a Soviet or Japanese trade and aid campaign also sparked Washington's response. Hence, US policy makers worked to expel the entire panoply of extra–Hemispheric influence in the Americas.

The successes of Fidel Castro in Cuba beginning in 1959 and the Sandinistas in Nicaragua in 1979 partially breached the principle by facilitating the expansion of Soviet military power and political influence in the Western Hemisphere. But, the principle remained inviolate as components of US anti–Soviet policies and programs multiplied. US policy makers strained to contain Soviet influence by confecting a continuum of declarations, military and developmental aid programs, assistance to ham–fisted dictatorships, manipulations of trading agreements, military threats, interventions by US surrogates and US troops, et cetera, ad nauseam. In the process, the US bullied the Latin American countries into following the US line, thereby putatively contributing to US security.[1]

While not deviating substantially from the defined principles, US security policy anent Mexico reflected a special spin. Mexico defined an exceptional case — it boasted a large population and significant wealth; it bordered the US. Most importantly, Mexico enjoyed unusual political stability, the sine qua non of US Latin American security policy. Hence, US policy makers tolerated Mexico's strain of independence. They suffered Mexico's opposition to US–sponsored anti–communist resolutions floated through the Organization of American States (OAS). They stood by as Mexico maintained diplomatic relations with Castro's Cuba from the mid–1960s through the late 1970s. United States policy makers even endured Mexico's occasional flirtations with the Soviet Union and the Socialist Bloc. All of that extraordinary forbearance of Mexico's posturing sprang from the United States infatuation with Mexican political stability

While US policy makers vehemently attacked Soviet totalitarianism, they never extended their democratic principles to opposing what Peru's Mario Vargas Llosa called Mexico's "perfect dictatorship," the guardian of the nation's political stability. In the early 1980s, US policy makers consciously decided against condemning the official Partido Revolucionario Institucional's (PRI) heavy–handed electoral fraud against the conservative opposition Partido Accion Nacional (PAN). In the same vein, US policy makers offered no succor to the left opposition's Partido de la Revolución Democratica (PRD) as it challenged the official party and the accepted dogma in the late 1980s. To repeat, US policy makers defined Mexican political stability as a basic principle of US security policy.

But, the end of the Cold War begot a context favoring a more creative security policy that included support for Mexico's fledgling democracy.[2] In the first place, the clear and present threat to US security disappeared, permitting US policy makers to evolve more sympathy with the forces of political change in Mexico. The Soviet peril had passed from the worldscene. As the Kremlin cut off financial assistance, Fidel Castro's

Cuba also lost all practical significance as a threat to the US. No longer compelled to emphasize the primacy of Mexican political stability as a counter to the supposed ambitions of Soviet imperialism or Cuban mischief, US policy inched toward tolerance of creative opposition in the Mexican polity.

Moreover, several economic influences worked to transform the bilateral relationship. Mexico's economic crises of 1982 and 1994 provided points of leverage for US diplomacy. When the US salvaged Mexico from financial collapse, US policy makers seized the opportunity to encourage the Mexican government to embrace political, as well as economic, reform. Furthermore, regional trading blocs forming in Europe and the Far East nudged both Mexico and the US toward economic cooperation culminating with NAFTA. In the process, the rise of Mexican Neo–Liberalism facilitated an ideological climate conducive to economic integration based on capitalistic, free market principles.[3]

Finally, several trends crystallized in the US to define drugs and illegal migration as national security issues. The trends included increasing drug consumption and growing xenophobic nativism. To be sure, the end of the Cold War also featured a US military establishment in search of a mission designed to ensure its continued viability.

## COMPONENTS OF CONTEMPORARY POLICY

Three components define the major thrust of contemporary US security policy on Mexico. They include: 1) encouraging a new definition of political stability evolving from the recognition of opposition forces playing a legitimate role in a participatory democracy; 2) cultivating North American economic cooperation through free trade in the NAFTA; 3) and scotching the flow of drugs and illegal migrants from the South.

### *Mexico's Democratic Political Stability*

US policy makers have changed their interpretation of Mexican political stability quite dramatically. Both the means to nurture political stability and the ends it serves differ from the representations of the Cold War period.

Semi–authoritarian rule channeled through the PRI formed the means for ensuring Mexican stability prior to the early 1990s. As the millennium approaches, US policy makers now strive to encourage a more pluralistic and democratic reality in Mexico. For example, official policy during the early 1980s interpreted the conservative PAN's challenge to the PRIista ruling elites as implying possible destabilization. But, in the late 1990s a vibrant PAN appears as a necessary component of a new design of political stability built upon democratic consensus. In the 1970s, US policy makers urged the eradication of guerrilla bands in Mexico's South. But, in the 1990s they encourage negotiation and conciliation with the Zapatistas in the state of Chiapas. In previous decades, US policy makers would have repudiated the social democratic reformers who organized the Alianza Civica. By the mid–1990s, Washington was dispatching public money to the Alianza to support its election monitoring and programs for electoral reform.

To be sure, many of Washington's policy makers continue to suspect and fear the nationalistic PRD. But their opposition is less ideologically rigid then in the 1980s when the PRD formed from a combination of dissident PRIistas, independent socialists, and communists. In truth, the PRD has also assumed a more moderate position. In the 1980s, the party called for a unilateral repudiation of the foreign debt; in the mid–1990s, it petitions for bilateral negotiations on the issue. In 1994, the PRD's Cuauhtémoc Cárdenas appeared to repudiate the NAFTA; by 1997 when he won the mayor's position in Mexico City, he had made peace with the trade agreement, although continuing to advise discussions to address weaknesses in the document. In response, Washington's policy makers inched toward accommodation with the PRD, adding even more legitimacy to Mexico's emerging democracy.

In sum, the end of the Cold War signals a substantially different US posture on a range of political actors in Mexico as they go hesitantly toward a new formulation of political stability based upon participatory democracy. American policies embrace the PAN, they deal with the Alianza Civica, they recognize the legitimacy of the PRD, and they even foresee a positive political role for the Zapatistas rebels.

Moreover, the new realities introduced by the termination of the Cold War led to the redefinition of the strategic considerations served by Mexico's political stability at about the same time that the PRIista regime suffered a crisis of legitimacy. In Cold War days, US policy makers urged authoritarian political stability to obviate the popular appeal of Mexico's communists and nationalists, or to suppress the challenge of the nation's left–wing guerrillas.

In the 1990s, a new pattern of democratic political stability serves other purposes. In the first instance, it combines with Neo–Liberal economic policies to foster an environment conducive to foreign and domestic private sector financing and investment. In the late 1990s, international bankers and investors interpret participatory democracy as contributing to long-term stability. For example, the Mexican stock market enjoyed measurable gains in the wake of the PRD's significant victories in Mexico's 1997 mid–summer elections. That is, the emerging new designs of democratic political stability in Mexico encourages US money and nurtures economic development. In turn, increasing investment provides a cushion to facilitate the move toward participatory democracy.

Beyond facilitating private sector investment, Mexican consensus–based political stability in the new millennium also significantly diminishes the threat of Mexican civil conflict triggering a massive movement of refugees invading the US. The specter of Mexico's millions overwhelming the US as they fled generalized violence in the wake of governmental breakdown has long haunted US policy makers. While certainly not obviated by the evolution of Mexican democracy in the late 1990s, the menace wanes as Mexican political consensus waxes.

### The North American Free Trade Agreement

The second principle of post-Cold War US security doctrine applied to Mexico fastens upon the cultivation of the NAFTA. The NAFTA counts a series of advantages for the United States. The advantages range from those diffusely and indirectly tied to US security to several principles more specifically and directly related to American national security doctrine.

At the diffuse end of the continuum, the North American trade pact promises to contribute to Mexican economic stability, a significant component of the nation's political stability. The NAFTA contributed measurably to Mexico's economic recovery beginning in 1996. Externally, it assured Mexico's access to the US market. Internally, it disciplined Mexican policy makers, encouraging them to stay the course and discouraging them from ill–conceived, radical, counterproductive solutions.

From the northern perspective, the NAFTA also contributes to US national security. It fortifies the US economy as it opens opportunities for US–based multinational corporations to expand operations and increase their profits. Indeed, the NAFTA is as much investment treaty as trade pact. Combined with other Neo–Liberal reforms in Mexico, for example, the NAFTA has forced open areas previously closed to foreign investment — the banking, energy, and mining sectors, as well as governmental procurement across the board.[4]

Inching even closer to security precisely defined, the NAFTA consciously seeks to sharpen the competitive edge of the US economy by facilitating productive specialization and increased division of labor. In fact, the fear that rival trading blocs would overwhelm the United States served as a mighty impetus for the NAFTA as it took form in the 1980s. When the European Union (EU) evolved coherency and the Asian Pacific Economic Cooperation pact (APEC) took form, US (and Mexican) policy makers grew apprehensive and embraced the NAFTA in economic self–defense, reflecting their concern for their national security, and for North American economic viability.

Finally, US security considerations fasten most directly on the geopolitical implications of the NAFTA. In 1993, US Ambassador to Mexico, John Negroponte, outraged Mexican nationalists in writing to Washington that NAFTA spelled the definitive inclusion of Mexico into the sphere of American hegemony. That is, the strategic significance of the trade pact signified that the NAFTA had finally and definitively brought Mexico into the US sphere and secured the soft underbelly of the US from potential enemies. The point is consistent with a long strain of US strategic thought and practice exemplified by the construction of the Panama Canal, the declaration of the Roosevelt Corollary to the Monroe Doctrine, the existence of the naval base at Guantanamo Bay, and interventions and/or occupations of Cuba, the Dominican Republic, Grenada, Haiti, Nicaragua, Panama, et al.

In sum, the first two principles of US security policy explaining contemporary relations with Mexico clearly involve extensions of traditional policy; neither are singular departures. The US search for political stability in Mexico is a variation on the basic theme. New actors play the parts, but the plot is unchanged: Mexican political stability contributes to US security. As for the NAFTA, it defines another variation on the traditional security theme of US economic control in the Western Hemisphere. The United States has exercised its economic hegemony in the Hemisphere by offering or refusing loans, by giving or withholding aid, and by selling arms or prohibiting their sale. In the area of international trade, the US has manipulated a continuum of trade benefits and punishments touching coffee, copper, sugar, tomatoes, and tuna; and encompassing most favored nation status and the US Generalized System of Preferences (GSP). Most recently, that traditional policy has embraced the NAFTA, assuredly a significant agreement for the United States, but perfectly consistent with a long strain of international economic policy dating from the nineteenth century.

But, the third principle of contemporary US security that pertains to Mexico forms a different matter. It is a notable new departure in US security policy, and it profoundly influences the bilateral relationship.

### Drugs and Undocumented Migrants

The third principle of US security policy applied to Mexico pertains to US drug and refugee/immigration policies. These policies and programs define the most contentious issues at controversy between the neighboring countries. They also signal new departures and novel conundrums for the application of United States security policy to its southern neighbor.

In the context of this book, they additionally define unconventional components of security doctrine germane to the post-Cold War period. Both are questionable propositions. The validity of defining drugs as a national security threat in the US is at least precarious; the charge that undocumented migrants threaten national security is close to preposterous.

In 1986, President Ronald Reagan declared drugs to be a national security issue, triggering a flurry of debate, followed by a series of apologies attempting to explain the connection between drugs and national security. The policy then produced the mustering of military might at the US–Mexican boundary line (and beyond) and ever increasing political and economic pressure on Mexico. The most dramatic and controversial manifestation of pressure took the form of yearly "certification" that Mexico was up to US–defined standards in its anti–drug campaigns. In the last years of the 1990s the shortcomings of the entire anti–drug effort along with growing charges of human rights abuses at the US–Mexican boundaryline combined to catalyze a reappraisal of the doctrine.

The initial debate in the 1980s focused upon the fact that the national security declaration signalled the use of the US military in the anti–drug campaign in the US–Mexican borderlands. During the debate, the Secretary of the Navy damned as "absurd" and "childish" the move to have the US military block the boundary line with Mexico. The Director of the

Immigration and Naturalization Service condemned the measure as "simplistic" and admonished the Congress about problems to come.[5]

The several criticisms of defining drugs as a national security threat gave rise to apologies designed to explain how drug cultivation, trafficking, and usage jeopardizes the national security of the United States.[6] The analytical foci range geographically from negative effects in Latin America (and Mexico, specifically) to the deleterious consequences in the United States heartland. Conceptually, the apologies range from the political to the moral realms. One facet of the charge holds that in Latin America's enormously rich and potent drug merchants corrupt governments. In the United States, huge amounts of money are frittered away on drugs. Moreover, drug usage is blamed for diminishing the effectiveness of US military and damaging society through "decayed morals, increased crime, the breakdown of family values..."[7]

All of those charges seem to carry a strain of validity, but the direct connection to national security is not clearly articulated. It may be that a Mexican government corrupted by drug lords will be less sympathetic to US interests, but no proof is proffered. In truth, the specific argument is not even broached. Moreover, the special and singular connection of drugs to national security wants careful treatment. A doctrine that defines marijuana as a national threat, but excludes alcohol from the same category clearly lacks consistency. Illegal drugs jeopardize public health, but they may not be so serious in their overall impact as cigarettes. Some drugs may lead to lethargy and contribute to physical frailty, but so does excessive television viewing.

Beyond drugs, undocumented migrants form another dimension of the new departures in defining threats to US national security. Undocumented migrants and refugees from Mexico and beyond are not officially defined as constituting a national security threat in the United States, but, their impact is often depicted as being quite negative. A leading study characterizes the debate on migrants and refugees as being "colored by national security concerns."[8]

Even more than the arguments about the national security implications of drugs, the putative links between undocumented migrants/refugees and national security challenge credibility. They extrapolate several levels beyond any imaginable clear and present danger. The supposed negative relationship between migrants and national security evolves from the charge that significant undocumented migration implies a series of economic, political, public health, and environmental consequences detrimental to national vitality and strength. The reasoning proposes that migrants and refugees overburden the economy, provoking social anxiety by contributing to unemployment, consuming public services, and increasing the welfare rolls. Environmentalists fasten upon the threat to national space, conjuring the image of over–population in the United States. The public health advocates invoke the image of malnourished and disease–ridden migrants crossing the line from Mexico and infecting the US population with exotic maladies.

Finally, the political nuances of the national security connection to migration emphasizes direct threats in the form of terrorists moving north from Mexico and an indirect menace to national unity arising from the expanding diverse (polyglot) ethnic, cultural, and racial characteristics of contemporary American society. President Ronald Reagan's cry in the early 1980s that the United States had "lost control of its borders" also played to the political subtheme of the national security argument.[9] The reality seemed to erode America's patriotic self–image; it defied the claim to sovereign control of the national territory. A former INS Commissioner's threat of a "silent invasion" struck the same theme.

Those arguments run the gamut from absurd to questionable, but all insinuate their way into the popular and semi–official apologies linking migrants and refugees to presumed threats to US national security. Not unlike the Soviet scare of the Cold War days, bureaucratic politics plays upon popular ignorance to contribute to public paranoia. As previously the Central Intelligence Agency (CIA) and the military prospered with the systematic exaggeration of the Soviet threat, so in late 1990s the Border Patrol, the INS, and the military benefit from the spectre of undocumented migrants and refugees overrunning the Republic.

Combined with the official doctrine that defines drugs as a security threat, the national fix on undocumented migrants and refugees has led to the militarization of the United States–Mexican border region and the annual certification of Mexico as meeting US standards on the drug issue — the two most conspicuous manifestations of these novel interpretations of US security policy and their controversial and negative impact on the US–Mexican relationship.

Indeed, the negative reaction of the Mexican government joined with ongoing opposition in the US to nudge the American government towards a reappraisal of both national security strategies. Beginning at least as early as 1997, Washington launched a review of certification and US military presence in the binational borderlands. A patrolling soldier in the rural Texas borderlands killed an apparently innocent young man, precipitating the review of military patrols in the area.

The certification policy is damned on two counts. First, it is inconsistently applied to varying countries; despite similar circumstances, Colombia was decertified in 1997, but Mexico gained conditional certification. Moreover, the sanctions tied to decertification are so draconian that it is highly unlikely that the US could ever impose them. Their imposition would severely damage the bilateral relationship. The price is too high.

In sum, the major principles of US post-Cold War security policy took on increasingly clear form as the 1990s advanced, but some components tended to be more problematic than others. US policy makers displayed earnest commitment to encouraging Mexico's moves toward pluralistic democratic participation. The policy makers interpreted the evolution toward democracy as the way to ensure political stability and, in the process, contribute to US security. Following the NAFTA, the Mexican and US economies moved inexorably toward integration as the millennium approached. The policy makers construed economic integration as a contribution to the competitive position of the US economy. Even more directly germane to national security doctrine, North American economic union also secured the southern flank of the United States, a security anxiety for more than 200 years.

But the final component of the post-war security policy became increasingly problematic. The security implications of undocumented migration and drugs remained ill–defined. The negative economic and political consequences of nativistic immigrant bashing plagued the policy makers. Contentious debate raged on the locus of the drug problem. The contradictory implications of the components of US policy slowly dawned on the policy makers and hesitant moves toward reformulation evolved.

## CONCLUSIONS: COMPLICATIONS AND CONTRADICTIONS

An analysis of United States post-Cold War security policy's application to Mexico suggest two analytical foci. The first centers upon the strengths and weaknesses of the several components of the formulation. The second looks to the relationship of its several parts to determine their consistency or contradiction. Shorter and longer term considerations also play into the analysis.

The first principle of United States policy centers upon US support for Mexico's contemporary democratic opening. The emergence of Mexican pluralistic democracy counts both longer and shorter term implications for US security. The longer term analysis strikes a clearly positive chord, but tends to the abstract. The shorter term focus introduces some complexity as it fastens more upon the concrete.

In the first instance, the evolution of a pluralistic democratic system in Mexico promises to serve US security interests. It contributes to firmly–grounded political stability. It discourages foreign penetration of the Mexican political elites. From an economic perspective, political democracy invites US investment, thereby strengthening the Mexican economy and linking it ever more closely to the United States. Finally, democratic political stability combined with economic growth dampens undocumented migration and refugee movement and may even diminish the attractions of the drug trade.

While all of that invites approbation, the shorter term brims with more complicated implications attendant to the transition from stability based upon a semi–authoritarian system to one founded upon democratic pluralism. US policy involves a calculated risk. The realization of Mexican democracy is uncertain. Transitions brim with potential for political disintegration and/or radicalization. As the numbers of political actors increases arithmetically, the potential for discord multiplies geometrically. For example, the emerging of the nationalistic PRD signalled by the 1997 Mexican elections implies potential tension in the bilateral relationship. While backing off its earlier repudiation of the NAFTA, the PRD and others continued to call for re–negotiation of selected components of the trade accord. Depending upon the positions defined and the attitudes assumed by critics of the NAFTA, an effect on trade and investment seems quite likely. The subsequent negative consequences for the Mexican economy follow in train. And, to complete the syllogism, the consequences for US security wax equally clear.

The point leads logically to a consideration of the second plank of US security policy's meaning for Mexico — economic integration symbolized by the North American Free Trade Agreement (NAFTA). Again, two analytical foci stand out. The first pertains to the direct economic implications in Mexico and the United States; the second relates to indirect political fallout in both countries.

The NAFTA offers economic advantage to the United States and Mexico, but in both countries' advocates exaggerated its positive impact and opponents damned it for a multitude of real and imagined sins. In the US, the resulting disillusion contributed to expanding political opposition that led to the US Congress in 1997 denying the President "Fast Track" authority to pursue additional trade agreements in Latin America. In Mexico, the NAFTA combined with other Neo–Liberal policies and programs like privatization and the reduction of subsidies to trigger widespread socio–economic dislocation ending in a similar political backlash. The Zapatista revolt in 1994 highlights the most bombastic example of the relationship between the NAFTA and opposition to the government; the expanding political influence of the PRD is more subtle, but unquestionably more significant.

In both cases, domestic political opposition spills over into the international arena to threaten the bilateral relationship. In Mexico and the US public and official opinion blames the respective partner country for the putative iniquity of the NAFTA. To be sure, cause and effect are frequently confused and the consequences of global trends and other programs and policies are erroneously blamed on the NAFTA. However unfortunate that may be, it is largely irrelevant to the political analysis of the NAFTA's efficacy for US security policy.

In somewhat the same way, the complex implications of the NAFTA and Mexico's modernization program secret their way into the migration and drugs issues — the third leg of the tripod of US security policy's application to Mexico. Mexico's economic crisis beginning in late 1994 certainly stimulated undocumented migration to the United States, but so did a continuum of NAFTA–related improvements to communications and transportation infrastructure.

Potential illegal migrants took advantage of those newly established facilities to be better informed and to travel more cheaply and efficiently. The ongoing success of Mexico's drug traffickers nest in the same setting. As more traffic flows North across the US boundary line, the opportunities for transporting illicit drugs multiplies.

But those examples touch only the margins of the migration and drugs components of United States security formulations. More directly, the basic doctrine betrays essential flaws. The doctrine is at least incomplete; it is probably ill–conceived; and it is partially counterproductive. First, the doctrine is incomplete, unfinished. In truth, the security doctrine does not deal, per se, with undocumented migration. It rather defines the security threat as a massive movement of refugees springing from economic collapse and political chaos in Mexico.

A policy based upon that premise is difficult to sustain. In the first place, the advocates muster no evidence stronger than fantasy to document the likelihood of massive refugee movement. Moreover, even large numbers of refugees fail to imply a threat to US security. They may entail measurable erosion of psychological well–being in America's Southwest and significant demands upon the national coffers, but neither of those define a security threat as that term is traditionally understood.

Beyond incomplete, US drug policy and its security correlatives are ill–conceived. The glaring confusion between supply and demand exemplifies the primary (and hypocritical) core of the policy's fallacious conception. If drug addiction in the United States were fundamentally the result of supply, it would form a traditional national security issue. The military would guard the boundary line against the invasion of the alien drug merchants.

While the problem is partly that, it is much more a domestic issue emanating from different causes. They derive from moral, psychological, social, economic, and political sources imbedded in the human condition in the United States. The remedies spring not from national security doctrines wrought by military strategists, but rather from the caring and healing arts and sciences and their practitioners — social workers, medical doctors, psychologists, counsellors, priests, ministers, rabbis; and, in the last analysis, from parents endowed with skills and touched with love.

As the migration and anti–drug components of US security policy are incomplete and ill–conceived, it is not surprising they are also counterproductive because they are flawed by internal contradiction. US self–righteous preaching and callous muscle flexing sparks a nationalistic backlash in Mexico. It endangers bilateral amity and often overrides the goodwill emanating from components of US support for Mexican political democracy and economic stability.

Mexican enmity for the US especially crystallizes about the yearly certification process. Each Spring, the American President is called to certify that Mexico's anti–drug efforts satisfy US standards. In this annual rite the Mexico bashers hold forth in the press and in the US Congress. The Mexicans rightly interpret the exercise to be insulting, degrading, and disrespectful of Mexico's legal sovereignty, political dignity, and socio–cultural integrity. "Respect" defines a profoundly significant concept in Mexico; impugning dignity and flaunting disrespectful attitudes eat away at the very core bilateral friendship.

President Clinton's 1997 state visit to Mexico illustrates the point. The President dedicated his entire visit to mending fences ripped asunder by the orgy of Mexico bashing concomitant to the annul certification debate.[10] He left untouched profoundly significant conundrums touching bilateral economic and political cooperation. The President devoted almost all of his efforts to assuring Mexicans of US "respect" in an effort to undo the harm wrought by a policy that defined drugs as a threat to national security and Mexican supply as the major cause of the millions of Americans addicted to illegal substances.

In sum, US support for Mexican democracy and its search for bilateral economic cooperation betray problems for US security policy not obviously apparent at first blush. These questions demand attention, but they seem amenable to political solutions guided by diplomatic skill. But, US programs in pursuit of the component of the policy defining undocumented migration and drugs as security threats appear destined for far less success. The premise is questionable at best and in every instance its implications are exaggerated and/or ill–defined. To add insult to injury, US governmental policy officially blames Mexico and other external suppliers as the most important cause of the US drug problem. As US security policy fosters that fantasy, it sabotages stable bilateral relations, thereby diminishing rather than enhancing US security.

To end on a slightly more optimistic note, the late 1990s did offer some glimpses of sanity in a couple of areas of US policy on undocumented migration and drugs. First, in the wake of the fatal shooting of the Texas youth near the boundary line the Pentagon in mid–1997 suspended all military ground patrols in the US border region as it reevaluated the policy. Second, small glimmers of a realistic evaluation of the US drug malady and intelligently conceived anti–drug strategies began to characterize policy statements. Both President Clinton and the coordinator of the US anti–drug program, General Barry McCaffrey, joined the issue in setting out two important principles. They emphasized several times over that US demand played a significant role in evoking drug production and trafficking from Mexico and other Latin American countries. They also began to back away from unilateral arrogance in advocating a bilateral approach. In the process, serious discussion emerged of abandoning the certification process.[11] To be sure, none of those principles evolved into concrete policies and programs, but all offered some small promise that the contradictory components of US security policy might be reconciled.

168                                              *Edward J. Williams*

## NOTES

1.  See Cole Blasier, *The Giant's Rival: The USSR and Latin America*, revised edition (Pittsburgh: University of Pittsburgh Press, 1987).

2.  For this and other themes discussed here, see John Bailey and Sergio Aguayo Quezada, eds., *Strategy and Security in U.S.-Mexican Relations Beyond the Cold War* (San Diego: Center for US-Mexican Relations, University of California, 1996); and Michael J. Dziedzic, *Mexico: Converging Challenges*, Adelphi Papers (London: Brassey's, 1989).

3.  See Judith A. Teichman, *Privatization and Political Change in Mexico* (Pittsburgh: University of Pittsburgh Press, 1995).

4.  For some documentation and discussion, see Teichman's Chapter Four, "Dismantling the State" in her *Privatization and Political Change...*, pp. 129-58.

5.  See Edward J. Williams and Irasema Coronado, "The Hardening of the United States-Mexican Borderlands: Causes and Consequences," *Boundary and Security Bulletin*, Vol. I, No. 4 (January 1995), pp. 69-74.

6.  See two analyses that appear in *Parameters*, the organ of the US Army War College: Michael H. Abbor, "The Army and the Drug War: Politics or National Security," and William W. Mendel and Murl D. Munger, "The Drug Threat: Getting Priorities Straight"; respectively, Vol. XVIII, No. 4 (December 1988), pp. 95-112; and Vol. XXVII, No. 2 (Summer 1997), pp. 110-24.

7.  Abbot, "The Army and the Drug War," p. 95.

8.  Timothy J. Dunn, *The Militarization of the U.S.-Mexico Border: 1978-1992* (Austin: Center for Mexican American Studies, University of Texas, 1996), p. 41.

9.  See Oscar Martinex, *Troublesome Border* (Tucson: University of Arizona Press, 1988), p. 1.

10.  See James Bennet, "For Mexicans, Clinton's Visit Is a Serenade," *New York Times* (8 May 1997), p. A7.

11.  For description and discussion of the new initiatives, see James Bennet, "Clinton and Mexico Chief Pledge Joint Effort on Border and Drugs," *New York Times* (7 May 1997), p. A1; "Clinton and Zedillo sign treaty to put lid on weapons smuggling," *Arizona Daily Star* (15 November 1997), p. A3; "End of 'certification' in sight?" *Latin American Weekly Report* (28 October 1997), p. 511; and "Troop withdrawal 'a tremendous victory'," *Quaker Service Bulletin*, Vol. 78, No. 2 (Winter 1997), p. 1.

# 9

# America and Regional Conflict in the Post-Cold War/Gulf War Era: Some Implications for the Future

*Grant T. Hammond*

The problem of change in the international system is a vexing one. There is seemingly no one way to avoid it, no particularly effective way to prepare for it, sometimes little means to contain it, and often great difficulty in coping with it. This is true not only for neighboring countries in the region where change occurs, but for the world as a whole. It is a particularly difficult circumstance for superpowers or great powers that see themselves as having greater influence than most. They are expected to do a certain amount of work to preserve the status quo or at least ensure that its transformation is, if not peaceful and calm, at least not terribly disruptive.

Alas, it is not necessarily a welcome nor an easy task, for regional hegemons, if there be any, or for the great powers of our era. This is particularly true for the US as the self-proclaimed "last remaining superpower." How change is permitted, encouraged, controlled or resisted is critical to the peace and stability of the planet. So too is whether it effects only one country, a region or the entire international community. But, there are no recipes for success. Though a number of similarities can be discerned, each case is unique and ultimately has to be confronted accordingly.

In that period since the end of the Cold War, the changed environment of world relations has been a novel and not well understood set of circumstances. The end of the Cold War, the dissolution of the Soviet Union and the end of the Gulf War, constitute a sort of triple dose of global change. Traditional enemies disappeared, new forces and countries have emerged, and the very ground rules for interstate relations have been modified. The comfortable bi-polarity of the Cold War, the threat of nuclear destruction, and the practice of détente have ended. They have given way to a torrid pace of states dividing and replicating, to frequent humanitarian impulses for intervention, and to experiments in democracy and capitalism all over the globe. The fetish of the moment is for collective security through the UN and if not, cooperative security through *ad hoc* coalitions. Unilateral actions are decidedly not seen as appropriate even if they were affordable — economically, morally or militarily.

This has been made more urgent and unclear by the urge to embrace the concept, if not the reality, of what Secretary General Boutros Boutros-Ghali called "preventive diplomacy."[1] Timely, appropriate, prophylactic intervention of a peaceful nature is seen as far preferable to belated, costly military efforts to redress change that has come to be seen as undesirable for whatever reasons. But, there is no litmus test for determining scope, scale, duration, significance and either intended or unintended consequences of transformations in the international system. The list of active interventions is roughly the same as those instances which the US and other major world powers studiously avoid. For every belated Bosnia, there is an East Timor, for every Somalia an Afghanistan under the Taliban, for every Haiti, a Zaire, for every Rwanda, a Sri Lanka. Neither the impulse for intervention nor the reality of regional conflict is universal.

## REGIONAL CONFLICT

What is regional conflict and why does it erupt in some places and not in others? Regional conflict is any violent disruption or sudden and significant political economic change within or among states that by its nature or likely expansion could lead to a significant rearrangement of the status quo in a particular region. Hence, domestic instability, a primary cause of regional conflict in many instances, is necessarily a potential threat to the region writ large. An insurgency or civil war that became internationalized could very well expand into a serious global conflict.

But regional conflict could also occur because of the breakdown of established principles of international order or the failure of cooperative regional security arrangements.

What determines the threshold for outside intervention in regional conflict? There are no easy answers but there appear to be some generally applicable insights, at least for the US. First, certain regions — most of Africa — are not of great enough concern to elicit outside intervention save for the protection or evacuation of foreign nationals. They are neither important enough as sole sources of resources nor large enough as markets that they are of great cost or consequence to those outside the area. Absent ideological rivalry and the zero sum game scoring of a bi-polar Cold War, they count for less than they once did. Second, other regions — the subcontinent and Indian Ocean — are large, distant, complex and increasingly left to their own devices by default if not design. India is the emerging regional hegemon and increasingly able to police the area. Third, still others — Latin America — for all the internal strife in given countries, are remarkably free from interstate conflict. That is a sizable chunk of the planet's states and peoples that are not likely to see foreign intervention in regional conflict.

This leaves four regions where regional conflict is, if not likely, at least serious in its implications: Europe, Central Asia, the Far East and the Middle East. These areas just happen to contain one or all of the following: important markets for major powers, important resources, rapidly expanding populations and economies, and domestic sources of political instability. They also contain the seeds of hegemonic rivalry in the region either among themselves or their neighbors. Germany is a *bete noire* in Europe as is Japan in the Far East and Russia in Central Asia. China is seen by most as the most rapidly developing power of the future by sheer size and the weight of over 5,000 years of cultural impact while the Turks, Persians and Arabs seem destined to replay their ancient struggles for dominance in the Middle East as well.

## ENGAGEMENT AND ENLARGEMENT VS. DISENGAGE-MENT AND CONTRACTION

The trend of the United States is not for engagement and enlargement, its national security strategy, but for disengagement and a narrowing of focus. Despite interventions from Panama to Somalia and Haiti to Bosnia, a concomitant reality of US policy is its massive and precipitous disengagement from both Europe and the Far East. US troops are coming home, bases are being closed, forces re-deployed and the US is preparing to project power not from bases overseas but from the continental United States (CONUS). Since 1989, US military forces stationed in Europe have shrunk from nearly 329,000 to 117,000 troops. That is a 65 per cent reduction.[2] Those stationed in the Far East have declined from over 124,000 to 94,000, a 24 per cent reduction.[3] Half of this cut came from the closure of Clark Field and Subic Bay in the Philippines. Counterintuitive though it may be, that is one of the major transformations in the post-Cold/Gulf War world. We are increasingly less likely to affect events abroad because we are not there, at least in the numbers that we used to be or in the bases, which we used to operate. There are also other forces with which to contend — a growing concern for social security rather than national security, signs of a resurgent isolationism, cuts in defense budgets, and a false notion of war engendered by CNN's images of the air campaign in the Gulf War.

A second major transformation is the diminished, rather than enlarged, area of policy concern for the United States. Aside from US Marines extracting American and other foreign nationals from a variety of trouble spots in Africa and modest humanitarian aid, the US has written off Africa as an area of major involvement or concern. The same is true for much of Latin America save for drug interdiction and arms sales. Indeed, the promotion of American business interests is the only real enlargement to be pursued. The notion that any real political commitment or policy concern follows in its wake is largely illusory. If enlargement is interpreted as the spread of democracy and capitalism, the emphasis is definitely on the latter. That is really defined by access of US businesses to domestic markets the world over, whatever the political flavor of the regime or the economic system which supports it. If there is any doubt in that, look at the record when decisions have to be made between human rights records and MFN status with China, or democratic political practices vs. arms sales in the Gulf region, or even unsavory regimes — including Iraq — and export trade of almost any kind. While we have preferences, we don't usually let them get in the way of pragmatic business concerns. In that regard, we are not very dissimilar to most other nations, rhetoric to the contrary notwithstanding.

The area where engagement and enlargement is seemingly boundless is in the arena of what is called popular culture. Though much of the rest of the world is not and does not want to be American, the pervasiveness of

Coca Cola, McDonald's, MTV, rock music, blue jeans, American movies and syndicated television shows belies the preference of the masses. According to the *New York Times*, most of the top movies playing in Brazil, Britain, Germany, Israel, South Africa and Japan in the Spring of 1997 were American.[4] Both Madonna in the Middle East and "The Chicago Red Oxen" ("da Bulls") in China are popular icons. In Croatia, one might encounter "Hard Rock Cafe — Zagreb" complete with a pink, 1956 Chevy in the lobby. Television itself may have a deleterious effect as knowledge of how others live and a desire to emulate them may well overwhelm the resources of the polity, economy and society to accommodate these desires.

A study reported in the *New York Times*, reviewed the top television shows and books being read around the world. The Germans were watching their version of "The Love Boat." South Africans watched the American soap opera "The Bold and the Beautiful." In the reading department, the Japanese were reading American psychiatrist's Scott Peck's *People of the Lie*, an 1983 study of evil people and the hope for healing them.[5] This predilection for things American, massive global advertising and a rise in the numbers of those under 20 make a volatile mixture. The major reality of the first quarter of the next century — the ubiquitous presence and massive numbers of global teenagers — and a desire for trappings of things American may cause major problems. Deferred gratification is not a hallmark of the young and their susceptibility to advertising and things American are legion.

## AN HISTORICAL OVERVIEW

Even in Europe, where we thought the world more civilized and war banished as a result of the carnage of both World War I and II, "regional conflict" has occurred. The wars of Yugoslav secession and succession have demonstrated that action by the US, NATO or individual nations in the area, was slow to occur and plagued with difficulties despite the willingness of major powers in the region to act, and the unquestioned capability to employ force to halt the spread of conflict. We watched for three years as war spread within 300 miles of both Rome and Budapest, 250,000 were killed and 2,000,000 became refugees.[6] The series of wars and conflicts in the former Yugoslavia are symptomatic of our confusion about the causes of war. Economic and legal integration have far less to do with it than stability. Social scientists have long known that the sources of war lie more with instability than the character of a state, be it democratic or totalitarian.[7]

Even more worrisome is the data which supports the proposition that far from adding to stability, periods of transition to democratic political systems tend to be particularly unstable.[8] The referenda approach to statehood is supported and condoned while we create a larger number of smaller states. Under a banner of peaceful change and international law, we create Slovakias and Slovenias, which are only the tail end of a process of state expansion. The state system has doubled in size in the last 30 years, and nearly quadrupled in the last fifty. Ominously, though, 75 per cent of these new countries are smaller than the US state of Massachusetts in both population and wealth. Even peaceful change is making things worse, not better. We now we have weak old states, marginalized by defections and even weaker ones newly created.[9]

At the end of World War I, the world saw the passing of four great empires, some of which had lasted for six hundred years: The Russian, the German, the Austro- Hungarian and the Ottoman. In their place emerged a large number of new states, most weak and unstable, themselves both a cause and consequence of what E. H. Carr has called "the twenty year truce"[10] between the Versailles settlement and the outbreak of World War II. Despite high hopes, the League of Nations, collective security and disarmament did not prevent war. At the end of World War II, in addition to the collapse of the Third Reich, there was the end of the Italian and Japanese delusions of imperial glory, the establishment of a growing Soviet Empire and the continuation of civil war interrupted by World War II in China. There was also the beginning of the end of colonial rule in the British, French, and Dutch empires as wars over colonial control began to afflict all three as territories from Israel to India gained their independence and others — Vietnam, Algeria, Indonesia, Malaysia — fought for theirs.

We find ourselves at the end of the Cold War/Gulf War in a no less enviable position. Both the international system and an increasingly larger percentage of its supposedly sovereign members are very unstable at the moment. Unlike the previous era from 1914 to 1991, it is not predatory totalitarianism of either the right or the left, which threatens the international system and individual states within it. Rather, it is the expansion of that system itself and the weakness and instability of many of the members of it that are responsible. The world seems to be littered with what have been called "failed states,"[11] lines on a map with a name and supposed independent existence which lack real sovereignty, economic viability or political stability. Lebanon, Bosnia, Liberia, Haiti, Rwanda, Nagorno Karabakh, Somalia, and a host of others all come to mind as lacking one or all of the requisites for true statehood and the prospects for a viable existence to continue as an independent entity.

Furthermore, we have, in the name of democracy and the avowed US National Security Strategy of "Engagement and Enlargement,"[12] and in keeping with the supposed principle of "self-determination" encouraged and abetted the creation of many unstable new political entities whose existence as states remains to be seen. These stretch from Slovakia and Bosnia in Europe to Abkhazia and Armenia in the former Soviet Republics of Central Asia. Indeed, the instability of regimes from the previous era — the Democratic People's Republic of Korea, Israel and a Palestinian entity, continue to haunt the Far East and Middle East respectively. We have seen the creation of many small, poor, unsustainable states under the aegis of self-determination. Woodrow Wilson may well come to be one of the most reviled men of the twentieth century for elevating such a notion to a principle of the international state system. Neither he, nor we, have determined how many people may self-determine their future nor on what basis such should be permitted to occur.

For those of us who are living through the perilous times of uncharted change in the international system without the comfort of bi-polar rivalries to simplify things, it seems unprecedented. We seem besieged by novelty and uncertainty with little in the way of experience to guide us. While that may seem to be the case, it is a false image. There are precedents.

The end of the Cold War occasioned the third major transformation in the international system in the twentieth century. We would do well to look at the two precedents offered by a like period of time after World War I and World War II. True, these were violent cataclysms that left most if not all of their participants exhausted and which were followed by efforts at comprehensive peace settlements and the creation of global security organizations. In that regard, our period is dissimilar, but the challenges we face are not.

The following chart compares the number of interventions in the six years following World War I, World War II and the end of the Gulf War by the United States.[13]

**Table 9.1**

|                     | 1919-1926 | 1945-1952 | 1991-1997 |
|---------------------|-----------|-----------|-----------|
| US Intervention     | 6         | 5         | 6 (14)*   |
| US NEOs/Protection  | 14        | 2         | 8         |

(NEO = Non-combatant Evacuation Operation)
* = Interventions in 6 places, 14 separate occasions in the time period.

What this chart reveals is that this period is not necessarily filled with more overseas deployments and employments of military force, be it in humanitarian, peace keeping or conflict situations than in previous periods of massive international change. It also points out how slow yet pervasive the Cold War rivalry was between the US and the USSR.

At the end of the Cold War/Gulf War, we have had independence movements in Armenia, Chechnya, Nagorno Karabakh, and the Yugoslav republics, not to mention civil wars in Somalia, Liberia and Zaire, and numerous military coups in Haiti, Rwanda, Burundi, and Sierra Leone. Interventions, however publicized and controversial have occurred in only half of those listed, however. What is different about these various regional conflicts to cause intervention in some cases and to be virtually ignored in others? What factors in regional conflict determine whether or not intervention will occur, and if it does, what kind of intervention it will be?

First and foremost is the issue of national interest. If the issue or region is not directly important to a major nation, it is not likely to intervene. There must be some political principle, some economic self-interest, some concern for widening instability to cause a great power to act. In the era of superpower bi-polar rivalry, there was a sort of self-fulfilling prophecy that if one side stood to gain in any way, the other should try and prevent it. Since we scored the Cold War as a zero sum game, it was treated as such and that is largely the way things played out.

But there is a secondary reason for intervention. Increasingly, we have intervened in regional conflicts for "humanitarian reasons:" to stop the killing of civilians, to end massive migrations of refugees, to assist with famine, disease and massive numbers of wounded which wars produce. While the so-called "CNN Factor" and public outrage make good news coverage, they may not make good policy. The US was forced to withdraw from Somalia, as eventually was the UN. The jury is still out on Haiti and Bosnia, and US forces are still in both countries. The danger is that it will prove hard to end an operation to assist the Kurds in Northern Iraq called "Provide Comfort" which originally was a 30 day mission which has now lasted over seven years. The UN has been in Cyprus on a peacekeeping mission for 34 years now. While there has been no war between Greek and Turkish factions — yet — there has been no political settlement of the dispute either. Does that make UNICYP a success or failure?

## REGIONAL CONFLICT AND INTERVENTION

What about the use of US military forces to intervene in the twenty years before WW I and WW II? How much of this occurred then? How do these figures compare with the period of the Cold War, which is almost twice as long? The following chart reveals the answers.[14]

**Table 9.2**

|                   | 1895-1917 | 1919-1941 | 1945-1991 |
|-------------------|-----------|-----------|-----------|
| US Intervention   | 8         | 11        | 32        |
| US NEO/Protection | 32        | 18        | 17        |
| TOTALS:           | 40        | 29        | 48        |

What this suggests is that the period known as the Cold War had three to four times the number of US military interventions in twice the time span. Thus it was roughly twice as likely to have US military interventions than the previous periods under review. On the other hand, the rate of NEO or protection operations of American citizens and assets abroad were only half as frequent as in the pre-WW I period and the same for the inter-war period, although the Cold War time frame is twice as long. That is to say, the incidence of NEO/protection operations was about the same as the inter-war period and about one fourth the number of the period before World War I.

What are we to make of this? Is the world becoming less stable or more so? What are our measure of merit of stability and just what does stability mean? Stability can mean either the capacity to resist change or the ability to absorb it. It would seem that the world is less stable than it was for much of the Cold War era, decolonization notwithstanding. It is both less resistant to change and less well able to absorb it without potential violence and socio-economic dislocation. Is the US less activist or interventionist than in its past in these regions, or more so? Why? The answers to these questions are not clear and may well be in flux depending on the administration in power, the locus of the conflict, the number of Military Operations Other Than War (MOOTW) already underway, and the alliance or coalition politics and partners involved. The short answer is that despite the Wilsonian/Clintonian rhetoric of a crusade for engagement and enlargement, the realities are far more limited and highly selective.

## STABILITY AND CHANGE

The sources of discontent, internal and external, in much of the world are not difficult to discern. They include political challenges to authority and legitimacy, corruption, authoritarian and totalitarian systems, irredentism, and multinational societies. Some of these are legacies of colonialism, others are home grown in more recent times. Nearly every independent country in Africa started out as a multi-party, parliamentary democracy and nearly all have become one party, military supported dictatorships. More vexing still are the social and economic difficulties faced by most countries of the so-called Cold War legacy euphemism, "the Third World." They are beset with a bewildering array of difficulties. These include rapidly expanding populations, increasing poverty and disease, huge debts and debt burdens, inadequate food supply or distribution of it, underdevelopment, massive unemployment and underemployment, mal-distribution of wealth, poor infrastructure, environmental degradation and religious divisions which both undergird and overlay all else.[15]

Under these circumstances, it should come as no surprise that there is internal violence in the form of civil wars, military coups, insurgent movements, and religious wars. Externally, there are competitions over territorial boundaries, access to water, economic exclusion zones, territorial waters, sanctuary and pursuit of insurgents, state sponsored terrorism, refugee migration, religious practices and affiliation and countless other issues in dispute with neighbors in the various regions. Most of these problems are of long standing and the sort which historically have been solved by force of arms, an imposed agreement by a regional hegemon, or international peace settlement guaranteed by those outside the region rather than by negotiation per se.

The difficult question is how to deal with change within a country or a region and not destabilize the region or the world? More particularly, how does the international system withdraw recognition of a sovereign nation and de-legitimize it peacefully? More pointedly still, how does the international system replace one governing faction with another without resort to force of arms? And, on whose authority is this done? These are not easy questions to answer and yet they lie at the heart of the problem of stability in the international system. Allowing for evolution but spurning revolution — or at least most of them — becomes very difficult for the motives of others both in the region and beyond are not necessarily in harmony.

## AMERICA'S DILEMMAS

Americans are caught in a dilemma. They are possessed of one of the most radical political philosophies on earth enshrined in their declaration of independence — a claim on "inalienable rights" to "life, liberty and the pursuit of happiness." Not property, not security, not wealth, but happiness is the goal of Americans. And they have a belief in technology, a faith in engineering, the wherewithal to throw money at problems to solve them and a belief in progress that comes as close to being their national religion as anything. This conviction in a better future and the pursuit of happiness makes them more capable than most cultures of embracing change. And change for America has been generally good.

But, as the world's sole remaining superpower, with the largest share of the planetary GDP (21 per cent), and an increasing concern for consumption rather than investment or protection, in Robert Gilpin's terms,[16] this natural affinity for change is tempered. The United States, as one of the wealthiest nations on earth, is enamored of the status quo. Change could bring instability and instability could threaten prosperity and prosperity and progress are what makes America what it is, at least for the bulk of her citizens. Most of the time we prefer the devil we know rather than the one we do not, stability, however flawed, and the status quo over change we cannot control. Controlled change, US initiated change, incremental change — fine, but not revolution, civil war or uncontrollable events with sweeping implications. Thus, the nation with the world's most liberal political philosophy finds itself as one of the most tenacious supporters of the status quo.

But America's liberal impulses and Utopian predilections are no less strong. Americans see themselves, in Ben Wattenberg's marvelous phrase, "the first universal nation."[17] We are a mongrel nation of immigrants, united by deeply held convictions rather than by shared experience, identities, habits and attachment to territory. We are a polity not on the basis of geography, ethnicity, race, religion, language, culture, or the usual combinations of such. Americans are united as Americans solely by their commitment to a set of political ideals — the rights of the individual, popular sovereignty, democratically elected representatives, toleration of others. Indeed, Samuel Huntington has gone so far as to proclaim that "the United States has no meaning, no identity, no political culture or even history apart from the ideals of liberty and democracy and the continuing effort of Americans to realize their ideals."[18] More than this, we *do see* the opportunity to achieve what Franklin Roosevelt proclaimed as World War II was ending. "We seek peace — enduring peace. More than an end to war. We want an end to the beginning of all wars. . . ."[19] This is an idealistic sentiment. However, it too is a part of the American dream.

The expansion of democracy and the avoidance of conflict are seen as inherently good things, not just for Americans, but for all peoples everywhere. From the precepts enshrined in our Declaration of Independence

> We hold these truths to be self evident, that all men are created equal, that they are endowed by their creator with certain inalienable Rights, that among these are Life, Liberty and the Pursuit of Happiness. That to secure these rights, governments are instituted among men, deriving their just powers from the consent of the governed.

to the Preamble of the Constitution of the United States

> We the People of the United States, in order to form a more perfect Union . . .

and the Preamble of the Charter of the United Nations,

> We the Peoples of the United Nations, determined to save
> succeeding generations from the scourge of war, which twice in our
> lifetime has brought untold sorrow to mankind . . .

the same themes emerge. It was on this basis that George Bush sought so
earnestly to see the establishment of a "New World Order — a phrase
printed on US currency in Latin as "Novus Ordo Seclorum" — a "New
Order of the Ages."

The problem is that states are the major actors in the international
arena and responsible for the order, or disorder, that occurs. As Charles
Tilly has noted, "States make war and wars make states."[20] The major
task that states are optimized to do, is to conduct war. And unless or until
they are replaced as the major agent of most of the world's peoples, that
reality will continue to exist. Such order as exists on the planet is due
largely to the actions, agreements, conflicts and disagreements of states.
The legitimacy of certain governments and the ability of an increasing
number of new, small, weak states to survive and prosper is at issue.
Which ones the major powers of the world decide to assist may make all
the difference in the world as was the case when France saw it as useful to
aid a fledgling United States of America because they shared a common
enemy — the British.

## PREVENTIVE DIPLOMACY AND COOPERATIVE SECURITY

Much of the future of regional conflict will be determined by the
involvement of the United States in particular and other great powers in
general. More directly, the level of their support for UN or regional
association efforts at collective security are likely to condition whether the
world enjoys a more stable period of relative peace or finds itself embroiled
once more in a series of conflicts both large and small. Of particular
concern is how best to avoid the internationalization of civil wars which
can become global cataclysms. The Balkans of 2014 may be just as
volatile as they were in 1914. Revanchist desires (Germany in 1939 and
North Korea in 1950), the desire for self determination and independence
(all the wars of decolonization in the 1940s, '50s, '60s and '70s, the
former Soviet and Yugoslav Republics in the 1990s), or simply good old-
fashioned territorial disputes and acts of aggression (the wars of the Middle
East, Iran-Iraq, the Gulf War) have all been prevalent and will no doubt

plague us still in the years to come.  Old habits die hard.  And conflict may become more likely, not less, because there are more states to engage in it, a world arms bazaar which feeds it, no end of supposed causes for it and little in the course of human history to suggest that peace is terribly long-lived.  As Philippe Delmas argues, why should war, which was once a daily occurrence, suddenly disappear only because ten per cent of humanity was able to avoid it for two generations?  The record is not good.  From 1500 to 1800, Europe was at war 270 years out of 300, with a new war every three years.[21]  It is likely that in the years of the twentieth century, war and revolution have caused the deaths of at least 300,000,000 people.  To think that these habits will change radically as the opportunities for conflict and the means to engage in it expand geometrically is simply not realistic.

So the world is likely to be a rather messy place with the sordid slaughter of Rwanda, Cambodia, Bosnia, Chechnya, Afghanistan, and more recently, the Congo, Republic of the Congo and Sierra Leone will likely to continue despite our wishes and even efforts to the contrary.  An new era of collective security led by the US under UN auspices might well emerge eventually.  But if it does, it will be under the banner of states seeking to impose stability by force of arms as has been the case in the past.  How then does one select which conflicts are worthy of intervention and those to which, in the words of Nancy Reagan's anti-drug campaign, we should "Just Say No?"  That is the real question the answer to which will largely determine whether the world becomes a more benign and peaceful place or not.  And there are no easy answers.

## INTO THE TWENTY-FIRST CENTURY

One of the more provocative visions of the future, and an explanation for it, is presented by Philippe Delmas:

> This world is without precedent. It is as different from the Cold War as it is from the Middle Ages, so the past offers no basis for comparison. The planet continues to become more and more unified and at the same time more and more fragmented, and the distinction between war and peace is getting lost. There are no more world wars, but instead we have local wars, which have increased in cruelty and multiplied in record numbers. . . But tomorrow's wars will not result from the ambitions of States, rather from their weaknesses. Not having taken this into account, the

principles and the rules of the system of international law, far from preventing war, will make sure that war has a rosy future.[22]

But, if the world's great powers, and its sole remaining superpower, are united in anything, it is probably reluctance to intervene in the regional conflicts of the future. Few affect them directly and most can be overlooked for some time, despite the moral discomfort this may cause. The recent past has made us all gun shy — literally. Russia got burned in Chechnya. The US was sullied in Somalia. France found the casualties high and the discord great in Bosnia. Britain still has Northern Ireland with which to contend. A $600 billion investment has not united East and West Germany nor improved the economy. China must absorb Hong Kong and create its version of economic progress amid tight political control. Japan's economic bubble has burst as has most of South East Asia. Saudi Arabia is in debt. Israel is torn from within. NATO, hence Europe, cannot act without American support, if not leadership.

Where is the incentive for suppressing regional conflict among the great powers? The only case where intervention to undo regional conflict seemed to be at hand was with Nigeria and other West African states trying to wrest the coup leaders from Freetown in Sierra Leone. The fact that more people were killed in Angola than in Bosnia is virtually irrelevant. The fact that the interlocking ethnic cleansing, set of coups and civil wars of Rwanda-Burundi-Zaire is regional conflict at its worst did not seem to motivate any real efforts to stop it. The after the fact investigations and shaking of fingers does little to discourage others from more of the same both there and elsewhere. We seem to have a highly developed skill for acceptance of Hobbesian realities in most of the world despite protestations to the contrary. We already miss the bad old days of the Cold War. We will come to miss them even more in an increasingly chaotic world of multiple regional conflicts conducted by both state and non-state actors that will erode whatever semblance of an international system still exists.

As Lenin asked, "what is to be done?" The answer is *not* a renewed commitment to humanitarian concern, economic integration, support for self-determination, democratic political systems and international law, pleasant though that prospect may sound. Rather, what is needed is a return to some rather cold, calculating politico-military assessments of what patterns of access, influence and control should be promotive of the most stable order over the longest period of time while we attempt to improve the mess in which we find ourselves. While we may get to a more benign, integrated, legally sanctioned environment eventually, the transition is likely to be long and painful in spreading these values from the First to the Third World. Those who doubt this are referred to Robert Kaplan's global version of "Bleak House" in his book *The Ends of the Earth: A Journey at the Dawn of the 21st Century*, or to Samuel Huntington's vision of the future in *The Clash of Civilizations and the Remaking of World Order*.[23]

We have ample evidence that economies can flourish for a long time in less than pristine examples of democracy and with more than a modicum of rampant corruption. South Korea, Indonesia, Taiwan, Singapore, and Hong Kong as well as most of the oil rich Middle East were all testimony to that. We have very little evidence that democratic systems can function and take root amid growing poverty. The experience of most of the states of Africa offer evidence to the contrary as does Haiti closer to home. Economic growth would appear to have more to do with stability than democratic political systems. A Marshall Plan for other areas of the world where there was neither the work ethic, skill level nor commitment to fair practices rather than institutionalized corruption would likely do little other than waste massive resources. Post World War II Europe was a unique environment. Humanitarian relief to the victims of regional conflict, the desire to feed the hungry, minister to the sick and wounded, assist the refugees who have fled conflict are all noble sentiments but serve to create new problems as well. It is nearly a quarter of a century since the end of the war in Vietnam and the "boat people" who fled that war are still living in camps in Hong Kong, Thailand, Cambodia and elsewhere causing problems for the states which have given them "temporary" succor for decades.

The debates will continue to rage among a host of academics, policy makers and professionals of various sorts.[24] Neither we nor they are likely to settle them one way or the other nor do so soon. But how do we approach the messy, uncertain and ever changing world we encounter? Carefully, selectively and in a manner to support principles of order and legitimacy while preserving a capacity for rapid adaptation. What do we do about regional conflict? The short answer is to apply the philosophy of the Cold War in a different way. Regional conflict must be contained. Its greatest danger is a global conflagration that may grow out of it. In some cases it can best be contained by ignoring it, in others by actively intervening to limit it and in others still be ending it by force of arms. As usual, knowing when to apply what means may well determine the ends, and hence the success or failure of the initiative.

The implications for the future are as follows. "Cooperative security"[25] may be no more effective than collective security. The test of intervention is still national self-interest. Somalia was the lesson and Rwanda and Zaire the proof. Preventive diplomacy may work, but rarely, and only when the signals of commitment — ground combat forces if necessary — are clear and unambiguous. Macedonia has been a rare success to date. Defining the situation and understanding what is at stake are critical to the type of response that is required and the success or failure of the operation. The inability of NATO powers to agree on these and the belated response this occasioned in Bosnia are a case in point. "Military Operations Other Than War" (MOOTW) is a dangerous euphemism which hides the fact that the deploying of armed forces carries with it the power and prestige of the nation(s) involved and risks the very thing it seeks to avoid — war. Military forces decay rapidly and may become more of a burden than an asset at times as the Russians discovered in Chechnya and the US is discovering in its myriad deployments about the globe. Most importantly, a determined, unified foe fighting for survival, willing to endure great sacrifices and wage a protracted war is a dangerous enemy and not to be taken lightly. Vietnam should have demonstrated that.

Ultimately, those who live in the region will have to settle things for themselves. Outside intervention in regional conflict may dampen hostilities for a time or control or constrict things to some degree, but it is not likely to settle the issues over which others are contending. They must do that themselves. We can provide assistance of various kinds, but we must not exceed our capabilities with the hubris of omnipotence. Regional conflict is not going to go away and is likely to increase. As it does, it will threaten most the minority of the players in the state system — the wealthier "haves" — who have a set of rules and expectations not shared by the majority. If regional conflict becomes pervasive enough, frequent enough, significant enough, it can destroy the international system as it nearly did in WW I. How well we avoid that possibility is more likely dependent on restraint than on the exercise of power to remake the world in our image. We should be an example always, an arbiter rarely, a standard, never. That will not be easy and may prove impossible.

The views expressed in this article are those of the author and do not necessarily reflect the official policy or position of the United States Air Force, Department of Defense, or the US government.

## NOTES

1. Boutros Boutros-Ghali, "An Agenda for Peace: Preventive Diplomacy, Peacemaking and Peacekeeping," Report of the Secretary-General pursuant to the statement adopted by the Summit Meeting of the Security Council on 31 January 1992 (New York: United Nations, 1992).

2. Data taken from US Department of Defense sources as of 31 March 1996 reprinted in "Active Duty U. S. Military Personnel Strengths, Worldwide," in *The World Almanac and Book of Facts, 1997* (Mahwah: World Almanac Books, 1996), p. 181 and from the International Institute of Strategic Studies data from 1989 reprinted in Gerard Chaliand and Jean-Pierre Rageau, *Strategic Atlas: Comparative Geopolitics of the World's Powers*, Revised Edition (New York: Harper & Row, 1990), p. 208.

3. Ibid.

4. "The Media Business: What's Playing in the Global Village?," *The New York Times* (26 May 1997), pp. C 8-9.

5. Ibid.

6. See Susan Woodward, *Balkan Tragedy: Chaos and Dissolution After the Cold War* (Washington DC: Brookings, 1995), especially pp. 1-20, 374-400.

7. See J. David Singer, *Resort to Arms: International and Civil Wars, 1816-1980* (Beverly Hills: Sage Publishing, 1982).

8. See Edward D. Mansfield and Jack Snyder, "Democratization and the Danger of War," *International Security*, Vol. 20, No. 1 (Summer 1995), pp. 5-38, especially pp. 12-17.

9. Philippe Delmas, *The Rosy Future of War* (New York: Free Press, 1997), p. 8.

10. E. H. Carr, *The Twenty Years' Crisis, 1919-1939* (New York: Macmillan, 1961).

11. See Gerald B. Helman and Steven R. Ratner, "Saving Failed States," *Foreign Policy*, No. 89 (Winter 1992-93), pp. 3-20.

12. *A National Security Strategy of Engagement and Enlargement* (Washington DC: The White House, February 1995).

13. Data compiled from Richard F. Grimmett, "Instances of Use of United States Armed Forces Abroad, 1798-1995," *CRS Report for Congress*, Congressional Research Service, The Library of Congress (6 February 1996) and current newspaper reports.

14. Ibid.

15. See Donald M. Snow, *Distant Thunder: Third World Conflict and the New International Order* (New York: St. Martin's Press, 1993), especially ch. 2, "Third World Problems in a First World Dominated System," pp. 25-56 and also ch. 6, "An Old Problem with New Teeth: Regional Conflict," pp. 136-66.

16. Robert Gilpin, *War and Change in the International System* (Princeton: Princeton University Press, 1982).

17. Ben Wattenberg, *The First Universal Nation: Leading Indicators and Ideas About the Surge of American Power in the 1990s* (New York: Free Press, 1991).

18. Samuel P. Huntington, *American Politics: The Promise of Disharmony* (Cambridge: Harvard University Press, 1981), p. 262.

19. Cited in Frank L. Klineberg, *Positive Expectations of America's World Role: Historical Cycles of Realistic Idealism* (Lanham: University Press of America, 1996), p. 423.

20. Charles Tilly, "Reflections on the History of European State Making," in Charles Tilly, ed., *The Formation of National States in Western Europe* (Princeton: Princeton University Press, 1975), p. 42. See too the marvelous commentary on this by Bruce D. Porter, *War and the Rise of the State: The Military Foundations of Modern Politics* (New York: Free Press, 1994.)

21. Philippe Delmas, *The Rosy Nature of War*, p. 148.

22. Ibid., p. 213.

23. Robert D. Kaplan, *The Ends of the Earth: A Journey at the Dawn of the 21st Century* (New York: Random House, 1996) and Samuel P. Huntington, *The Clash of Civilizations and the Remaking of World Order* (New York: Free Press, 1996).

24. See Sean M. Lynn Jones and Steven E. Miller, eds., *The Cold War and After: Prospects for Peace*, Expanded Edition (Cambridge: The MIT Press, 1994) and Michael E. Brown, Sean M. Lynn Jones and Steven E. Miller, *The Perils of Anarchy: Contemporary Realism and International Security* (Cambridge: The MIT Press, 1995). Most recently, see the section on "US Foreign Policy: Out of This World?" *International Security*, Vol. 21, No. 4 (Spring 1997).

25. See Stephanie Lawson, ed., *The New Agenda for Global Security: Cooperating for Peace and Beyond* (St. Leonards, NSW, Australia: Allen & Unwin, in association with the Department of International Relations, RSPAS, Australian National University, Canberra, 1995), especially ch. 1, "From Collective Security to Cooperative Security? The Gareth Evans Vision of the United Nations" by Ramesh Thakur, pp. 19-38.

# 10

## The Balkan Quagmire: Clash of Civilizations?

*Vladimir K. Volkov*

In the transnational international community of today, information flows at an unprecedented rate. However, though technological advances have facilitated instantaneous transmission of information around the world, this information is not always free from misunderstandings or myths deliberately propagated by the mass media. Citizens of the global community can still be left with distorted perceptions of reality based upon unfounded stereotypes and erroneous assessments. The widespread use of inadequate and biased concepts are now, and will certainly remain in the twenty-first century, a source for fueling tensions on the world stage. In this regard, the contemporary Balkan crisis serves as an interesting case study particularly given that perceptions of the origins and consequences of this conflict differ so dramatically in Russia and the United States.

The twentieth century saw two Balkan wars in its early period (1912-13), and the end of the century is marked by a Balkan crisis which flared up in 1991 and remains in progress. The Balkan wars of the early twentieth century, which erupted after almost four decades of peace in Europe, riveted worldwide attention. Both wars, especially the second one, were accompanied by military crimes committed by various sides against civilians. The Balkans had suffered a tradition of violence in the form of massacres of the residents of Christian regions by the Turks, and this pattern of violence continued in the region encompassing other ethnic groups as well.

To investigate the sources of conflict and crimes, the US Carnegie Endowment sent a fact finding mission to the Balkans comprised of representatives of a number of European countries. The commission submitted a report, written in late 1913 and published in July 1914, a few days after the assassination in Sarajevo and the outbreak of World War I. Some eighty years later, at the close of the twentieth century, the Carnegie Endowment published a new edition of the commission's voluminous report comparing the developments of the past with the present-day processes. The new edition was published under the title *The Other Balkan Wars*. It was preceded by an introduction penned by George F. Kennan entitled "The Balkan Crises: 1913 and 1993."

George Kennan, an outstanding US diplomat and a recognized authority in the history of US-Soviet relations, had embarked upon a new area of study. His debut demonstrates that any author may experience not only successes but also failures. His central point was to reiterate that the contemporary conflict had deep roots; he emphasizes the similarity of developments in the early and closing decades of the century. Kennan contends that developments in the Balkans in the periods prior to and during Turkish domination had the effect of thrusting a non-European civilization into the Southeastern portion of the European continent. He contends that the inhabitants of the Balkans have preserved many of their non-European characteristics, including features that correspond less with the world of today than with that of eighty years ago.[1]

In essence, Kennan is suggesting that the Balkan peoples were banished from European civilization. All that is taking place today in this region is the product of non-European civilization and is unique to the Balkans. It is no wonder that his explanation met with objections and criticism. One of the strongest critiques was offered by Maria Todorova. Todorova contends that Kennan's perspective was based upon a false ideological stereotypical image that could not be supported by historical facts.[2]

What was revealed by World War I? In 1914, the Carnegie Endowment sent yet another commission to investigate the atrocities committed by German troops against the Belgian population, but this report was not published in the difficult conditions of hostilities. There were so many examples of similar military crimes that references to the "Balkanization" of Europe became increasingly widespread. This reference inseparably bound the Balkan region with images of extreme nationalism and violence.

World War II produced similar examples, not the least of which were the Nazi practices of mass extermination and genocide and of pitting individual ethnic groups against each other.  Were the Balkans the birthplace of the Holocaust?  In reviewing Kennan's introduction, Todorova stressed that one might think that there had been nothing of the sort in Europe.  Thus, Kennan produced a mythical stereotypical image of the Balkans as a region where, as distinct from Europe, nothing had changed.  Such an ideological construction was built according to the following dichotomous principle:  the west (Europe) and other countries.  This perspective was evident in much of the thinking during the Cold War.

## THE BALKAN POWDER KEG:  HISTORICAL SOURCES OF CONFLICT

The expression "The Balkans-Europe's Powder Keg" is usually associated with the assertion that it was the Balkan developments of the early twentieth century and the assassination of the Austrian Archduke Franz Ferdinand on 28 June 1914 in Sarajevo that led to the outbreak of World War I.  Although such views, quite often set forth even in history textbooks, are widespread, they produce an erroneous view of the actual course of events.

In the early twentieth century, the Balkan countries found themselves in the midst of political struggle between the two military-political blocs — the Entente (Great Britain, Russia, France) and the Triple Union (Germany, Austro-Hungary, Italy).  This confrontation added new features to the old Eastern Question associated with the Balkan people's national liberation struggle against the Turkish domination, and with the struggle waged among the great European powers for influence in the region.  As a result, confrontation in the region has ever since been affected by that of intrabloc relations.

Within the Triple Union, the interests of Germany and Austro-Hungary were identical.  Both were pursuing the policy of economic and political expansion in the Balkans and in the Ottoman Empire thereby creating apprehension on the part of Great Britain and Russia.  In those conditions, Germany supported Austro-Hungary's annexation of Bosnia and Herzegovina in October 1908.  Russia's attempts to convene an international conference to discuss problems in the Balkans were fruitless because of lack of support by Russia's Entente allies, Great Britain and France.

The 1908 Bosnian crisis led to greater international tensions and stimulated growing ethnic contradictions in the Balkans. The national movement gained strength not only in the lands incorporated in the Ottoman Empire, but also in the Yugoslav regions of Austro-Hungary where the Croat-Serb political coalition had been formed. However, the primary factor was that the two military blocs of great powers clashed for the first time in the Balkans leading to continued active involvement in subsequent developments. The Balkan Union, which united Greece, Bulgaria, Serbia and Montenegro, was formed with the support of Entente countries, and the Union defeated the Ottoman Empire in the first Balkan War (October 1912 - May 1913). Austro-German diplomatic efforts were directed toward prompting Bulgaria's decision to review the results of the war by force of arms, for it regarded them as unacceptable. As a result, Bulgarian Tsar Ferdinand unleashed a war among the allies (the second Balkan war).[3]

However, the root cause of war would be found elsewhere. The German political analysts and the German General Staff had concluded by that time that the situation had not developed in favor of the Triple Union. Austro-Hungary, its member, was growing weaker as a result of the internal national struggle which was gaining momentum. In contrast, Russia's rapid economic development buttressed the Entente's position and consequently, weakened the Triple Union's positions. The use of force, waging a preventive war, was viewed as the solution. The positions of the Entente countries differed with respect to the Balkans. Consequently, the German leaders believed that the Balkans provided the opportunity to split the united front among the Entente countries.

Documentation provided by West German scholar Fritz Fischer revealed the strategic calculations of the German Imperial leadership.[4] According to Fischer, the decision to unleash a preventive war had been made in principle in December 1912 as soon as the preparations could be completed and an appropriate pretext was supplied. They proceeded from the idea that the external pretext for war should offer the hope of breaking Russia away from Great Britain and destroying the Entente. Such a pretext was supplied in June 1914 after the assassination in Sarajevo. Thus, Europe's "powder keg" was actually in the heart of the continent; the Balkans only provided the desired spark for those holding the fuse.

All Balkan countries eventually became involved in the maelstrom of World War I. Serbia, Montenegro, Greece and Romania fought on the side on the Entente, while Turkey and Bulgaria sided with Germany and Austro-

Hungary. Italy initially took a neutral stand and later joined the Entente. Such an alignment of forces later split the Balkan countries into the victors and the defeated. At the close of the hostilities, a new state was formed (1 December 1918) on the ruins of the Hapsburg Empire — Yugoslavia (originally it was called the Kingdom of Serbs, Croats and Slovenes) which united, by decision of their political representations, all Yugoslav peoples of former Austro-Hungary and also Serbia and Montenegro. The emergence of new states on the territory from the Baltic to the Adriatic seas (Poland, Czechoslovakia, Hungary, Austria) produced a new political map of Central and Southeastern Europe.

The break-up of Austro-Hungary, the collapse of the Ottoman and of the Russian Empires, and the emergence of a number of new states gave rise to many issues of contention including territorial questions and the position of national minorities. It was then that the term "Balkanization of Europe" gained influence among politicians fixing the negative stereotype image of the Balkans. The international relations system in Europe developed as a consequence of the Versailles Peace Settlement, engineered by Great Britain, France and the United States. That system was spearheaded against Soviet Russia and the defeated Germany, while the Balkan countries did not have much importance in European affairs.

As tension in Europe grew in the period preceding World War II, the general situation inevitably affected the nations of the Balkans. They were shocked by the Munich Agreement and the fate of Czechoslovakia.[5] Their common desire was to avoid involvement in the conflicts of great powers. However, the region's strategic position and the actions of fascist Italy and Nazi Germany made it impossible to remain outside the conflict. Italy's occupation of Albania (April 1939) and attack against Greece (October 1940) extended the zone of hostilities to the Balkans as well. Nazi Germany convinced first, Romania (November 1940) and later, Bulgaria (March 1941) to join the fascist Triple Pact. In April 1941, Germany invaded, occupied and dismembered Yugoslavia.

In short, hostilities were brought to the Balkans from the outside, by the great powers, primarily by the fascist states which recarved the political map of the region establishing Great Albania and Great Bulgaria. Under German guidance, the Croat fascists set up the so-called Independent State of Croatia which became the main tool of Hitler's occupation policy in Yugoslav lands. The Hitlerites were the inspiration behind the policy of genocide against Jews, Gypsies and Serbs. The resistance movement involuntarily assumed the features of an ethnic conflict (the Serb Chetnik movement), although the revolutionary tendencies soon prevailed in the partisan movement under the communist guidance. Among the Balkan peoples, the greatest losses were sustained in wartime by the Yugoslav peoples and among the latter, by Serbs.

## THE BALKANS DURING THE COLD WAR

The Balkan countries were directly affected by the results of World War II. Communist regimes were established in a number of those countries (Yugoslavia, Bulgaria, Romania, Albania). The landing of British troops prevented the communists from taking power in Greece. However, that policy led to civil war in Greece (1946-1949) which served as an impetus to the Cold War. The Truman Doctrine, set forth on 12 March 1947, became one of the main elements of the Cold War policy. The German issue (the Berlin Problem) and the Korean War added to the tensions and led to global confrontation between two superpowers and two blocs — NATO and the Warsaw Treaty Organization. The Balkans remained in the forefront at the outset of Cold War in the period of formation of a bipolar world.[6]

The establishment of the Cominform Bureau (September 1947) stepped up the process of Sovietization of East European countries. In that context, the Soviet-Yugoslav conflict (the Spring of 1948), rooted largely in the conflict between Stalin and Tito, had consequences transcending the framework of bilateral relations. Yugoslavia was ostracized (especially after the decision, adopted at the Cominform meeting, held in Hungary in November 1949) by the USSR and other socialist countries. Yugoslavia was subjected to gross political pressure accompanied by saber-rattling. It was only after Stalin's death, and the Soviet delegation's visit to Belgrade in 1955, that relations were normalized.

The first period of detente in the mid-1950s proved to be more enduring in the Balkans than in other regions of the world. Apart from the normalization of relations with Yugoslavia, the USSR took steps to ease tensions in its relations with Turkey, which had a favorable effect on the situation in the entire Balkan region. In the second half of the 1950s, Bulgaria and Romania proposed that the Balkans be transformed into a nuclear-free zone of peace. Regardless of the propaganda effect and certain elements of verbiage, that policy reflected the common desire of the Warsaw Treaty Organization member countries and of the USSR to rule out the Balkans as targets for the East-West competition. That line was tacitly accepted also by NATO, with the result that in the 1960s an original situation was formed in the Balkans characterized by the formula 2+2+2. That formula implied that two of the Balkan countries were NATO members (Greece and Turkey), two of them were members of the Warsaw Treaty Organization (Bulgaria and Romania) and two represented nonaligned states (Yugoslavia and Albania).

That alignment of forces proved to be stable enough to produce the longest period of peaceful development for the Balkans in the past three centuries. Before the Summer of 1991, there were no interstate clashes in the region, while those crises that did occur were settled rapidly. This situation demonstrated the desire of the two blocs to regard the non-aligned countries (Yugoslavia and Albania) as a grey zones between them. That understanding fostered stability in the region. Individual conflict situations (the most serious proved to be the conflict between the Cypriot Greek and Turkish communities) were settled along diplomatic channels. The key to regional security seemed to have been found. The development of bilateral economic and cultural relations between the nations of the Balkans was not hindered by their membership in opposing blocs (NATO and the WTO, the European Union with its Common Market and the Council for Mutual Economic Assistance).

However, gradually, processes were developing in the socialist camp countries which had no precedent in world history. The communist regimes in those countries, after having gained notable successes in their economic and cultural development in the first postwar decade, started manifesting signs of stagnation. In conditions of the developing scientific and technical revolution (STR), the socialist countries began to lag behind the leading capitalist powers in levels and rates of development. Those processes, in the late 1950s-early 1960s, revealed that the socialist countries were unable to implement the economic and political reforms in the new spirit of the times. Those processes led in the 1960s to crisis situations in a number of countries resulting in harsh measures, adopted by all communist regimes, especially after the Soviet occupation of Czechoslovakia in 1968.

Similar tendencies took place in the Balkan socialist countries. They were accompanied by increasingly administrative methods in economic management, in the spheres of party control and in political and cultural life. As the influence of communist ideology began to dwindle, leaders of these countries came to rely increasingly on national sentiment as a means of legitimizing their power. Albania, under the leadership of Enver Hozha, in continuing its anti-Yugoslav policy of the past, isolated the country from the rest of the world. The regime ruptured relations with the other socialist countries and engaged in promoting irredentist propaganda among the Albanian population in Yugoslavia. The Romanian leadership, with Nicolae Ceaucescu at the helm, deliberately whipped up nationalist feelings to distract the public from setbacks in the country. Infringement of the national rights of Transylvania's Hungarian minority was among the levers of such a policy which periodically led to disputes with Hungary and tensions in Romanian-Hungarian relations. The same role was played by the Macedonian issue in Bulgarian-Yugoslav relations. However, the most profound changes were taking place in Yugoslavia, as a result of the effort to create a new model of socialism under the leadership of Josip Broz Tito.

The differences between the Yugoslav and the Soviet systems were more evident in theory than in practice. True, the Yugoslav system somewhat ameliorated the communist regime, especially in the sphere of culture, mass media and expanded contacts with the rest of the world. However, it preserved the one-party political monopoly (although Yugoslavia's Communist Party had been renamed as the League of Communists of Yugoslavia) and authoritarian features. Bureaucratic centralism was lowered in Yugoslavia from the federal to the republican level, thus making it possible for Yugoslavia to outstrip the USSR in the process of formation of ethnocratic (ethnic/bureaucratic) clans or, to be more precise, in Yugoslavia they were manifested earlier than in the USSR. This social strata did not vanish together with the communist regimes. On the contrary, following the collapse of these regimes, they preserved real power, discarded old ideology and, by making use of nationalist verbiage, transformed themselves into a new ruling stratum-- ethnocracy. Such metamorphoses were especially noticeable in multinational states.[7]

National contradictions became increasingly sharp in Yugoslavia beginning in the late 1960-early 1970 period eventually spreading to many regions of the country (Kosovo, among others, with its prevailing Albanian population). The nationalist divisions were especially strong in Croatia, where in 1971 a crisis situation arose threatening to erupt into civil war. The conflict was prevented by the authoritarian intervention of President Tito who had replaced the Croat republican leadership. The subsequent steps, especially the adoption of the 1974 Constitution, accelerated the process of decentralization of the Yugoslav state and paved the way for the further consolidation of the local ethnocratic clans.

Since the 1980s, after Tito's death, the Yugoslav Federation began to assume the features of a confederation. The country was swept by a wave of struggle among ethnocratic clans for spheres of jurisdictional influence and power. This led to the crisis of the state system which increasingly took the form of separatism. The struggle was concentrated in the contradictions between the Croat and Serb party-bureaucratic groupings, each of which sought to win the support of the nationalist strata of intellectuals and attract other social forces to their side. The mass media representing the republics carried endless mutual accusations generating an atmosphere of national intolerance. The struggle grew increasingly acute as the communist regime disintegrated. The ethnocratic clans, having consolidated their positions in the process of that struggle, acted as the main motive force.

## THE CONTEMPORARY YUGOSLAV CRISIS

The Yugoslav crisis developed against the background of the *perestroika* process in the Soviet Union and post-Cold War global situation. The velvet revolutions in late 1989 in a number of socialist countries acted as a mighty catalyst for the developments in Yugoslavia (especially the overthrow of communist regimes in neighboring Bulgaria and Romania).

At the 14th LCY Extraordinary Congress in January 1990, the delegations of Slovenia and Croatia proclaimed the independence of the republican Leagues of Communists. Thus the unity of the party as the guiding structure of the communist regime was destroyed, which was followed by the escalation of separatist actions. Elections were held in Slovenia and Croatia and the newly elected bodies declared their sovereign status and introduced changes in names and state symbols. Those actions had an especially demonstrative anti-Serb nature in Croatia where in the Summer of 1990 the state symbols used by Ustash fascists in the years of World War II were adopted. Croatia was proclaimed to be the state of exclusively Croat people (previously it was regarded as the state of Croats and Serbs). The Serb population was denied the right to cultural autonomy. These actions evoked a negative reaction among the Serbs in Croatia and gave rise to irredentist trends among them. Finally, on 26 June 1991, Slovenia and Croatia proclaimed by mutual agreement their full independence and separation from Yugoslavia. The crisis was transformed into a conflict.

It cannot be determined with any certainty what nature the conflict could have assumed or what solution might have been reached had it not been for interference of the European powers in Yugoslav affairs, primarily on the part of the newly united Germany.[8] The first secret and later open support added a certain aggressive and demonstrative nature to the Slovenian and the Croat leaderships' separatist actions. From the outset, they launched a virulent anti-Serb propaganda campaign in the mass media. Under German pressure, a meeting of Foreign Ministers of the European Union member countries was held in Brussels on 17 December 1991, which passed a Declaration on the Criteria of Recognition of New States in Eastern Europe and the Soviet Union and also a Declaration on Yugoslavia. They stated that the European Union was prepared to extend recognition to the Yugoslav republics and confirmed their support for the obligations stated in the document on the criteria of recognition of new states.[9] In keeping with the terms of the documents, on 15 January 1992, the European Union countries, and several other states, extended recognition of the independence of Slovenia and Croatia and later, also of other Yugoslav republics.

The steps taken by the European Union directly affected the problems of security on the European continent, and because of its significance in international affairs, the actions had global implications as well. Those steps deserve analysis both in terms of international law and geopolitical consequences. Such actions could only take place in an atmosphere of intoxicating euphoria which reigned in the West after the self-dismemberment of the Eastern Bloc and especially following the collapse of the Soviet Union and after the stunning triumph of the Desert Storm operation in Iraq. However, there was no unity among the great European powers. In fact, Germany was behind the declarations; for France and Great Britain those steps looked more like a sacrifice to the altar of the Maastricht Treaty and EU unity.

From the viewpoint of international law, the EU declarations represented a gross violation of the 1975 Helsinki Act stipulating respect for the territorial integrity of each state signatory. The declarations in question withdrew Yugoslavia (and also partially the USSR) from the sphere of the international legal jurisdiction of the act.[10] Further, the twelve EU countries assumed the functions for which no one had authorized them, willfully misappropriating the Organization for Security and Cooperation in Europe (OSCE) and UN decision-making prerogatives concerning the destiny of a sovereign and independent state. Finally, the EU declarations confused the notions of state borders, guaranteed by the Helsinki Act, with the administrative interrepublican borders within the Yugoslav Federation, which were thus granted the status of state borders. This conflicted with the rights of other nations to self-determination and offered an opportunity for the application of double standards for the solution of many problems. These developments led one Italian scholar to conclude that the emergence of new states on the territory of the USSR and Yugoslavia had taken place outside the framework of internal and international law.[11]

From a geopolitical viewpoint, the EU Brussels resolutions implied active political interference by West European states, primarily by Germany, not only in the internal political affairs of a country that was not a EU member, but also in the grey zone that once divided the two blocs. Since almost all EU countries were NATO members, this represented the first time that the world's only remaining bloc exceeded the limits of its responsibility. In terms of history, it constituted the first step toward the establishment of a new world order based upon the strengthening of global unipolar influence. This involved expansion of the definition of NATO's responsibilities followed by the growth of the bloc itself at the expense of the grey zone and of certain former member countries of the Warsaw Treaty Organization. The Brussels resolutions of December 1991 served as the impetus for this new direction.

The Yugoslav (Balkan) crisis naturally was not the cause behind the changes taking place in the world, but it acted as a catalyst in bringing about transformation of the entire system of international relations. The EU decision actually stripped the OSCE of its rightful authority to deal with such problems. Subsequently, the UN peacekeeping forces receded to the background to be replaced by NATO troops. Thus, NATO moved to center stage in the Balkan quagmire for the first time displaying its military force in the post-Cold War international arena.

In the Balkans, and especially in Yugoslavia, the EU Brussels resolutions (December 1991) prompted the development of separatism not only in Slovenia and Croatia but also in other Yugoslav republics. The resolutions created the prerequisites for spreading the crisis beyond the former Yugoslav borders, blocked the negotiation process between the republics and gave an anti-Serb slant to the crisis. Interference from the outside, although initially under the UN cover, made the crisis more acute and protracted. Developments took an especially tragic turn in Bosnia and Herzegovina, with sharp clashes among its three ethnic communities — Muslim, Serb and Croat. After NATO replaced the blue helmets in 1994, NATO became a participant in the Bosnian conflict by offering support to the Muslim and Croat communities in carrying out air strikes against the Serb community (the Bosnian Republica Srbska). The Dayton Agreement, orchestrated by US diplomacy in 1995, put an end to the bloodbath, but it did not offer solutions to the cardinal problems of the Yugoslav crisis. Moreover, in addition to the old issues (Macedonian, Albanian), the Dayton Agreement created a new problem — the Serb issue in the Balkans. This came about as a result of the favoritism displayed toward one side (Croat-Muslim), and infringement on the interests of the other side. US policy has been described as Clinton's undeclared war against the Serbs.[12]

As in the past, the current Balkan crisis is profoundly tied to major restructuring of the entire international system. The 1991-95 Yugoslav crisis ensued as global tectonic shifts were occurring as a result of the dismemberment of the Warsaw Treaty Organization and the collapse of the Soviet Union. The developments of early 1997 in Serbia, Bulgaria and Albania indicate that the region is still plagued with political instability. The elections, held in 1997 in the Federal Republic of Yugoslavia, Croatia and Bosnia, served as a conclusive testimony that these nations may enter the twenty-first century with the same leaders, respectively, with Slobodan Milosevic, Franjo Tudjman and Alija Izetbegovic.

## A CLASH OF CIVILIZATIONS?

As a geopolitical area, the Balkans, throughout its long history, has been a crossroads or "contact zone" of various civilizations. Nevertheless, in all its parameters, the Balkan region (to be more precise, Southeastern Europe) is an integral part of European civilization. Samuel Huntington's theory of the clash of civilizations has many weak points and it is quite justly criticized from various sides. His demarcation of the borders dividing the civilizations is a central point of contention. Where are the dividing lines in European civilization? On what basis does Huntington separate Western Europe from Eastern Europe? If we consider the difference between Catholicism and Protestantism, on the one hand, and Orthodox Christianity, on the other, then why is it not also appropriate to divide the Muslim world into its Sunnite and Shiite areas?

The European civilization should not be reduced to only one subregion—Western Europe. No one will deny the fact that the North American subregion belongs to this civilization. After the break-up of the Soviet bloc, the Central European subregion was defined to include the Balkan subregion (incorporating both the former Warsaw Treaty countries and some of the NATO countries and non-aligned states) and the East European subregion (Russia, Belarus, Ukraine). There is every reason to contend that Europe now stretches from Lisbon to Vladivostok.

The achilles heel of Huntington's theory consists in the fact that history offers only a few examples of clashes of civilizations. One may cite the campaign of Alexander the Great that extended to India, the Muslim rulers' campaigns of conquest in the Middle ages, and the invasion of the American continent by European conquistadors. The colonial policies of European powers in the modern era had the features of political and economic subordination rather than of civilizational cataclysms, while a great number of wars were waged within the framework of the same civilizations. European history may serve as the best case in point. Suffice it to recall the two world wars of the twentieth century. It is the conflicts within the same civilization that pose the primary threat to the security of the modern world. Humankind has so far had no other experience.

The contemporary Balkan conflict is based on the struggle of ethnocratic clans, created in the years of communist rule, for power, territory and property. That was the last crime committed by the communist regimes against their peoples. The ethnocrats managed to provoke ethnic strife and intolerance among a broad strata of the population by making use of past experience, relying on the nationalist ideology and portraying the neighboring people as the enemy. The result is that on the territory of former multinational Yugoslavia, where communists proclaimed the policy of brotherhood and unity, new state formations have emerged with ethnic cleansing as a stated policy objective. Ethnic minorities are subjected to various kinds of discrimination throughout former Yugoslavia. The Serb population has been nearly entirely driven from Croatia. A similar picture may be found in Bosnia's national communities which came into being after Bosnia was divided under the Dayton Agreements. Numerous Albanian and other ethnic minorities now live in Serbia (Federal Republic of Yugoslavia).

The ethnocivil war has claimed thousands of lives (the exact figure can hardly be determined) and resulted in displacing in excess of 2.5 million people from their permanent place of residence. Ethnic cleansing was by no means something accidental or unintentional. It represented a deliberate goal, led by ethnocratic clans whose purpose was to foment ethnic strife. The leadership of various republics and regions spare no effort to prevent the refugees from returning to their former places of residence. Moreover, the process of ousting what remains of minority populations continues.

The real picture of Bosnian reality on the territory where the most tragic developments took place is far removed from the notion of clash of civilizations. Before Yugoslavia's break-up, Bosnia and Herzegovina, especially its capital city of Sarajevo, presented an idyllic picture of the peaceful cohabitation of people of various religious faiths. There were many mixed marriages and people quite definitely defined their nationality as Yugoslav. Such a situation was facilitated by their common ethnic origin (all of them had Slav roots), common Serb-Croat language and similar way of life and mores. The Muslim nation was built by the communist regime and the local ethnocracy (the latter — in order to justify their claims to power) in the course of all postwar decades. The Croat-Serb confrontation and the slogans of establishment of an Islamic state in Bosnia led to explosion in that peaceful region. In the quest to preserve and perpetuate power, these ethnocratic clans now spare no effort in attempting to transform minor distinctions into major differences or to spill blood on the newly established borders.

## SECURITY IN THE BALKANS BEYOND THE MILLENNIUM

Since the beginning of 1997, there has been an exacerbation of tensions in the Balkans (the crisis in Albania, the struggle waged between the opposition and the governments in Bulgaria and Serbia). The threat of new ethnic clashes has only increased in Bosnia. Having brought an end to the bloodbath, the Dayton Agreements have failed to establish lasting peaceful resolution of conflict. The old question is still relevant: how is peace to be ensured in the Balkans?

The conference convened in Paris in February 1997 by the French Institute of International Relations (IFRI) and the Peace and Crisis Management Foundation (Chairman B. Vikobrat) concluded that the process of consolidation of separatism in each of the newly-constituted countries of former Yugoslavia is underway. The primary goal of the ruling nationalistic clans, led by those responsible for having unleashed the ethnocivil war, is to consolidate their power. Opposition forces, also acting under the influence of ultranationalism, cannot offer a democratic alternative. Ethnic intolerance prevails in the activity of all state formations, and serves as an obstacle to the solution of the problem of returning refugees to their places of residence. The refugees encounter hatred and rejection and are thereby prevented from returning to settle and live in normal conditions.

The situation is especially alarming in Bosnia and Herzegovina where the Dayton Agreements have fixed the ethnic division. In the Muslim-Croat area, to which NATO offers its economic and political support, the Muslim army is being rapidly re-equipped with up-to-date heavy computerized military hardware and Muslim officers have trained under the guidance of retired US military officers affiliated with the US peacekeeping program. The development of such military capability far exceeds the defense requirements of Bosnia's Muslim population.

The situation in the Bosnian Serb Republic is entirely different. The political leadership is torn by discord. The replacement of the military leadership and demobilization have demoralized the army. The potential of the military has been to a considerable extent destroyed as a result of NATO air strikes. The economy continues to suffer the consequences of economic sanctions, and as distinct from other Bosnian communities, the Serb Republic also receives no significant outside economic aid. The configuration of the republic's territory, assigned to it under the Dayton Agreements, has disrupted contact among various sections.

The imbalance of forces has resulted in the upsurge of revanchist sentiment among the Muslim leadership in Bosnia. The Bosnian Muslims encounter no opposition from NATO forces, especially from US representatives who have become increasingly aware that the Dayton Agreements will operate only as long as the NATO peacekeeping force remains on Bosnia's territory. There have been expressions of concern that if Western forces did leave Bosnia, Muslim troops might launch an offensive occupying the territory of the Serb Republic and driving the Serb population from the area. The propaganda campaign supporting such an offensive has already been launched by citing accusations of failure to extradite those guilty of military crimes to be tried by the Hague Tribunal[13] and obstacles preventing the return of Muslim refugees to the territory of the Serb community. Those accusations are supported by the Western mass media stirring animosity against Bosnia's Serb community. The latter cannot count on the support by the Federal Republic of

Yugoslavia, since it has been ruined by the economic sanctions and is openly threatened by NATO. In a word, following the withdrawal of the peacekeeping force, Bosnia and Herzegovina may be divided between the Muslims and Croats (the section populated by them would be incorporated into Croatia), accompanied by a large-scale campaign of ethnic cleansing of Serbs.

The Bosnian problem and its Dayton solution have produced a stalemate. It is only too obvious that the situation is paradoxical: After contributing to the break-up of multinational Yugoslavia, the Western powers, and now NATO, aim to revive multinational Bosnia and Herzegovina and reintegrate its three communities, while the latter are not prepared to maintain cooperation and their relations show no signs of improvement. Diplomatic and military pressure exerted from the outside has not been productive. The promise of economic cooperation may prove to be the most promising force for bringing some resolution to conflicts in this war-torn region, though the prevailing spirit of mistrust may even limit the effectiveness of this incentive.

The Balkan countries (former Yugoslavia, Bulgaria, Albania, Romania) are a region of economic disaster. In a number of these countries, the Gross Domestic Product (GDP) has dropped by 50 per cent, and the unemployment rate is exceedingly high. Entire sectors of the national economy are idle. Establishment of economic cooperation between the countries of the region is of vital importance. No results have so far been produced by projects such as the European Union's Regional Approach or the New American Initiative on Cooperation in Southeastern Europe. It is obvious that what is necessary is initiative on the part of the Balkan countries, taking into account their own realities, toward opening opportunities for economic cooperation with traditional partners.

The alleviation of regional economic problems is of primary importance for security in Southeastern Europe. Political restructuring and consolidation of democratic institutions and norms will be achieved only by improving economic conditions in the region. It would be no exaggeration to say that the Balkan countries' means for cooperation with the European Union, which is the desire of most of them, will be through the establishment of regional cooperation, primarily economic cooperation.

Resolution of the Balkan crisis also requires the commitment to create forms of cooperation within the framework of a unified greater European civilization. Such cooperation must involve participation on the part of all the subregions of Europe. The attempt to solve this conflict through the bilateral European Union-Balkan relationship has yielded no results.

Concerted action on the part of the United States and Russia might be very significant for breaking through the mass of contradictions in Europe. Yet, thus far, the two countries are constantly subjected to new challenges in building such a relationship. In order to cooperate in working toward resolution of this crisis, and in other critical post-Cold War international security issues, the two countries must first develop mutual trust. While a US-Russian security partnership might be a vital factor for long-term resolution of tension in the Balkans, it is difficult to construct the foundation for such a relationship in light of initiatives such as expansion the NATO alliance to the East.

By introducing troops in Bosnia, NATO assumed the moral commitment to maintain peace in the region.[14] This problem is likely to occupy center stage in European security for a long time to come and there will be no easy exit for those external powers embroiled in the situation.

## NOTES

1. George F. Kennan, *The Other Balkan Wars: A 1913 Carnegie Endowment Inquiry in Retrospect with a New Introduction and Reflections on the Present Conflict* (Washington DC: Carnegie Endowment, 1993), p. 13.

2. Maria Todorova, "Balkans: From Discovery to Intention," *Slavic Review*, Vol. 53, No. 2 (Summer 1994), pp. 453-82.

3. Yu. A., Pisarev, *The Great Powers and the Balkans Before World War I* (Moscow: Nauka, 1985).

4. This school is represented by many scholars. Most important, the works of Fritz Fischer should be mentioned. See Fritz Fischer, *Germany's Aims in the First World War* (New York: WW Norton, 1967); Fritz Fischer, *World Power or Decline: The Controversy over Germany's Aims in the First World War* (New York: WW Norton, 1974); and Fritz Fischer, *War of Illusions: German Policies from 1911 to 1914* (New York: WW Norton, 1974).

5. V. K. Volkov, *The Munich Agreement and the Balkan Countries* (Moscow: Nauka, 1978).

6. See B. Kuniholm, *The Origin of the Cold War in the Near East: Great Power Conflict and Diplomacy in Iran, Turkey and Greece* (New York: Princeton University Press, 1980) and Dean Acheson, *Present at the Creation* (New York: Norton, 1969).

7. V. K. Volkov, "Ethnocracy - an Unforeseen Phenomenon of the Post-Totalitarian World," *Politicheskiye issledovaniya*, No. 2 (1993).

8. H. J. Axt, "Hat Genscher Jugoslawien entzweit?"*Europea-Archiv*, No. 12 (1993), p. 353.

9. "Yugoslavia on Fire. Documents, Facts, Comments (1990-1992)," in *Modern History of Yugoslavia in Documents*, Vol. 1 (Moscow: Slavyanskaya letopis, 1992), pp. 192-94.

10. As a matter of fact, the same may be said also about the Soviet Union, although the signing on 8 December 1991 of the Belovezhsky Agreement somewhat ameliorated the situation.

11. Antonio Cassese, *Self-Determination of Peoples: A Legal Reappraisal* (New York: Cambridge University Press, 1995).

12. R. K. Kent, "Contextualizing Hate: The Hague Tribunal, the Clinton Administration and the Serbs," *Dialogue. Revue trimestrielle d'art et de sciences,* Vol. 5, No. 20 (December 1996), pp. 16-32.

13. Much has been written about the illegal and propagandist nature of the Hague Tribunal's activity. See Kent, "Contextualizing Hate."

14. In my opinion, the best among the studies devoted to the Balkan contradictions is the book by Smilja Avramova, *The West's Unheroic War against Yugoslavia.* At present, it is published only in Serbo-Croat, see Smilja Avramov, *Postherojski rat Zapada protiv Jugoslavije* (Novi Sad: LDI Veternik, 1997).

# 11

## Visions of the Battlefields of the Future and America's Response

*Barry R. Schneider and Victor P. Budura*

What vision do the leaders of the United States military have concerning the threats they will face in future wars and the kind of strategies and capabilities they must have to win on the battlefields of the future? How might that US official vision be countered by asymmetrical strategies adopted by regional opponents? How might the United States counter such asymmetrical strategies in future wars?

### THE OFFICIAL US VISION

The grand strategy of the United States under the Clinton Administration can be found in published form in several documents including *A National Security Strategy for a New Century* and *A National Security Strategy of Engagement and Enlargement*.[1] In these official statements, the United States is to prepare for various types of threats by possessing the capability to:

- Deter and defeat aggression in major regional conflicts (MRCs);
- Counter the activities of terrorist organizations and state-sponsors of international terrorism;
- Stem the proliferation of nuclear, biological and chemical (NBC) weapons and their means of delivery.[2]

Who are the enemies that the United States might fight in future major theater conflicts? The US Government has no official "enemies list." Such adversaries will select themselves, but there are indications of their identity. First, they will likely come from the ranks of radical regimes that have declared themselves the avowed enemy of the United States or one of its major allies. Second, they are likely to be states that sponsor international terrorist organizations. Third, they probably will have a previous record of aggression in their home region. Fourth, they will be of special concern if they are arming with nuclear, biological, or chemical weapons and the means of delivering such weapons of mass destruction. If these criteria are applied there are a handful of potential adversaries the United States might face with all these characteristics: Iraq, Iran, Syria, Libya, and North Korea. China might also qualify if you pay attention to the words of some of their military leaders and foreign policy elites. However, the overall relations with China appear to be improving in the 1990s.

Where does Russia and the other newly independent states of the former Soviet Union fit into this picture? Since 1991, relations with these 15 states and the United States have dramatically improved and friendly relations now prevail between the leaderships. The official view and posture of the United States is that these states are our friends and future trading partners and will be treated as such unless events prove differently. And yet, no US leader can be unaware of the recent hostility of the Cold War era when the Soviet Union and its Warsaw Pact allies posed an overwhelming threat to the liberties and life of the people of the United States and their allies. One spark could have destroyed both East and West in a nuclear holocaust in less than a day. Despite the success of the Strategic Arms Reduction I (START I) Treaty and economic pressures in reducing arsenals, despite the mutual signing of the Chemical Weapons Convention and Biological Weapons Convention, and the willingness of the superpowers to work together in the Cooperative Threat Reduction programs — the two sides still work in the nuclear shadow.

US leaders fear that a dramatic change in the Russian leadership after Boris Yeltsin leaves office could put the Russian strategic arsenal into less friendly hands. US leaders fear the return of the Russian cocked nuclear pistol aimed once again at targets in North America. For that reason, US leaders are reluctant to discard their own nuclear deterrent force on less than a reciprocal basis. Indeed, they are eager to reduce the nuclear threats to both sides via nuclear negotiations (START II, III and beyond) before that threat can be resurrected to put them once again into a mutual hostage relationship.

The *US National Security Strategy of Engagement and Enlargement* states that the United States military should be postured to be able to fight and win two nearly simultaneous major regional conflicts (MRCs).[3] For example, the US military would be simultaneously tasked with: 1) Re-fighting Desert Storm if Saddam Hussein's forces were ever again to march into Kuwait and/or Saudi Arabia; and 2) Defeating the North Korean Army if it should attack across the DMZ separating the two Koreas.

Critics of this two-MRC tasking point out shortfalls in the US capability to implement this grand strategy, particularly in the logistics support area. This two-MRC plan is put into considerable jeopardy by the stepped up operational tempo driven by heavy commitments of forces to operations other than war, and by reductions of US force structure by approximately 40 per cent, and military personnel by 32 per cent, since the end of the Cold War.[4]

To maintain its worldwide commitments, the US Air Force alone stations over 80,000 people abroad on an average day.[5] These are assigned to a multitude of tasks. In Fiscal Years 1996 and 1997, US military personnel assisted in humanitarian and other military missions other than war (MOOTW) in Bosnia, Germany, Macedonia, Haiti, Panama, Japan, Albania, the Virgin Islands, Liberia, Mongolia, Zaire, Rwanda, and elsewhere.

US military aircraft patrol the skies of Iraq in Operations Northern Watch and Southern Watch,[6] and US military specialists protect and assist the UN Special Commission (UNSCOM) and International Atomic Energy Agency (IAEA) inspectors who are in charge of ferreting out and dismantling the Iraqi nuclear, biological, chemical and missile programs. As of July 1997, there had already been 600 such inspections inside Iraq.

Other US military personnel are assigned the job of participating in counter-drug operations especially in South and Central America. Meanwhile, many of the assets of US Transportation Command, particularly of the US Air Force Air Mobility Command are dedicated many days of the year in transporting equipment, supplies, and international personnel to and from areas where United Nations peace operations are at work. In 1996, there were about 20 such UN missions on several different continents.

Such far-flung commitments divert US forces and their resources from preparation for their main task, fighting and winning the projected two near-simultaneous major regional conflicts should they occur.

What would it take for the United States to fight and win two such overlapping conflicts? Clearly, this would depend on the capabilities, strategy, and weapons chosen by the enemy states or groups. The vision statement of the US Chairman of the Joint Chiefs of Staff, *Joint Vision 2010 (JV2010)*,[7] was published to create a broad framework for understanding joint warfare in the future and to direct US armed services acquisition programs toward acquiring the capabilities to carry out four types of operations: precision engagement; dominant maneuvers; focused logistics; and full-dimensional protection of forces and assets.

Note that *JV2010* is not a strategy per se, but, rather, is a set of capabilities that the Chairman of the Joint Chiefs of Staff (CJCS) and Joint Staff envision as necessary to achieve maximum results, or in the words of *JV2010*, "full spectrum dominance" in the coming era.[8] Each of the US military services (Army, Navy, Marines, Air Force) is tasked with supporting this joint vision. For example, the US Air Force has emphasized the need to develop six core competencies including:

- Air and space superiority
- Information Superiority
- Global Attack
- Precision Engagement
- Rapid Global Mobility
- Agile Combat Support[9]

These USAF core capabilities are put at the disposal of the warfighting commanders in chief (CINCs) as they develop their theater warfare strategy and concepts of operations plans (CONPLANs). The regional CINCs, supposedly inspired by the same ideas as those in *Joint Vision 2010*, would implement this air arm support to help achieve the combined force *JV2010* capabilities of dominant maneuver, precision engagement, full dimensional protection, and focused logistics. These capabilities, harnessed to a good strategy and operational plan, are designed to bring an enemy force to its knees and to secure US and allied war aims in future conflicts.

It should be clear that the US Air Force and the Chairman of the Joint Chiefs of Staff have both bought into the idea that there is an on-going "revolution in military affairs." Both place emphasis on achieving information dominance and are dependent on operating from space as a means of achieving force multiplication via improved communications, surveillance and reconnaissance, and navigational inputs. Both articulate the need for battlefield agility and emphasize the importance of precision in targeting and placing the right forces against enemy forces and assets. These characteristics, taken together, are what some US defense analysts say will create a revolution in military affairs, creating, in combination, an unprecedented future military capability.[10]

It is to be noted that each of the US armed services may have somewhat differing notions and doctrines for fighting future wars, despite the lip service given to jointness and joint visions. Moreover, none of the armed services per se are assigned the job of devising future US military strategy. That is the job assigned to the regional warfighting commanders in chief such as the CINC for US Pacific Command for a war in Korea, or the CINC for US Central Command for a conflict in the Persian Gulf arena. Their concept of operations plans (CONPLANs) will drive US military strategy in a given area of responsibility in the world, and can be over-ridden only by direct orders of the US President.

Thus, *JV2010* must be implemented into strategic reality by the warfighting CINCs on future battlefields, and may be ignored if the situation warrants, and the CINCs entertain a contrary vision. As written, *JV2010* is very broadly conceived and could be implemented in radically different ways. It is open to multiple interpretations as to what actions, acquisitions, and plans provide the necessary means to achieve full spectrum dominance through focused logistics, precision engagements, dominant maneuvers, and full dimensional protection.

In fact, some readers might consider *JV2010* to be heavy on slogans and catch phrases without spelling out with much precision the likely winning strategies and capabilities to be employed against the probable threats to be encountered in future wars.

The CJCS vision statement about the US capabilities needed for the year 2010 is congruent with the President's grand strategy paper in one way. It would address, at least, the first three of his major future threats perceived, that is, that of a major regional adversary threatening US citizens, interests, and/or allies. It is incomplete, however, in addressing the other threats mentioned in the President's statement on grand national strategy, namely the NBC proliferation and terrorist threats and how the US military plans to respond to them.

Even in looking at how to respond to a major regional conflict, *JV2010* is backward looking rather than forward looking. Indeed, despite the many historical warnings about the need to prepare for the next war rather than attempting to fight the last one, *JV2010* is more a vehicle for refighting Desert Storm than a way to cope with the likely asymmetrical strategies of opponents in the years ahead.

The *JV2010* "Precision engagement" requirement is reflected in the ability of allied forces in the Gulf War to achieve bombing goals with precision-guided munitions delivered from a variety of platforms. This increased lethality from far fewer sorties is one form of precision engagement envisioned for the future.

The *JV2010* requirement for a "dominant maneuver capability" is a quest for a future flank attack capability similar to the unanticipated "left hook" attack employed by General Schwarzkopf's ground forces against Saddam Hussein's forces in Desert Storm. It presupposes that allied forces will face an opponent as blind as Saddam Hussein and as unprepared for countering such an attack. However, it cannot be ruled out that a flank attack waged against an adversary in the future might be anticipated, recognized by adversary satellites or unmanned aerial vehicles (UAVs) or reconnaissance aircraft. Such an attack might be intercepted by enemy NBC weapons barrages. In a future conflict, an enemy might choose to protect his flanks by creating lethal keep-out zones. These zones or flank areas might be seeded with radiological, chemical, or biological agents to deter or prevent US forces from transiting them.

*JV2010* is wise to include the call for "full dimensional protection" in future wars, but this goal is difficult to reach. It is possible, however, that a future adversary may acquire the means of penetrating defenses and causing great damage on US and allied expeditionary forces in future campaigns.

At present, US and allied active and passive defenses are very insufficient to cope with enemy NBC weapons mounted on ballistic and cruise missiles and other platforms if the use of such weapons is not deterred. US military communications may be in for major disruptions from adversaries skilled at information warfare (IW). It is possible that a future adversary will be able to jam or destroy some important US satellite transmissions. Future enemy IW capabilities may be able to disrupt high-tech allied armies, navies and air forces that are dependent on massive and sophisticated transmissions of data and commands.

It is likely that some future adversaries will recognize the folly of directly pitting its conventional arms against that of the world's existing superpower and its allies. Instead, it is likely that adversaries will adopt asymmetrical strategies such as NBC use or information warfare.

Finally, *JV2010* rightly elevates the need for "focused logistics" in future combat, recognizing that Desert Storm/Desert Shield was probably a historical aberration, never to be repeated again in our lifetimes by another adversary. It is unlikely that the United States would ever be so fortunate again to confront another rogue state in war where the enemy allows a six-month uninterrupted buildup of US and allied arms before the fighting begins. Nor is the United States so likely in the future to have such a stockpile of advanced weaponry and troops in place in Europe for transfer to a nearby theater of war.

However, what the authors of *JV2010* do not tell us is how to achieve just-in-time delivery of reinforcements, supplies and equipment to win a major theater war against the next aggressor who does not cooperate in his own demise. The US sealift and airlift is not presently available in magnitudes equal to the task of quick projection of hundreds of thousands of troops and their weapons, ammunition and supplies. It could be weeks or even months before adequate numbers of supporting units from the continental United States arrived in the theater of war to stop a sizeable invading force. This is particularly a problem if it does not halt itself as did the Iraqi military in 1990-91. It is also unlikely that a future enemy will allow the United States and its allies free entry into nearby sea bases or air bases.

The *JV2010* vision statement also identifies the threat to the United States as being a regional aggressor that engages in fighting large-unit battles with the United States and allied power projection forces. However, an enemy might not choose to fight such massed battles pitting rival conventional forces against each other. Rather, a future opponent, fearing the conventional firepower of the United States, as demonstrated in the 1990-91 Gulf War, might choose instead an asymmetrical strategy where their forces and weapons strengths might be pitted against specific areas of US vulnerability.

## FUTURE ENEMY ASYMMETRICAL STRATEGIES: THREATS AND RESPONSES

There are several asymmetrical strategies that a future regional niche competitor might adopt in future fights with the US military:

- Low Intensity Warfare
- State-Sponsored Terrorism
- NBC Battlefield Employment
- Information Warfare
- Counter-Space Asset Attacks

### *Low Intensity Conflict*

One such asymmetrical strategy is low intensity combat. The Viet Cong, and to some degree, the North Vietnamese, used guerrilla tactics to wear down a superior military adversary and inflict sufficient casualties so that the United States would face increasing political opposition to the war from the public at home. Ultimately, this unpopular war was terminated short of US victory because it lost the support of the American people, the Congress, the media and from some of the Administration's own decision-makers. This was the first televised US war and the American withdrawal was forced because the war was lost in the living rooms of the American people. One way to defeat a superpower is to inflict a political defeat on it on the home front, even if outright victory cannot be achieved on the military battlefield.

Mao Tse-tung once said of his approach to war was to use superior intelligence, mobility, and tactics to wear down a superior enemy force. His forces fought a political battle to win the hearts and minds of the people to his side in a protracted war of attrition. He once said, "my strategic situation is one against ten, but my tactics are to pit ten against one." He also said the relationship of his guerrilla forces to the people was as of the fish to the sea. With their support he had a constant reservoir of fresh recruits, intelligence information, supplies and sanctuary.

In his protracted war against the Kuomingtang forces of Chiang Kai Shek, Mao's forces gave up land for time to reorganize and build. The long march into the interior of China bought such time and new recruits. Slowly, utilizing many local victories where he had gained local if not overall superiority, his forces grew and those of his adversary dwindled. Finally, he was able to move from the guerrilla level to the conventional force level of combat where his final victories were won in China. The Kuomingtang forces were finally forced off the mainland and withdrew to offshore islands, principally to Taiwan, in 1947.

Faced with an adversary superior in conventional arms and numbers of troops, Mao used an asymmetrical approach. His guerrilla strategy eventually turned the tide of the Chinese civil war, wore down the enemy, and led to victory and control of the world's most populous state, one with roughly the same territorial size of the United States and four times as many citizens.

There are numerous areas of the world where such a low intensity warfare approach might give the United States a great deal of trouble. An adversary might be successful if he were to adopt guerrilla strategy and tactics, if he had the support of much of the local population, and had the necessary leadership and patience for prolonged war. Other factors favoring a guerrilla campaign are the presence of rough terrain or jungles that offered concealment. Such a low intensity combat strategy would also be facilitated if the adversary was lucky enough to be located in a region where the US vital interests were not clearly seen to be engaged. Guerrilla tactics might also work against the United States where the cost of suffering significant US casualties was not seen as being worth the benefit of winning that conflict. Low intensity combat is one of the asymmetrical strategies that the weak might employ to neutralize the conventional combat advantages of the stronger state or coalition.

*JV2010*, with its emphasis on high-technology solutions to future combat, is silent on how to re-fight Vietnam or any future guerrilla conflict where low-intensity combat is emphasized. It is also possible that US and United Nations forces might be caught in the crossfire from an on-going low intensity civil war while conducting a military operation other than war (MOOTW).[11]

Therefore, it might be well for the US military to reemphasize in its doctrine, training, acquisition, strategy and planning, the necessity to prepare to fight a counter-guerrilla conflict, particularly in an urban environment (Sarajevo, Mogadishu, Beiruit, Kuwait City) since more and more of the Third World is becoming urbanized.

### State-Sponsored Terrorism

Another threat to US national security that *JV2010* fails to address is the problem of independent or state-sponsored terrorism. This is a threat best met by excellent intelligence and small elite units rather than by army divisions, air force wings, or US naval convoys.

In an era where chemical and biological agents and weapons may be within reach of high-tech terrorists, we may be increasingly at risk from such assassins. It is not impossible that the United States might face a regional enemy who might use chemical or biological terrorists under their control to inflict large-scale casualties in US or allied cities during a crisis or conflict. Such NBC use might be intended to weaken the US and allied public resolve to fight a regional conflict to victory at such high costs.

This asymmetrical terror approach could also easily backfire as the American and allied publics might demand severe retribution for mass civilian losses at home. The state sponsoring terrorism might trigger US public rage that would push for military escalation if New York or Washington, London, Paris, or another major US or allied metropolitan center were struck heavily by chemical or biological terrorists in the midst of a major regional conflict.

The US Department of Defense has been active in both antiterrorism (defensive measures used to reduce the vulnerability of individuals and property to terrorist acts) and in counterterrorism (offensive measures to prevent, deter, and respond to terrorism). As Secretary of Defense William Cohen has recently reported to the US Congress, "in response to the recent tragedies in Saudi Arabia (the bombing at Khobar Towers), the Joint Staff has established a Deputy Directorate for Combating Terrorism under the Director of Operations, Joint Staff."[12]

As Secretary of Defense William S. Cohen has stated: "US counterterrorism forces receive the most advanced and diverse training available and continually exercise to develop new skills. They regularly train with their foreign counterparts to maximize coordination and effectiveness."[13]

In response to the recent spate of terrorist acts inside the United States and abroad, quite a number of antiterrorism units are being formed by different agencies.[14] The Federal Bureau of Investigation has formed a new Domestic Emergency Support Team (DEST). The State Department has created the Foreign Emergency Support Team (FEST). The Public

Health Service has initiated planning for Metropolitan Medical Strike Teams (MMSTs) for a hundred US cities. The Department of Energy has, since the 1970s, had a Nuclear Emergency Search Team (NEST) to counter nuclear terrorists and is presently planning to form a Biological Emergency Search Team (BEST) and a Chemical Emergency Search Team (CEST). The US Army has in place its Tech Escort Units to cope with a chem-bio incident on foreign soil. Its counterpart is the newly formed US Marine Chem-Bio Incident Response Force (CBIRF).

### NBC for Use on the Battlefield

Another asymmetrical approach to countering the United States and its allies in regional theaters of war, might be the use of nuclear, biological and chemical (NBC) arms and missile delivery systems on the battlefield. As General K. Sundarji, former Indian Army Chief of Staff, has concluded, "the lesson of Desert Storm is don't mess with the United States without nuclear weapons."[15]

What might tempt a leader of a rogue state equipped with either nuclear, biological or chemical weapons and the means to deliver them to use such weapons of mass destruction? What use are NBC and missile assets to such leaders?

It is important to understand the enemy if one is to counter his potential NBC strategies. One use of NBC weapons might simply be to deter the United States from projecting power into the region occupied by that enemy state either through active or implied threats. Possession of weapons of mass destruction and an indicated willingness to use them could put the adversary in the position to inflict mass US and allied casualties. This threat or the actual employment of such weapons could trigger an outcry among the US public to avoid such a conflict with such heavily armed aggressors in a regional war very far from the homeland. Leaders in places like Iran, Iraq, Libya, Syria, or North Korea may try to win not so much by a direct military exchange but, mostly, by strongly influencing US public opinion.

NBC-armed opponents might also brandish such weapons to discourage potential US allies from joining regional coalitions against them or to discourage them from offering base rights and other help to such a coalition. For example, it is a fact that in the Middle East, most states only have one, two or three major cities, the loss of which would decapitate their governments and shatter their economies. An NBC threat against any of them would be a powerful disincentive to get involved in a regional war if that was not already forced upon a state located there. NBC-armed adversaries also might gamble that they could destroy or annihilate most of the forward-deployed US forces in their area by using weapons of mass destruction at the inception of a war. Such early NBC use could also disable or make unavailable major seaports and air bases to prevent US and allied reinforcements from entering the region. Finally, NBC opponents might keep their weapons of mass destruction in reserve during a major theater conflict to prevent being overrun or dictated to in the conflict's end game.

US military planners thinking about countering such enemy strategies would want to adopt appropriate countermeasures to negate them. This would likely include a full-blown US counterproliferation program featuring such measures as:

- Development and deployment of advanced conventional counterforce options including the ability to strike and destroy mobile missiles and deeply buried underground bunkers. Such counterforce capabilities must be able to seize, disable, destroy, disrupt, interdict, neutralize, or deny an opponent the use of its weapons of mass destruction in times of war or unambiguous warning of an impending nuclear, biological, or chemical weapons attack.
- Development and deployment of advanced conventional forces and maintenance of nuclear weapons capable of maintaining escalation dominance and a sound deterrent, hopefully one that can work short of crossing the nuclear threshold.
- Development of adequate national technical means and human intelligence to discover key targets nodes of an adversary, and to provide insight into the goals and thinking of future wartime adversaries. Knowing the enemy will be very important to defeating him at acceptable costs. Knowing where all, or nearly all, his weapons of mass destruction are located can turn them into weapons of limited destructive capability, if such intelligence is mated with highly effective counterforce options.
- Development and deployment of long-range precision-guided conventional capabilities that can be targeted on enemy NBC assets from launch points outside the enemy striking power, and capable of effectively penetrating and neutralizing enemy air and missile defenses.

- Development and deployment of effective multi-layered air, cruise missile, and ballistic missile defenses to provide a protective bubble over allied forces in the field during combat.
- Development and deployment of effective force protection capabilities against enemy main force units and special operations forces on the ground.
- Equipping US and allied forces with early warning detectors that can determine when enemy chemical and biological attacks have been initiated. Such detectors must provide adequate time for donning protective gear and taking defensive measures before the chemical or biological attack can inflict mass casualties and substantially disrupt allied operations.
- Developing and deploying adequate passive defense equipment, supplies and training to US and allied forces in the theater of operations. This should include vaccinations against lethal known biological agents and adequate supplies of antidotes and medicines. Adequate amounts of individual and collective protection equipment must be provided to the forces. Large area decontamination procedures and equipment must be designed and provided to keep air and sea bases of embarkation operating at full capacity for as long as necessary to win the conflict.
- Developing and deploying a survivable and timely logistics stream into the battle areas without providing mass targets for enemy WMD to destroy. Means also have to be found to decontaminate air bases and aircraft, ports and ships that have to operate in a dirty NBC environment to prevent air and sea bases of embarkation vulnerabilities from becoming wartime "show stoppers."
- Following a plan of military operations that optimizes the dispersal and movement of forces and the means of supply to complicate enemy targeting.[16]

It is likely that the US and its allies would retaliate against an enemy use of nuclear weapons with a response in kind. But, how should the United States and its allies respond if an enemy used chemical or biological weapons? This is a policy question that is still being debated. Should the United States have a declaratory policy of using its only weapons of mass destruction (nuclear weapons) if an adversary uses WMD first, even if it is non-nuclear in nature? Or should the United States start with an advanced conventional weapons response, knowing that it can probably predominate anyway by staying conventional? At what cost in casualties or outcomes should the United States and its allies be willing to remain conventional in order to achieve its post-war nonproliferation aims that might be shattered if nuclear weapons were used? These are all questions currently under considerable debate.

Another dilemma to be faced once NBC weapons of any type have been employed in a conflict is that of how far the United States and its allies take their counterforce campaign in search of a military victory. Too effective an offensive campaign might force the rogue nation leader to initiate use of his NBC forces before he loses them to US and allied air strikes, missile strikes, and special forces operations. Here, there is a question of how far to prosecute a war with an NBC-armed adversary, particularly in the end game.

Can allied forces neutralize all or most enemy NBC assets before they are used? Can allied forces strike quickly enough and effectively enough to disarm him before he strikes? If not, will not effective counterforce operations simply guarantee that he will "use rather than lose" his weapons of mass destruction as allied offensive measures become more and more effective? At what point will a rogue leader initiate NBC use in the end game? When he has lost 30 per cent of his weapons of mass destruction? 50 per cent? 70 per cent? Where is his likely decision point or the threshold where he would decide to "use" rather than "lose" his remaining WMD capability?

If effective counterforce operations are not mated with very effective active and passive defenses at this "use or lose" decision point, all allied offensive strikes will have accomplished will be forcing the adversary to use his mass destruction weapons. The likely victims will be US and allied forces, nearby noncombatants, and allied urban centers within reach of his forces.

One lesson is not to try to do the entire job with offensive forces. Effective defenses are needed to intercept whatever the offense cannot neutralize. The package of a good offense combined with a good defense at the receiving end of an enemy's NBC weapons is necessary if any campaign against such a heavily armed enemy is not to result in a pyrrhic victory at best and a horrific defeat at worst.

### Information Warfare

Another asymmetrical strategy that an adversary might adopt to counter the conventional advantages of the United States and its allies might be information warfare (IW) techniques. An adversary might attempt to "level the playing field" by using electromagnetic pulse (EMP) bursts, resulting in burning out circuitries, potentially disrupting the advantages that the US and its allies might enjoy in space assets such as communications satellites, weather satellites, the Global Positioning Navigational satellites, reconnaissance satellites, early warning satellites, and any space strike capabilities that might be deployed in the future. Such EMP bursts might also knock out major US and allied air, ground, and sea assets, and disrupt the command, control, and communications of such forces.

Less spectacular, but bothersome, information warfare (IW) tactics might also be to attack asymmetrically US and allied non-defense, but important, economic databases of banks, stock markets, corporate records, air traffic control systems, power grid electronics, and telephone exchanges. Here enemy hackers and jammers might play an important role.

A systematic attack on data bases used to run the US Time-Phased Force Deployment List (TPFDL), the mobilization plan for getting US forces to the fight, could create havoc. An IW attack on key defense communications nodes might delay, distort, and destroy the Air Tasking Orders communicated from the continental United States to coalition air forces in the field in time of war. With effective IW attacks an enemy might be able to shut down the digitalized battlefield approach of the US forces of the future. Unless such forces also trained without all its high-tech capabilities, they might be rendered far less effective than if they remained "wired."

Secretary of Defense William S. Cohen has stated that he is aware of the threat to US forces and society from information warfare attacks. He states that "DOD...has been a leader in recognizing the vulnerability of the national infrastructure."[17] In March 1995, an Infrastructure Policy Directorate was formed to investigate the vulnerabilities and to determine how to best protect them from IW attacks.[18] In August 1996, a Critical Infrastructure Protection Working Group (CIPWG) was created to address means for implementing improvements in protection of the US infrastructure.

In 1960, the Defense Communications Agency (DCA) was created to consolidate the communications functions of the Department of Defense. As one summary states:

> ...the name changed to the Defense Information Systems Agency (DISA) in 1991... The Agency is responsible for providing a seamless web of communications networks, computers, software, databases, applications, and other capabilities that meet the information processing and transport needs of DOD users in peace and all crisis, conflict, humanitarian support and wartime roles. DISA's main objective is to anticipate and respond to the needs of its customers, the warfighters, by providing seamless, end-to-end, innovative and integrated information services which provide a fused picture of the battlefield.[19]

In order to carry out its mission, DISA oversees programs to protect the delivery of such information and communications to the regional CINCs in a hostile information warfare environment. For example, it coordinates with a number of new DOD organizations and programs to prepare the US military for both offensive and defensive applications of information operations that have recently begun at Kelly Air Force Base in San Antonio, Texas. This includes the Joint Command and Control Warfare Center,[20] the US Air Force Information Warfare Center, and the Information Warfare Battlelab at the Air Intelligence Center, all located on Kelly's "security hill."

### *Attacking or Offsetting US Space Assets*

One final asymmetrical approach would be to recognize the United States dependence on space systems as its Achilles Heel, and to degrade or disrupt these important space-based force enhancement capabilities. There are less risky options than using a nuclear EMP burst. These enemy "space control" options would not invite a truly asymmetric nuclear response by the world's sole superpower.

The classic definition of space systems recognizes that they are composed of at least three elements: the ground control site, the link between antennas on the ground and those on orbit, and the satellite itself. The notion of using an anti-satellite system to destroy or disable a US satellite is provocative and as fraught with risk as using a nuclear weapon to knock out unshielded electronics by an EMP burst.

A better approach would be to disable or disrupt the telemetry, tracking and commanding sites which are not on US territory, but which are near the enemy's theater of operations. This does not require actual destruction of the site, but rather, a disruption of its usefulness during a critical satellite maneuver or the downloading of pertinent data collected from the satellite transmission. This would deny useful information to US forces and disrupt the decision process.

Another option, which never receives enough attention, is disruption of the electronic link between the ground segment antenna and the receiver or transmitting antennas on the spacecraft. Typically, people talk about jamming but it is usually easy to detect and to identify the source so that such actions would become an attributable act of war. Meaningful discussions of how to perform space control rapidly become classified and compartmentalized, however, our adversaries will probably know more about the "how to" because they already know more about our capabilities in space than the average joint warfighter.

In using space assets to augment their own future military operations, the best option for a future adversary is to go to an almost totally commercial architecture for their space/information needs. Except for missile warning functions and the collection of signal intelligence, almost all other space-based information of military significance can be obtained in the future commercial market place. The United States uses space as a force multiplier for unilateral advantage in conflicts. It is possible that a future opponent can offset this US space advantage by acquiring space hardware and services in the commercial marketplace and obtain similar force multiplier capabilities against US forces in the future.

For example, the requirement for military satellite communications can be met via international consortia such as INTELSAT and IRIDIUM.[21] Navigational needs can be met by purchasing dual-use receivers that can use either the US Global Positioning Satellite or the Russian GLOSNASS satellite navigational systems. Reliable weather data is available from multiple sources, and launch services can be purchased from a number of countries and companies.

Multi-spectral imagery and data is available from many suppliers and in resolutions and revisit times that meet timelines for provision of militarily significant information. Therefore, relying on commercial space assets in any future conflict with the United States would complicate the situation and diminish the capability to exercise space control when the space-based systems are not the property of the aggressor state.

If one accepts the Tofflers' premise that forms of warfare follow the way that wealth is created, then it is no great leap of imagination to propose that either space warfare or information warfare which utilizes space systems are a real possibility in the near future. Currently, the United States possesses a large asymmetric space advantage, which will diminish rapidly as the number of nations acquiring space capabilities increases year by year.

## FIGHTING FUTURE WARS

The separate US armed forces each may have a somewhat different view concerning how to fight and win future conflicts, despite the push for jointness in operations. It is conceivable that *JV2010* will be paid lip service, but might be observed only in its very general form. However, as it is sometimes said, the devil will be in the details.

The problem is that the United States and its allies are not yet fully prepared for these asymmetrical enemy strategies. Enemy strategies of low intensity warfare, state-sponsored terrorism, use or threats of use of weapons of mass destruction, information warfare and disruption of US space assets provide potential for inflicting harm.

It is clear that much more work must be done to meet these asymmetrical challenges of the future since it is possible that few adversaries would want to meet the United States head-to-head in conventional large-unit battles. Rather, they may have learned from the US conventional success in Desert Storm that the best means of fighting the United States, perhaps the only effective means, is through such asymmetrical strategies.

Thus, it is important that a corresponding amount of effort must be made to prepare the United States and its allies against both the major regional conflict contingency that could occur, *and* the asymmetrical challenges that are even more likely to emerge. *Joint Vision 2010* already is in need of annexes and extensive modifications if it is to ever become a complete and adequate blueprint for effective future US military preparedness.

---

## NOTES

1. William J. Clinton, President of the United States, *A National Security Strategy of Engagement and Enlargement* (Washington DC: US Government Printing Office, February 1996), pp. 1-45. A more recent version, highly similar in content, has been released by a new title, *A National Security Strategy for a New Century* (Washington DC: US Government Printing Office, May 1997), pp. 1-29.

2. *Ibid*, p. 13.

3. *Ibid*, p. 14.

4. *US Air Forces Issues Book* (Washington DC: USAF, 1997), p. 18.

5. *Ibid*.

6. Since the end of the Gulf War in 1991, until June 1997, the USAF had flown over 28,800 sorties in support of Southern Watch. In 1997, over 6,000 USAF personnel were employed in support of that mission. In 1996, the USAF flew over 4,500 sorties in support of Northern Watch.

7. Chairman of the Joint Chiefs of Staff, *Joint Vision 2010 (JV2010)* (Washington DC: US Department of Defense, 1996), p. 21.

8. This full spectrum dominance, in turn, is thought by many in the top echelons of military planning to require information supremacy over an adversary where the United States and its allies embrace their ability to collect, analyze, and transmit accurate information while denying and disrupting enemy information and decision systems.

9. US National Space Policy tasks the Defense Space Sector to "develop, operate and maintain space control capabilities to ensure freedom of action in space."

10. See Jeffrey McKitrick, James Blackwell, Fred Littlepage, George Kraus, Richard Blanchfield and Dale Hill, "The Revolution in Military Affairs" in Barry R. Schneider and Lawrence E. Grinter, eds., *Battlefield of the Future: 21st Century Warfare Issues* (Maxwell AFB, Alabama: Air University Press, 1995), pp. 65-98.

11. Nor does *JV2010* address the need of the US military to better prepare for the many military operations other than war (MOOTW) that have increasingly become its major day-to-day business. At any given time in the 1990s, there are 30 to 35 wars being fought in different regions of the world. Most of these are civil wars, ethnic conflicts and border brawls. During the 1990s, there have been no major interstate conflicts other than the 1990-91 Persian Gulf War where an US-led coalition defeated the Iraqi military and forced it to withdraw from Kuwait. However, in the 1990s, US forces have been mostly occupied with MOOTWs such as its participation in Bosnian peace operations, its operation in Haiti, and the ill-fated peacekeeping

mission to Somalia. US forces have also been engaged in policing the peace imposed on Iraq, providing an "air occupation" of that state, enforcing no-fly zones, and backing IAEA and UNSCOM inspectors in their missions to locate and destroy the Iraqi nuclear, biological, chemical and missile programs. MOOTW operations are not addressed in *JV2010*.

12. William S. Cohen, Secretary of Defense, *Annual Report to the President and the Congress, April 1997* (Washington DC: US Department of Defense, 1997), p. 77.

13. *Ibid*, p. 78.

14. David E. Kaplan, "Everyone Gets into the Terrorism Game, Too Many SWAT Teams Spells Confusion," *US News and World Report* (17 November 1997), p. 32.

15. See quotation in Dean Wilkenling and Kenneth Watman, "Nuclear Deterrence in a Regional Context," *RAND Report* (Santa Monica: RAND Corporation, 1995), p. 33.

16. See Barry R. Schneider, "Summary and Conclusions: An Agenda for Defeating the Enemy's Military Strategy," in *Future War and Counterproliferation: Military Responses to NBC Proliferation Threats* (New York: Praeger Publishers, forthcoming in 1998).

17. Cohen, *Annual Report to the President and the Congress*, p. 77.

18. *Ibid*.

19. "A Guide to the Defense Information Systems Agency," *Defense News*, Marketing Supplement (Fall 1997), p. 3.

20. For more detailed information on the Joint Command and Control Warfare Center see *Cyber Sword, The Professional Journal of Information Operations*, Vol. 1, No. 2 ( Fall 1997), pp. 1-51

21. INTELSTAT (International Telecommunications Satellite Organization) is an international consortium for coordinating global satellite communication established in 1964. The title for IRIDIUM, headed by Motorola, was derived from the fact that there were originally 77 satellites as #77 in the periodic table of elements. GLOSNASS (Global Navigation Satellite System) is the Russian navigation satellite system that is quite similar to the US Global Positioning System (GPS).

# 12

# Russian Military Doctrine/Strategy, Future Security Threats and Warfare

*Valentin V. Larionov*

In offering a Russian perspective on the questions of military strategy and future war, a few preliminary remarks should be set forth concerning basic concepts in Russian military studies. In the Russian tradition, military doctrine encompasses: a) war and the probability of its occurrence; b) preparation of the nation and armed forces for war; c) the possibility of averting war; d) and methods of waging war if aversion is unsuccessful. The doctrine changes in response to both external and internal conditions. While military strategy is constantly developing in accordance with circumstances, the essential elements of military doctrine are only periodically re-evaluated or altered. Military doctrine represents the sum total of the government's routine steps in organization of the military. These routine steps correspond with the goal of protecting national security. There is a direct functional connection between military doctrine and strategy since the composition of military doctrine is formulated on the basis of the conclusions and propositions of military strategy.

In the Russian tradition, military strategy, the systematized body of knowledge of the theory and practice of armed conflict, is considered one of the forms of war. It is understood that besides armed combat, there are other types of warfare — political, economic, ideological, diversionary, and so forth. Military strategy is considered the highest level of the theory of military art. Military art is classified as an integral part of military science. Military strategy relies on the objective laws of armed combat which are valid for relatively long periods of time.[1]

## THE EVOLUTION OF RUSSIAN MILITARY DOCTRINE AND STRATEGY

The end of the Cold War, dissolution of the Warsaw Pact and the disintegration of the Soviet Union also led to the partitioning of the Soviet armed forces. Russia, which became the successor to the USSR, inherited a mere two-thirds of the numerical composition of the Soviet armed forces. Eight of fourteen military districts went to Russia. Four of the six most technologically battle-ready strategic first echelon districts, including the Belorussian, Carpathian, Odessa and Kiev Military Districts, were transferred to other governments. Two districts were liquidated including the Baltic and Caucasus Military Districts. These changes radically altered Russia's national security situation and the importance of the USSR's successor, the new Russian Federation, in Europe.

In order to grasp the extent of the changes which took place in the character and content of military doctrine and strategy of Russia after the end of the Cold War, it is necessary to recall the legacy of the world view inherited from the communist past. The global Soviet-American confrontation, based on the ideological incompatibility of the two social systems, was the principal motive force behind Soviet military thinking and organization during the 40 years following the end of the Second World War. It was not until the introduction of Mikhail Gorbachev's *perestroika* that the motives in Soviet foreign and military strategy began to change. This shift in the form of political thinking included the repudiation of the openly hostile relationship with the United States as a class enemy. The priority concern in guiding relations with nations of the global community moved from focus on class conflict to emphasis on shared human values. This new foreign policy perspective was expressed in the character and content of military doctrine.

Corresponding with the dissolution of the Warsaw Pact, by the initiative of the Soviet leadership, a defensive doctrine was accepted by all Warsaw Pact governments in Berlin on 31 May 1989. The main points included the renunciation of preparation and implementation of offensive plans for WTO (Warsaw Treaty Organization) military units, the acknowledgment of the fundamental concept of "non-offensive defense," and the principle of "defensive sufficiency" in military production.

The subsequent development of the process of arms control and the reexamination of the structure of the armed forces was instituted by the leadership of the new government of the Russian Federation. In terms of Russian military doctrine, promulgated internally in 1993-94, the process of modernization went even further. The basic propositions of this doctrine included the following:

- Non-use of the armed forces of the Russian Federation against any state, except for individual or collective self-defense;
- Continued advancement of world-wide cooperation in avoidance of war and armed conflicts along with support or restoration of peace;
- Non-use of nuclear weapons against any signatory of the Agreement on the Non-Proliferation of Nuclear Weapons of 1 July 1968, or against any state not possessing nuclear weapons, except in the following cases: a) an armed attack by any state allied with a nuclear-armed country; b) an action by such a state in concert with a nuclear-armed country;
- Striving for a reduction of nuclear forces to a minimal level which would guarantee a ban on nuclear war, support for strategic stability, and eventually, complete elimination of nuclear arms.

The propositions of the military doctrine were approved by the Security Council and enacted by order of the President of the Russian Federation on 2 November 1993.[2] As an integral part of Russia's concept of security, the doctrine became the governing document for state organs on all levels during the transition period. The doctrine is consistent with the emerging post-Cold War US-Russian bilateral relationship. In January 1994, during President Bill Clinton's visit to Moscow, the US-Russian partnership was termed "mature." This was affirmed during the Halifax Summit and at the Anniversary Session of the United Nations in September 1995.

The understanding between the Russian and American defense ministries concerning participation of the Russian armed forces in the Bosnian peacekeeping operation and mechanisms for similar operations in the future represented confirmation of the doctrine. This will contribute to setting the foundation for creation of a post-Cold War security architecture in Europe. It follows that the process of reform of the system of national security within the new Russia is developing in the direction of overcoming the Cold War confrontation.

After the end of the Cold War, Russia's military doctrine underwent two reviews with the aim of achieving greater moderation. Russian troops were removed from foreign territories, a continuing process of reduction of the armed forces and the military budget is in progress and military-civilian industrial conversion continues. However, the process of reform is in no way complete. The government and military leadership, taking into account budgeting restrictions, are confronted with the necessity for modernization of military doctrine and the creation and introduction of new military reforms. Given economic resource limitations, it is difficult to devote the desired priority to the armed forces and procurement of quality armaments. The central question is how to ensure a high degree of military readiness in this new security situation and condition of resource limitations.

While military doctrine is changing in accordance with circumstances, military strategy has not been altered to such a degree. Being largely dependent on the development of and changes in the weapons used in armed conflict, strategy went through two important stages after the Second World War. The first was in the 1950s and 1960s, when the Soviet Union broke the American nuclear monopoly and attained superiority in space and rocket technology. The second stage, in the 1970s and 1980s, was a period of Soviet-American parity and recognition of the fact that nuclear war was not profitable. The transition from the first to the second stage strategy can be seen in the growth of the USSR nuclear missile capacity, the creation of the Strategic Rocket Forces, the reorganization of the structure of the armed forces, and the reduction in the number of motorized rifle divisions, heavy cruisers and long-range bombers.

In terms of theory of military strategy, forecasting the character of nuclear war was central during those years. The book *Military Strategy*, edited by Marshal Sokolovskii, played a major role in the interpretation at this stage.[3] Given that I co-authored the book, and prepared the three editions (1962, 1963, 1968) for publication, I would like to recall the principles on the conduct of nuclear war declared in this series. It was considered a matter of course that the United States and the NATO alliance were the main antagonists of the USSR. The nature of any future war, and the means of waging such war, were projected in the following manner:

- A future war would in all likelihood have been a general nuclear war which would settle the fight between socialism and imperialism;
- Nuclear strikes by the strategic forces and the action to repel strikes by the air defense and missile defense forces were to be the basic form of strategic action in such a war;
- Strategic operations in the land theaters were to have become both the means of exploitation of the results of the nuclear strikes and, in their own way, the occupation;
- The war was to have been primarily short-lived and lightning-fast;
- The conclusion of the war would have been completely dependent upon the country's and army's pre-war preparation, since the expectation of a high mobilization capacity in the course of the war would have been unjustifiable.

From today's perspective, such thinking concerning war with the West represented an unjustifiable intoxication with power. But in that romantic period of nuclear strategic development, it seemed to be an objective rule of military-technical development. The result of this objective rule was the realization of the long sought-after dream of politicians and commanders: the day when military strategy would become capable of fulfilling the goals of politics.

It is true that the "intoxication with power" did not last long. Having created an arsenal of nuclear weapons at the end of the 1960s, dozens of times greater than the level of the 1950s, and leveling the balance of forces between the Soviet Union and the United States, the hope of providing national security in the course of a mutual nuclear arms race was perceived as illusory. The politics of mutual threat proved that the price of unleashing a nuclear war was too great to allow it to become the only option.

This was expressed in the agreements between the USSR and United States in negotiations on limiting nuclear arms. The process began in 1969, long before the end of the Cold War. It led to the Anti-Ballistic Missile (ABM) Treaty, to the agreements on prohibition of nuclear testing and on non-proliferation, and to the Paris Accord limiting conventional forces in Europe. Under these conditions, the re-examination of strategy focused on the prognosis for the military-technical character of future wars, which had always been considered the first topic in any academic course on strategy. The probability of nuclear war, like general large-scale war, was for the first time forecast as low.

In the current period, and during the first quarter of the twenty-first century, regional and local wars, interstate wars and armed conflicts are considered to be more likely than a global conflict. Russia's participation in wars of this type will be dependent upon concrete conditions and most probably will be in the vicinity of the borders of the Russian Federation when direct threats to its national security arise. In regions far from Russia's borders, the participation of the armed forces in peacekeeping operations under multi-national command is foreseen.

In Russian strategy, it is normal to differentiate regional local wars and armed conflicts by their military and technical character. The first type would be a regional conflict in which multi-national forces might be equipped with the latest types of conventional weapons. Among the newest weapons are the highly accurate "smart" weapons, which allow a "non-contact" war to be waged with an opponent on the ground, in the air and at sea. The significance of such technology was demonstrated in Operation Desert Storm. The second type are those local and interstate conflicts which temporarily spill over national borders or become protracted civil conflicts. These conflicts usually take place using old weapons and massive armies. The third type of military operation of the future is the peacekeeping operation.

In concluding the topic on the character and composition of modern military doctrine and strategy, one marked tendency of recent years must be noted. Military strategy, like the art and science of war forecasting, planning, and leadership, is conspicuously losing its purely professional military character and is becoming an instrument dependent upon the corrupt interests of certain groups of politicians and businessmen. The motives for engaging in the Chechen conflict and for the strategic decisions made in this situation represents a striking example. The root economic source for this corruption gradually supplants the ideological motivation for the use of military force. It is possible that this trend toward the influence of economic corruption in determining the use of military force could become irreversible.

## ASSESSING RUSSIA'S SECURITY CAPABILITY

The historical experience of great nations irrefutably proves that it is possible to determine readiness to counter threats to national security only by means of the outcome or the war itself. The wars of the twentieth century have proven that most strategic forecasts concerning readiness turned out to be ill-founded. It was predicted that WWI would be a short skirmish in bordering regions. Although the antagonists prepared for such a war, WWI became a protracted trench war on extended fronts. In WWII, Hitler prepared a blitzkrieg against the USSR, but was forced to wage a prolonged war for which he was not prepared. Stalin predicted that the Red Army would be prepared to respond to "every blow" of the instigators of war "with one twice as strong," and to carry the war into foreign territory. However, not only was Stalin unable to deliver on his promise to retaliate, but he even lost the first phase of the war.

In order to avoid repeating the mistakes of history, one must not attempt to offer predictions with certainty concerning Russia's preparedness to repel external attack, violations of territorial integrity or threats to domestic stability. Nevertheless, though it is not possible to assess readiness with precision, one can identify both temporary and constant political and military factors likely to be significant. In order to explain this methodology, I will refer to an example from recent history.

It is known that the initial period of the Great Patriotic War (1941-45) went badly for the Soviet Union. Though mistaken in assessing the danger of an attack by Hitler, in the final stage of the initial period of the war, Stalin alluded to the influence of both temporary and constant factors which would determine the various phases and outcome of the war. From Stalin's explanation, it followed that the result of the initial period was determined by the suddenness of the attack by Hitlerite Germany and the lack of preparation of the Red Army to repel such an attack. At the end of 1942, when Stalin became convinced that these short-term factors were no longer operative, the constant factors began to determine the military might of the country and its means of exit: logistical endurance, the morale of the army, the quantity and quality of its divisions, the organizational ability and degree of preparedness of the command structure.

In terms of a system of evaluation relevant for the contemporary period, this example is probably not sufficiently illustrative. Nevertheless, we can not discount the fact that the readiness of any country for meeting the demands of national and global security must be evaluated in terms of both short- and long-term considerations. Moreover, security today includes not only military strength, but also such indicators as economic, ecological, law-enforcement and anti-terrorist security.

To assess Russia's preparation for meeting future national and global security challenges from this perspective it is necessary to emphasize several factors. First, it is important to consider the fact that the Russian people have throughout their history been capable of rising to defend the homeland when threatened. It is true that as distinct from the recent past, the present is notable for a lack of cohesion between the army and society. However, this is not to say that there is a conflict between the army and the people. Rather, the conflict is more likely to be observed in relations between the army and the political authorities. Second, Russia's vast territory, which creates favorable conditions for maneuvers, remains an operative factor in its military strength. Russia has, in comparison with any probable opponent, incomparable reserves of strategic raw materials and scientific-technical potential. Even in an age of modern weaponry and taking into account the introduction of new weaponry of the future, one must not fail to consider this factor. Third, in the steps it takes to avert world war, Russia relies on its nuclear potential, which will be a stabilizing factor at the beginning of the twenty-first century. At present, Russia is undergoing a crisis in preparing its general-purpose forces for repelling external threats. The lack of a clearly articulated conception of national security and the prolonged process of military reform are undoubtedly damaging the nation's defense capacity. However, Russia still has the fundamental capacity to protect its national security just as it has more than once in the past in response to dramatic and even unexpected turns of events.

## RUSSIA'S POTENTIAL ANTAGONISTS AND SECURITY THREATS OF THE FUTURE

At present, and for the foreseeable future, Russia does not regard any state as its enemy or as a potential antagonist. This view is based on the conviction that 1) the democratic course of Russia's internal development will remain unchanged, 2) the Russian people are peace-loving, non-malicious and endowed with Christian forbearance toward other peoples of other cultures and religions, and 3) Russia has no serious territorial or economic disputes with any distant nation or nations in the near abroad.

At the same time, we must not discount the existence of an anti-Russian attitude, even among our closest neighbors. They recall the imperial foreign policy of the Soviet Union, which professed a course directed toward achieving the victory of communism throughout the entire

world. The events in Hungary in 1956 and in Czechoslovakia in 1968
serve as reminders. Because of this, the neighboring states of Europe
remain guarded in their relations with Russia. The former members of the
Warsaw Pact belong to this group of states. A certain amount of strain
is observable in relations with the former republics of the USSR.

With regard to the nations of NATO, Western Europe and America,
there are varying evaluations. One view is that the countries of NATO, as
before, will occupy the leading place in world affairs, in spite of the
growing influence of peripheral regions in the global arena. Furthermore,
Russia must come to terms with its role as a second-tier power and must
search for forms of partnership with the members of the NATO alliance
under the conditions of the new situation. Another view posits that the
history of relations among nations in Europe provides no basis to
anticipate a long post-Cold War period and predicts a new division of
Europe. Is it not valid to assert that NATO's plan for eastward expansion
causing tensions with Russia points to the beginning of a future division
of Europe?

In spite of the lessons of history, the potential for a peaceful
partnership in Europe is far from exhausted and searching for Russia's
probable Western antagonists is not productive. However, those who
would revive NATO must finally acknowledge that the unraveling of the
Warsaw Pact eliminated NATO's major mission and suggests the need for
restructuring the alliance in accordance with political, economic,
ecological, and peace-keeping functions.

History has proven that military alliances develop from war and
establish the circumstances for the next war. How can one question the
threat of war from the East, when in the next fifteen to twenty years the
balance of military forces, by all measurements, will amount to a 3:1
advantage in favor of NATO? To alter that advantage to Russia's favor
within this period would be impossible. It is more realistic to suggest a
change in the axis of confrontation from East-West to North-South. It is
precisely in this sense that it will be possible to expect to find the
security challenges for both Russia and the West in the near term.

It is possible to envision a global situation in which the major
divisions of the future would involve conflict between the industrialized
nations of the North, including Russia, and the less developed South,
primarily the Islamic world. Nationalist and/or religious extremist leaders
of the South emphasize the fact that the Muslim peoples of the Near and
Middle East, Africa and Asia were undeservedly cheated by history as a

result of colonialism. Today, the Islamic world remains unstable and divided. Vast numbers of those practicing Islam throughout the world seek peace and present no security threat to non-Muslim nations. Nevertheless, it is important to remember that Islam presently has more than one billion adherents and Muslims constitute the majority of the population in nearly fifty nations.

The threat of wars either provoked by or exacerbated by religious or cultural differences can not be discounted by Russia. It is important to recall that Chechen leader, Dzhokar Dudayev, depicted the war waged in Chechnya as a Russian-Western conspiracy against Islam. Dudayev is still viewed as a martyr by many Muslims.

Russia, the United States, and other Western nations share an interest in preventing the future expansion of Islamic nations, and are equally threatened by the potential for terrorism perpetrated by certain extremist Islamic fundamentalist sects. Avoidance of direct or indirect conflict with the nations of the South will present a serious challenge for Russian security and strategy in the future.

For Russia, there is one more potential danger looming in the geostrategic security environment: a temporarily peaceful conflict between North and South in the Asian portion of the Eurasian continent. For the sparsely populated territories of Siberia and Northern Central Asia, this involves the threat of peaceful infiltration of large masses of people from the South. The process has already begun, although without the official sanction of our Asian neighbors.

Finally, it should be mentioned that the geopolitical map of the world began to change quite rapidly after the failure of the communist experiment in restructuring societal relations. It can not be ruled out that this experiment might be resurrected in another area of the world, and the possibility for the emergence of a threat to security as a result of resurgent communism can not be dismissed in this chaotic global environment.

## US-RUSSIAN MILITARY COOPERATION AFTER THE COLD WAR

US-Russian cooperation in the field of military technology began in the 1960s or long before the end of the Cold War. Even then, the two sides acknowledged the necessity of arms limitations and technical control of weapons systems and reductions. In 1963, the Nuclear Test Ban Treaty was signed establishing the beginning of the American-Russian cooperation in military technology. In subsequent years, the two countries would achieve even greater levels of cooperation.

It must be admitted that the process of broadening the cooperation and the achievement of mutual trust was difficult at the beginning. The USSR's position remained conservative until the mid-1980s. Priority was given to maintaining national technical means of control.

Decisive upheavals in this field occurred beginning in the mid-1980's. It was acknowledged that without local inspections, verification of compliance with certain agreements was ineffective. Russia began to permit independent, on-site inspections of the destruction of chemical weapons, the ban on nuclear testing, and the down-sizing of the armed forces and conventional arms. During the first three years of the Intermediate Range Nuclear Forces Agreement, 550 and 250 inspections, correspondingly, were carried out. There are ten types of inspections envisaged in the Strategic Arms Reduction I (START I) Treaty.

With the introduction of a new type of control over agreement compliance, corresponding technical organizational structures emerged in the United States and Russia. In the United States, the On-Site Inspection Agency was formed, and in Russia these tasks were performed by the National Inspection Service for the Reduction of Nuclear Danger. These organizations work in concert, demonstrating a new type of joint technical cooperation in the sphere of arms limitation and reduction.

Other critical areas of military-technical cooperation between the United States and Russia include:

• The exchange of information between Russian and American scientists in the field of nuclear and chemical technology and in the creation and destruction of weapons of mass destruction;
• Joint efforts on the means of technical control over armament and disarmament;
• Cooperation in mutual notification of unsanctioned incidents on the ground, at sea and in the air.

Of all the spheres of military-technical cooperation listed, the technology of arms control is, of course, the priority. It is not accidental that the strategic analysts in Russia and the United States confirm that it is essential to take into account the character and content of this process. They agree that it is wrong that limited care is given to the term "arms control" when it is connected to the development of the "rules" of the arms race and reductions in its cost.

Current and future technological advances challenge the long-term survival and development of humanity, potentially threatening the destruction of life. Consequently, arms control must become a distinctive form of coordinated decision-making in the field of security, primarily in questions of military-technical politics and strategy during the period of transition from confrontation to cooperation. In the final analysis, arms control must develop into military cooperation with a prevalence of joint decision-making in the key questions of military development.

Cooperation between the United States and Russia in military technology assumes that relations between the two countries will continue to develop according to the manner in which they took shape at the beginning of the 1990's. James Baker, while serving as US Secretary of State, characterized the fundamental changes in American-Russian relations: "...cooperation can become the norm, and differences of opinion can be reduced to concrete arguments . . . we have arrived at a normal and genuine partnership, where we can agree to dare to look into the future."[4] However, such a relationship will be contingent upon the commitment of those making the long-term strategic decisions in both countries. We must not fail to take into account the fact that some symptoms of discord have recently appeared owing to tensions in relations between the two countries. If these attitudes spill over to the areas of arms control and war preparation, it will threaten not only Russia and the United States, but also international security.

## POTENTIAL ADVERSE CONSEQUENCES OF RENEWED US-RUSSIAN MILITARY CONFRONTATION

In considering the potential adverse consequences of a renewed US-Russian military confrontation, it is necessary to discuss the relationship of the production cycle for the development of new weaponry and arms limitation. The cycle for the development of new weapons occurs in two stages: the creation/production phase and the implementation/deployment phase. The first stage involves the development of the idea for a design, laboratory research and creation of a prototype, field testing, and assembly-line production. The second phase includes the various stages of deployment or the study of the type of weapon and its particular make-up, deployment of the weapon in accordance with military doctrine and methods, development of the strategy and tactics of use, modernization of the weapon and its exploitation under battle conditions, and, finally, removal from the army's inventory.

In the twentieth century, the relationship between the stages of creation and deployment of weaponry has constantly changed in favor of shorter lengths of time to deployment, even if the weapon has not yet been utilized. It is also a given that as soon as a weapon prototype is operationally deployed, this fact immediately becomes moot as the search for new modifications or for the creation of a follow-on generation of the weapons class begins in the recesses of the scientific laboratories. Quantitative limitations, in reality, have been targeted at the second stage of a weapon's life or in the deployment phase. However, in order to achieve greater success in arms limitation, more active control is necessitated during the initial creation/production phase. Simply imposing quantitative limitations in the deployment phase is not sufficient when research and development continues to proceed unabated.

It is also important to consider the fact that progress in the development of new technologies in weapons production, including rapid advances in computer or information technology, will constitute a new stage in the intellectualization of weaponry. If this process is not disrupted by political decisions, it will lead to an even greater dependence of man upon machine, and toward an irreversible weakening of human control over the creation and use of weaponry ultimately increasing the probability of accidental war.

The weapons development process consumes a massive amount of scientific potential and financial resources. Undoubtedly, these resources could be better used in other scientific endeavors or directed toward meeting the needs of the population and state. The end result is heightening of the arms race with adverse consequences for global security. This was clearly corroborated when the USSR depleted its economic resources in the military-technical competition with the United States. In the case of a renewal of the competition, and a return to confrontation, the consequences can not but affect the fate of Russia and the United States.

Another issue of significance related to the issue of consequences of a renewal of the arms race is the temptation to consciously adopt a strategy aimed toward economic depletion of a probable antagonist. Some high echelon American military strategists and analysts have considered the desirability of a strategy directed toward bringing Russia to collapse by means of renewing expenditures on military weaponry. The consequences of such a foreign policy course are not entirely predictable. This could result not only in threatening Russia with a mass exodus of the population to the West, but also with a weakening, even without any evil intent, of control over nuclear materials and the nuclear button. A decline in the level of Russia's economic activity, below the level Russia presently maintains, threatens the economic security of the entire world — a fact which has not yet been taken into account within the pinnacles of power of financial organizations and the International Monetary Fund. The dark prognosis for renewal of the American-Russian confrontation and arms race is consciously speculative as is posing the question. Hopefully, there is no basis for such speculation.

## RUSSIA'S MILITARY FORCES AND MISSIONS OF THE FUTURE

The danger of nuclear conflict still remains, as do the nuclear ambitions of certain leaders of the Third World. Therefore, Russia must maintain deterrent strategic nuclear forces. Also, Russia must have a well-equipped professional army.[5] This is required to deter potential antagonists and to support global and regional security, not for offensive purposes.

Regional local wars are not to be excluded in the future. However, participation of the Russian Army or Navy in these distant wars is problematic. First, the prior political/ideological motive for Soviet participation in such wars, forcible imposition of communism throughout the world, no longer is an operative motive force. Second, again, Russia considers no state or people as its potential enemy. Third, the search for solution to Russia's current domestic crisis and the urgent need to complete the costly reform of the military are the priority concerns for both the political and military leadership.

The capacity to engage in peacekeeping operations such as in the case of Bosnia or Georgia-Abkhazia will continue to be important for Russia. In addition to executing the mission of protecting the security of the nation, Russia's army must be capable of participating in joint peacekeeping operations outside Russia and the Commonwealth of Independent States (CIS) in conjunction with the United Nations, the Organization for Security and Cooperation in Europe (OSCE) and other organizations. Russia must be prepared to perform functions atypical of armed forces in regional conflict situations, peacekeeping and peace enforcement missions including carrying out surgical air strikes against aggressors, conducting peace talks with warring sides, separating combatants and aiding in the delivery of humanitarian aid. The forces and their command must have prior preparation for performing these tasks, and the organizational structure of units must be consistent with the given peacekeeping mission. Also, equipment will be an essential factor in future warfare. In carrying out punitive operations against future aggressors, the armed forces of developed states will use new models of high precision weapons including guided bombs and missiles and electronic warfare.

Given Russia's current domestic instability, the question of the participation of the armed forces in internal conflicts arises. This is an unnatural role for the military. The CPSU program stated that: "From the standpoint of internal conditions, the Soviet Union does not need an army." This same interpretation is clear in the constitution of the Russian Federation. The primary mission for the armed forces is to protect the nation against external or foreign threats. In this context, one must question why such a substantial number of military forces were committed in the Chechen conflict. Furthermore, considering the outcome of the Chechen operation, and the human losses and material costs, it becomes clear that the individuals who made the decision to commit troops to Chechnya were out of touch with the most basic elements of political and military strategy. Russia must be prepared to deal with internal crises and tensions until the nation is firmly set on the path to developing a genuinely democratic state. At the same time, it must be realized that no army, no military art, even the most perfect, can correct the errors and miscalculations of politicians.

---

The perspective of the author is based on professional military experience spanning the period from WWII through the decades of the Cold War and its aftermath. The author has served in the General Staff Academies of the Soviet and Russian Armed Forces. The views expressed here are those of the author and do not represent the conclusions or judgments of officials of the Russian government.

## NOTES

1. The following sources provide reference for the point: I. Michnevich *Strategiya* (1899); A. Svechin, *Strategiya* (1926); and V. Sokolovskii, ed.,

*Voennaya strategiya* (Moscow: Voennaya izdatel'stvo MO SSSR, 1962, 1963, 1968).

2. The military doctrine was approved by Presidential decree on 2 November 1993. See *U Kazy Presidenta Rossiiskoi Federatsii* (Moscow: Progress, 1994).

3. *Military Strategy* (Moscow: The Military Publishing House, 1962, 1963, 1968).

4. Valentin V. Larionov and Sergei Rogov, *From Military Confrontation to Military Cooperation: Perspectives on Arms Control in the 1990* (Moscow: Institute of USA and Canada, 1989).

5. Recommendations for the future development of Russia's armed forces are discussed further in Valentin V. Larionov, "The Type of Army Russia Needs," *Nezavisimoye voennoye obozreniye,* Vol. 23 (28 June - 4 July 1997).

# About the Editors and Contributors

**Sharyl Cross** is Associate Professor of Political Science at San Jose State University. She holds a PhD in Political Science from the University of California, Los Angeles and was formerly a Graduate Fellowship Scholar at the RAND/UCLA Center for Soviet Studies and Post-Doctoral Fellowship Scholar at the Hoover Institution at Stanford University. Dr. Cross recently served as Visiting Professor of International Security and Transregional Studies at the United States Force, Air War College, Air University at Maxwell AFB. She has published numerous articles in scholarly journals and books on Russian foreign policy, US-Russian relations and security issues, and has been the recipient of many grant awards (IREX, US State Department, California State University) to support her research in Russia. Dr. Cross is co-editor of *The New Chapter in United States-Russian Relations: Opportunities and Challenges* (Praeger, 1994). She was recently awarded the Fulbright Scholarship and will be Visiting Research Scholar and Professor at the Institute of USA and Canada Studies of the Russian Academy of Sciences in 1999.

**Igor A. Zevelev** is Head Research Associate and former Deputy Director for the Center for Comparative Studies at the Institute of World Economy and International Relations (IMEMO) of the Russian Academy of Sciences. He holds a PhD from Moscow State University and Doctor of Sciences degree from IMEMO. Dr. Zevelev was Visiting Professor at the Henry M. Jackson School of International Studies at the University of Washington, University of California Berkeley and San Jose State University. Currently, he is Senior Fellow at the United States Institute of Peace. During 1996-97, he was a Fellow as the Woodrow Wilson International Center for Scholars. Dr. Zevelev has published several books and many articles on human rights, political development and international security issues. His most recent book is *Russia and the New*

*Russian Diasporas: The Road to Domination in Eurasia?* (US Institute of Peace Press, Woodrow Wilson Center Press and Johns Hopkins University Press, forthcoming).

**Victor A. Kremenyuk** is Deputy Director of the Institute of USA and Canada Studies of the Russian Academy of Sciences. He graduated from the Moscow Institute for Foreign Relations and holds PhD and Doctor of Sciences degrees in International Relations and Economics and Diplomatic History. He is Professor of Political Science at the Institute of USA and Canada Studies. Dr. Kremenyuk has also been Professor at the Diplomatic Academy in Moscow and Vienna and at the George C. Marshall European Center for Security Studies in Garmisch Germany. He has published six books in Russia on American foreign policy and US-Soviet relations, and has authored many monographs and articles on these topics published both in the United States and Russia. Dr. Kremenyuk has also published two books in the United States including *International Negotiations: Analysis, Approaches and Issues* (Jossey-Bass, 1991) and *Conflicts in and Around Russia* (Greenwood, 1994).

**Vagan M. Gevorgian** is Senior Editor of *USA: Politics, Economy and Ideology* published by the Institute of USA and Canada Studies of the Russian Academy of Sciences. He graduated from the Institute of International Relations in Moscow in 1951 and received a law degree from the Soviet Academy of Sciences Institute of Law in 1955. Mr. Gevorgian formerly worked as foreign correspondent in London and Brussels. He was a Research Scholar at the Institute of World Economy and International Relations (IMEMO) of the Soviet Academy of Sciences from 1962-70. He has published several books and many articles on a wide range of security topics.

**Sergei A. Baburkin** is Associate Professor of Contemporary History and Politics at the Yaroslav Pedagogical University, Yaroslav, Russia. He holds a PhD in History from the Institute of Latin America of the Academy of Sciences of the USSR and a Doctor of Sciences degree in Political Science from the Diplomatic Academy of the Russian Foreign Ministry. He has been Visiting Scholar at the Brookings Institute and the Kennan Institute for Advanced Russian Studies at the Woodrow Wilson International Center for Scholars. Dr. Baburkin's research interests include civil-military relations, international security issues and foreign policy.  His most recent book is entitled *Armed Forces in the Political Process* (1997).

**Victor P. Budura** is Colonel in the United States Air Force and presently works in the Department of Future Conflict Studies at the United States Air Force, Air War College, Air University, Maxwell AFB. Colonel Budura served on the faculty of the Air War College and as the Air Force Space Research Chair.  He has taught courses dealing with space in contemporary and future conflict at the Air War College.  His current research interests include space policy issues and operations and alternative security futures.  His operational experience includes tours as a Minuteman Launch Officer, NORAD Missile Warning Center, Space Watch Officer in the National Military Command Center and Commander of the Third Satellite Control Squadron which provided military communications to US forces during Desert Storm.

**Anna S. Bukharova** is Lt. Colonel in the Russian Armed Forces and a Post-Doctoral Candidate in the Department of Philosophy and History of Religion in the Higher Military College of Humanities.  Colonel Bukharova is a member of the Presidium of the Armed Forces and Society Association in Moscow.  She teaches Philosophy and is a Scientific Studies Associate in Politico-Military Studies at the Military University of the Russian Armed Forces.  Her current research deals with professionalization of the Armed Forces of the Russian Federation.

**Constantine P. Danopoulos** is presently serving as President of the Research Committee on Armed Forces and Society of the International Political Science Association, and teaches Political Science at San Jose State University.  He holds a PhD in Political Science from the University of Missouri, Columbia. Dr. Danopoulos was formerly the Editor of the *Journal of Political and Military Sociology*, and has served as a consultant on civil-military conversion in Russia. Dr. Danopoulos is the author of many books and articles dealing with civil-military relations and international security topics.  His most recent books include *Civil-Military Relations in the Soviet Union and Yugoslav Successor States* (Westview 1996), *The Political Role of the Military* (Greenwood, 1996) and *Crisis in the Balkans: Views from the Participants* (Westview, 1997).

**Grant T. Hammond** is Professor of International Relations at the United States Air Force, Air War College, Air University at Maxwell AFB. Dr. Hammond served as Chair of the Department of National Security Studies at the Air War College from 1991-94. He holds a PhD in International Relations from the Paul H. Nitze School of Advanced International Studies at The Johns Hopkins University. He has held fellowships from the US Government (NDEA), Woodrow Wilson Foundation, American Council on Education and Pew Foundation. Dr. Hammond has been a principal participant in two major studies devoted to forecasting the future strategic military environment and US capabilities (SPACECAST 2020 and Air Force 2025) commissioned by the Chief of Staff of the Air Force. He is the author of *Plowshares Into Swords: Arms Races in International Politics, 1840-1991* (University of South Carolina Press, 1993) as well as other books and numerous articles dealing with military strategy, operations other than war, recent wars, future conflict and other international security issues.

**Barbara Jancar-Webster** is Professor of Political Science at the State University of New York at Brockport. She holds a PhD in Political Science from Columbia University. Dr. Jancar-Webster has been Visiting Research Scholar at Moscow State University in the Departments of Environmental Resources Use and Environmental Law. She has served as Chair of both the Post-Communist Systems and Environmental Studies Sections of the International Studies Association (ISA) and represented the ISA at the UN International Women's Conference in Beijing in 1995. She has published several books and many articles on environmental policy, political-economic systems and the status of women in the former Soviet Union and East-Central Europe, and has received grants from the Woodrow Wilson Center and IREX. Her book entitled *Environmental Management in the Soviet Union and Yugoslavia: Structure and Regulation in Former Communist States* (Duke University Press, 1987) was awarded the International Studies Association Harold and Margaret Sprout Book Award.

**Valentin V. Larionov,** Major General (ret.), is Doctor of Historical Sciences and Military Consultant and Professor at the Institute of USA and Canada Studies of the Russian Academy of Sciences. He received his PhD in the Military Academy of the General Staff in 1955 and Doctor of Sciences degree from the Institute of USA and Canada Studies in 1970.

General Larionov served in the General Staff and was Professor in the military academies of the Soviet and Russian Armed Forces. He has published many books and articles dealing with Russian military strategy and doctrine, warfare, military art and international security.

**William C. Potter** is Professor and Director of the Center for Nonproliferation Studies at the Monterey Institute of International Studies (MIIS). He also directs the MIIS Center for Russian and Eurasian Studies. His current research focuses on nuclear exports, nuclear safety and nonproliferation involving the post-Soviet states. His most recent books are *Nuclear Profiles of the Soviet Successor States* (1993) and *International Missile Bazaar: The New Suppliers Network* (1994). Dr. Potter has served as a consultant to the Arms Control and Disarmament Agency, Lawrence Livermore National Laboratory, the RAND Corporation and Jet Propulsion Laboratory. He serves on the International Advisory Board of both the Center for Policy Studies in Moscow and the International Institute for Policy Studies in Minsk.

**Barry R. Schneider** is Professor of International Relations at the United States Air Force, Air War College, Air University at Maxwell AFB. He holds a PhD in International Relations from Columbia University. He formerly served as a Foreign Affairs Officer at the US Arms Control and Disarmament Agency and worked as an arms control and defense consultant to the Congressional Arms Control and Foreign Policy Caucus. Dr. Schneider has authored numerous publications on issues concerning future warfare, regional conflict and weapons proliferation issues. His most recent books include *Battlefield of the Future: 21st Century Warfare Issues* (Air University Press, 1995), *Pulling Back from the Nuclear Brink: Reducing and Countering Nuclear Threats* (Frank Cass, 1998) and *Future War and Counterproliferation: US Military Responses to NBC Proliferation Threats* (Praeger, forthcoming).

**Vassily I. Sokolov** holds a PhD degree in International Environmental Economics from the Institute of USA and Canada Studies of the Russian Academy of Sciences. Since 1975, he has been Senior Research Fellow and Head of the Environmental Research Group at the Institute of USA and Canada Studies. He has served as a consultant on environmental issues to the Russian Council of Ministers, Russian Ministry of Foreign Affairs, Ministry of Natural Resources and other governmental organizations. Dr. Sokolov is also Professor of International Environmental Studies at the Moscow International University. He is the author of *Environmental Protection and Resource Management: Economic Aspects* (Nauka, 1991) and many other publications in both Russia and the United States dealing with a range of international environmental issues. Dr. Sokolov has been the recipient of research support from the MacArthur Foundation and the Russian Federation's Presidential Award for Outstanding National Scientists.

**Timothy L. Thomas** is an analyst with the Foreign Military Studies Office at Fort Leavenworth Kansas which provides advisory support to the United States Army on regional military and security issues. Mr. Thomas previously served as the Director of the Soviet Studies Department of the US Army Russian Institute. He is a graduate of the US Military Academy and holds an MA degree in International Relations from the University of Southern California. He presently serves as Adjunct Professor at the Institute for Eurasian Studies at the George C. Marshall European Center for Security Studies and is a member of the Russian International Information Academy. He has published many articles on US and Russian developments in information technology, Russian military-political affairs, local wars and peacekeeping operations.

**Vladimir K. Volkov** is Director of the Institute of Slavic and Balkan Studies of the Russian Academy of Sciences and serves on the Presidential Council of the Russian Federation. Dr. Volkov also served as Professor and Head of the Department of International Relations in East-Central Europe at the Institute of Slavic and Balkan Studies. Dr. Volkov received his PhD in History from the Institute of Slavic and Balkan Studies in 1964. He has written several books and more than 200 articles on twentieth-century East-Central European and Balkan history and post-communist nationalism, political development and international relations in the region. He has been the recipient of several major academic research grants including the Ministry of Research and Technology Fellowship in France and the Woodrow Wilson Fellowship in the United States.

**Edward J. Williams** is Professor of Political Science at the University of Arizona. He holds a PhD in Political Science from The Johns Hopkins University. Dr. Williams has served as a Rockefeller Foundation

Research Fellow, a Fulbright Senior Lecturer at El Colegio de Mexico, and as a Visiting Research Scholar with the Strategic Studies Institute of the US Army War College. He has acted as a consultant with the US State, Defense and Labor Departments. Professor Williams has also served as President of the Association for Borderland Studies. He has authored many books and articles on United States Policy in Latin America, Mexican politics and foreign policy and border security issues. His most recent book is *Mexico Faces the 21st Century* (Westview, 1995).

# Index